The Ze
AGREEMENT

"Julie Tallard Johnson's *The Zero Point Agreement* is a brilliant resource for deep and lasting change. I have used the zero point agreement in my own life and have shared it with clients and students. It is not another pie-in-the-sky promise of change. It is straightforward and effective."

TAMAR ZICK, LPC, RYT, LICENSED PSYCHOTHERAPIST
AND REGISTERED YOGA TEACHER

"What a generous, wise, and useful book this is! Each chapter is so filled with quotes, anecdotes, hands-on exercises and more that help and inspire us to fully claim our own lives. There's enough here to guide and inform you for many years to come."

RUTH L. SCHWARTZ, PH.D., AWARD-WINNING POET,
AND AUTHOR OF *SOUL ON EARTH: A GUIDE TO LIVING &
LOVING YOUR HUMAN LIFE*

"A delightful companion for those of us seeking greater levels of balance, meaning, and joy—this book offers many gems of inspiration as well as the welcomed reminder that the journey toward wholeness always begins within."

KAREN HORNEFFER-GINTER, PH.D., AUTHOR OF
FULL CUP, THIRSTY SPIRIT

"*The Zero Point Agreement* is not only a book it's also a beautifully written love letter to the essence of who we really are."

RADIAH NUNEZ, HOSTESS OF THE H₂O NETWORK

"Julie's new book goes to the sinew from the beginning, reminding us of who we really are. She invites us to listen to ourselves, especially our demons, and shows us how to navigate from desire to the dreams that comprise our core. "Living life from my side" is an inspired, pragmatic concept that will change lives. Imagine a world where each of us takes 100% responsibility for our experience. This is Julie's offering: a spark of hope and a path of light."

PRUDENCE TIPPINS, OWNER/DIRECTOR OF
THE CALLIOPE CENTER FOR REFLECTION AND RENEWAL
AND WHEEL OF INITIATION COURSE FACILITATOR

"In this resource-rich book of practical wisdom and wise practices, Julie Tallard Johnson offers readers multidimensional insights, inspiration, and skills for living with greater authenticity, creativity, and happiness. Integrating science, spirituality, and art in an engaging and deeply thoughtful approach to becoming who you already are, this gifted teacher demonstrates how each of us can create more meaning and joy in our lives—in ourselves, in the world around us, and for our power to create and shape the stories we tell ourselves and others."

AMBER AULT, PH.D., CLINICAL SOCIOLOGIST
AND PSYCHOTHERAPIST

"Julie Tallard Johnson's *The Zero Point Agreement* is full of wisdom. We are invited to challenge our beliefs, habits, and assumptions and make ourselves vulnerable so that we can easily access the truth within our lives and experiences. Julie teaches us that by becoming our own meaning maker, we transform ourselves and the world in which we live. A true gift!"

AMY DELONG, M.D., HO-CHUNK NATION
DEPARTMENT OF HEALTH

"I love that the big beautiful zero is a central tenet of this book. What I see is a big round open door through which we can all walk on our journey toward wholeness. It's a journey with no destination, of course, since wholeness is not a place as much as a perspective, ever-shifting. Put on your dancing shoes; this is not a book to be read propped up in your La-Z-Boy!"

CLAUDIA SCHMIDT, SINGER-SONGWRITER

The Zero Point AGREEMENT

HOW TO BE WHO YOU ALREADY ARE

JULIE TALLARD JOHNSON

Destiny Books
Rochester, Vermont • Toronto, Canada

Destiny Books
One Park Street
Rochester, Vermont 05767
www.DestinyBooks.com

Text stock is SFI certified

Destiny Books is a division of Inner Traditions International

Library of Congress Cataloging-in-Publication Data
Johnson, Julie Tallard.
  The zero point agreement : how to be who you already are / Julie Tallard Johnson.
     pages cm
  Includes bibliographical references and index.
  Summary: "A practical guide to stop searching for meaning by creating meaning from within"—Provided by publisher.
  ISBN 978-1-62055-177-6 (pbk.) — ISBN 978-1-62055-178-3 (e-book)
  1. Self-realization. 2. Conduct of life. 3. Spiritual life. 4. Meaning (Philosophy) I. Title.
  BJ1470.J58 2013
  158.1—dc23
                                                                          2013015385

Printed and bound in the United States by Lake Book Manufacturing, Inc.
The text stock is SFI certified. The Sustainable Forestry Initiative. program promotes sustainable forest management.

10 9 8 7 6 5 4 3 2 1

Text design by Priscilla H. Baker and layout by Virginia Scott Bowman
This book was typeset in Garamond Premier Pro and Gill Sans with Avant Garde used as the display typeface

Quotations from pages 16, 20, 22, 62, 114, 163, 182, 190, 191, 215, and 262 of *A Joseph Campbell Companion: Reflections on the Art of Living* by Joseph Campbell. Copyright © 1991. Reprinted by permission of Joseph Campbell Foundation (jcf.org).

"Bad People" from *Morning Poems* by Robert Bly. Copyright © 1997 by Robert Bly. Reprinted by permission of HarperCollins Publishers.

William Stafford, "Thinking about Being Called Simple by a Critic" and excerpts from "Believer" and "You Don't Avoid the End" from *The Way It Is: New and Selected Poems*. Copyright © 1966, 1986, 1991, 1998 by William Stafford and the Estate of William Stafford. Reprinted with the permission of The Permissions Company, Inc., on behalf of Graywolf Press, Minneapolis, Minnesota, www.graywolfpress.org.

Excerpt from "The Winter of Listening" and "Start Close In" from *River Flow: New and Selected Poems* by David Whyte © 2007 Many Rivers Press, Langley, Washington, printed with permission from Many Rivers Press, www.davidwhyte.com.

"The White Bird" from *Mythical Journeys, Legendary Quests* by Moyra Caldecott used by permission of The Orion Publishing Group, London. Copyright ©1996 by Moyra Caldecott.

To send correspondence to the author of this book, mail a first-class letter to the author c/o Inner Traditions • Bear & Company, One Park Street, Rochester, VT 05767, and we will forward the communication, or contact the author directly at **www.julietallardjohnson.com**.

To my Creative Manifestation partners—Bert Stitt, Anne Forbes, and Erik Frydenlund and to the memory and efforts of David Bohm.

Life is without meaning.
You bring the meaning to it.
The meaning of life is
whatever you ascribe it to be.
Being alive is the meaning.

JOSEPH CAMPBELL,
A JOSEPH CAMPBELL COMPANION

In Lakota framework everyone is a meaning maker; everyone must make sense of his or her experience. Woableza has been translated as "realization." It has always seemed to me that this word acknowledges that each person has a capacity to make meaning; that understanding is very personal, is timed by him or her, and is not predictable; and for woableza to exist, a change in the person should take place.

GERALD MOHATT, *THE PRICE OF A GIFT*

Suppose we were able to share meanings freely, without a compulsive urge to impose our view or conform to those of others, and without distortion and self-deception. Would this not constitute a real revolution in culture?

DAVID JOSEPH BOHM, QUANTUM PHYSICIST,
UNFOLDING MEANING

Contents

Daiju visited the master Baso in China. Baso asked: What do you seek?

"Enlightenment," replied Daiju.

"You have your own treasure house. Why do you search outside?" Baso asked.

Daiju inquired: "Where is my treasure house?"

Baso answered: "What you are asking is your treasure house."

Daiju was enlightened! Ever after he urged his friends: "Open your own treasure house and use those treasures."

PAUL REPS AND NYOGEN SENZAKI,
ZEN FLESH, ZEN BONES

Reaching for Meaning

One of the illusions of life is that the present hour is not the critical, decisive one.

RALPH WALDO EMERSON

No snowflake in an avalanche ever feels responsible.

STANISLAW JERZY LEC, POET AND APHORIST

In the story on the facing page, Daiju comes to understand that what he seeks is carried within. He understands that his innate curiosity is a treasure in itself. He comes home to himself but cannot contain himself; he must share his gift in service to others. He finds his treasure house. Daiju comes full circle, as each of us can—we begin by wondering where our treasures are. Where is yours? What, up until now, have you been searching for? Where have you been looking for meaning? It's human nature to want to make our lives fulfilling personally, vocationally, and in our relationships. We all want to feel good about what we are doing with our lives. Most of us, however, are in one of two camps: those searching for meaning, or those who have given up the search. But there is a third option that is reemerging, a new myth as it were, which is to give up *the*

1

search for meaning in order to *make* meaning within all the circumstances of one's precious life.

There is an underlying science to living an inspired and meaningful life. This book is a template for those ready to fully engage in making meaning from all of life's situations. The zero point agreement and the techniques within this book are reliable methods for awakening yourself to the world around you and to your fullest potential (to your treasure house), no matter your circumstances. These methods offer an interior science of transformation that is established and proven, a spiritual technology for meaning makers. We can only discover the truth for ourselves by living life from *our* side (the zero point). In living life *from your side* you not only find lasting happiness and satisfaction but personal awakening. And through this personal awakening we directly benefit all life on this planet.

No one else can run the race, enjoy the fine meal, write the novel, or love your partner in your place. This life is yours to live. Too often, however, we rely on outside circumstances and resources to bring us happiness and fulfillment. Many wait on the sidelines of life for that opportune moment when circumstances will be just right for them. However, external conditions never bring us lasting happiness (as we will see in the discussion of the focusing illusion beginning on page 166). This search outside ourselves only strengthens our feelings of separation and dissatisfaction as we search for our happiness in this way. And our religious institutions and leaders, pop gurus, spiritual and economic con artists, big box chain stores, pharmaceutical companies, and many politicians depend on your search for meaning—for they will happily supply it to you.

> *As an adult, you must discover the moving power of your*
> *life. Tension, a lack of honesty, and a sense of unreality*
> *come from following the wrong force in your life.*
> JOSEPH CAMPBELL, *A JOSEPH CAMPBELL COMPANION*

Life happens when you realize that you are the meaning maker. Life isn't meaningful *until* you bring the meaning to it. Your happiness, creativity, and success all come down to living life *from your side* no matter what the circumstances. When each of us realizes that we are our own meaning maker and that we participate in the world from *our* place, we will find the meaning in *making* the meaning. Life then becomes a series of inspirational moments, bursts of insight, eruptions of creativity, and even personal revelation. Each moment becomes alive with opportunity, possibilities, and rewards. As Daniel Kahneman writes in his book *Thinking, Fast and Slow,* "When you analyze happiness, it turns out that the way you spend your time is extremely important."

Life is a journey of discovery and belonging. It is about making meaning from our experiences for ourselves while allowing the meaning we have made to change. The active life is about being able to *create and discover meaning in an ongoing way* and not hold on to one meaning or we may miss an opportunity at hand. As Joseph Campbell put it, "If we are hanging on to the form now, we are not going to have the form next."

When we review our life and recall times that we experienced an awakening or an epiphany (either through someone else's teachings or our own experience), what changed was some meaning we held. Our "aha" moment arrived from a shift in meaning; something we can only do from our side, from within ourselves.

✦✦✦

Teaching Story: Reaching for Meaning

There was a monk who appreciated his long walks along a cliff that overlooked the vast ocean. One day he slipped and fell, grabbing onto a small branch of a tree that hung out from the cliff. He was close enough to maneuver his way back up. But when he looked up he saw a tiger hungrily looking down at him. If he were to go up, he would be eaten. If he were to let go, he would fall to his death. He looked around for other options and saw a beautiful strawberry growing alone on a cliff vine within reach. Oh, how beautiful and sweet it looked to him!

He glanced up again to see the tiger waiting patiently. He looked below at his fall. He smiled, took a breath, reached for the strawberry, enjoyed it, and then let go.

✦✦✦

I first heard this story at eight years old from a progressive Lutheran minister, who later left the ministry to pursue other dreams. Like all good stories, it has stuck with me ever since. Looking back, I recognize this young minister as one of my teachers. He was a meaning maker. Now, in the remembrance of this story, I see us individually and collectively on this cliff. We often perceive ourselves as being caught between two unfavorable options. Fortunately, integral within such moments is always a third option—an opportunity to define the moment with what we reach for.

Typically there exists a multitude of possibilities unfolding within every given moment; no matter how limited our perception of our situation may be. Because we have not looked for the third possibility (the strawberry) we have not opened ourselves up to the vast potential of the situation. (The strawberry represents the immeasurable third option.) We are always given a third option of reaching for something within the moment that will define and frame our experience. When we know how to widen our perceptions to the multitude of our possibilities, and not get caught up in just solving a problem, real possibilities emerge. When our perspective is narrowed down to *the* problem, we often lose sight of the myriad opportunities to make meaning with our experience. Furthermore, our ability to be creative within this particular circumstance also increases with this widening view.

The way we become aware of this manifold "third option" is through the engagement of the underlying paradigm behind this entire book—the zero point agreement, which I developed to offer you the ability to live a meaningful and active life. "I live life from my side" is the personal expression of the zero point agreement, and it means to live from within as a meaning maker. All other agreements and possibilities come down to understanding this core agreement—to live life consciously and purposefully from our side. This agreement makes it possible to harvest personal meaning from all of life's circumstances. We can only make meaning, live creatively, be of real benefit, when we do so from the zero point, from our side.

The only secure truth men have is that which they themselves create and dramatize; to live is to play at the meaning of life.

ERNEST BECKER, CULTURAL ANTHROPOLOGIST

Similarly there is no point in asking the meaning of life, as life too is the meaning, which is self-referential and capable of changing, basically when this meaning changes through a creative perception of a new and more encompassing meaning.

DAVID BOHM, "SOMA-SIGNIFICANCE AND
THE ACTIVITY OF MEANING" FROM
THE ESSENTIAL DAVID BOHM

The Power of Agreements

Back in 1989, when my first book was published (*Hidden Victims, Hidden Healers: An Eight Stage Healing Process for Friends and Family of the Mentally Ill*) my initial title was *Silent Agreements*. I point this out because I have a long history and familiarity with how agreements form our lives. Agreements are attitudinal contracts that are in alignment with unconscious and consciously held intentions and beliefs. As it turns out, most agreements are unspoken and reside in our unconscious. Every act, every choice, every experience expresses what we are in agreement with and what we are not in agreement with. Basically, what you experience in the outer world is based in part on what you are in agreement with internally. Wherever there is a decision or action, there is an agreement; wherever there is an agreement, there are beliefs and assumptions sustaining it. Agreements are the reason we do what we do. Each and every decision we make is acting out or supporting an agreement that we have made. Therefore, to make these unconscious agreements conscious increases our human potential.

In some Buddhist traditions, teachers may suggest their students take jobs that help them lose their self-absorption. The challenging environment is understood as a means to deepen one's spiritual and ethical commitments. One point the teacher hopes to make is that it is not the environment and its conditions that determine our experience but the agreements and intentions we bring to it. Furthermore, living life from our side challenges a solipsistic and egoistic state by developing our understanding that we are one drop in the vast ocean and that the vast ocean is truly in us.

We can establish conscious agreements to direct our experiences like the wind directs a boat. We engage the zero point agreement to consciously facilitate more meaning, to live life to its fullest, and to harvest the potentiality inherent in our lives and to better benefit others.

> It's your life—but only if you make it so. The standards by which you live must be your own standards, your own values, your own convictions in regard to what is right and wrong, what is true and false, what is important and what is trivial. When you adopt the standards and the values of someone else . . . you surrender your own integrity. You become, to the extent of your surrender, less of a human being.
>
> ELEANOR ROOSEVELT

The Zero Point Agreement:
Living Life from Your Side

Later in the mid-90s I began offering the Initiation Course. The Initiation Course (and book, *Wheel of Initiation,* 2010) offers a spiritual template to explore and then dismantle agreements that sustain one's pain stories and habitual self through designing conscious agreements. To live creatively is to live an active spiritual life built on conscious agreements and intentions. To make meaning from your life and its circumstances is to live actively and consciously. To harvest the most potential from a situation or contribute the most to any given situation is to live life from the zero point, from your side. An initiated adult is a meaning maker.

Over the years of study and experience, I expanded and deepened the initiatory process presented in *Wheel of Initiation* to include the zero point agreement. My background in general systems theory,* transpersonal psychology, group dynamics, Buddhist principles, and reliance on observable nature comes together in this book, *The Zero Point Agreement*. In living the zero point agreement we recognize the potential within each experience. Life is about reaching for and enjoying the strawberry, which of course is really a metaphor for the multitude of possibilities that want to offer themselves up to us.

The zero point agreement is based on the science of interdependence (a mutual dependence between all living things) and on the Buddhist principle of dependent co-arising (everything comes into existence dependent upon other things). This science underlying the zero point agreement shows up in the natural world (how we are part of the whole). This systematic wisdom of connection is the foundation of the zero point agreement and the life of a meaning maker.

In your life, you are the zero point. I use a dream catcher to help visualize this concept. The dream catcher is a metaphor for the web of life in which we are at the center point, the zero point. At the catcher's center (its zero point) is an opening through which everything comes into the web and everything moves out from the web. Everything in our lives comes through us or from us.

Imagine having your life open up to the greatest potentiality of any moment, of having the ability to make meaning from any given situation, as well as having a tangible way to transform personal and global wounds. A global awakening can only take place on a personal level through a collection of individuals activating their zero points—just as each snowflake in a blizzard makes up the storm.

The zero point agreement states that you take one hundred percent responsibility for your experiences. You don't "surrender your integrity" to others as Eleanor Roosevelt mentions above. You don't blame others,

---

*General systems theory points to an underlying reciprocity and influence through all of life. Each and every thing is part of a system. General systems theory relies on the life sciences by exposing the natural law of causality and relationships through the observable universe.

God, or outside circumstances for your predicaments. Imagine your-self getting shot with a poison dart. How will it help you to blame the shooter or the arrow? Who does that serve? What is likely to happen if you say to yourself, "Why me? Why is this happening to me?" You had best put your energy into removing the dart and finding an antidote. Wasting time on blame and shame could ultimately kill you. As long as you assign credit or blame to someone or something outside yourself, lasting happiness will always elude you.

> *We must be our own before we can be another's.*
> RALPH WALDO EMERSON

Imagine This

Take a moment now and close your eyes. Take a deep breath and rest your awareness in the physical sensation of your breath. Just watch your breath as it moves in and out of the body. Notice the physical sensations of your body breathing and sitting. Don't add any spin to it; just notice the sensations of sitting and breathing. From this place of calm, imagine that you are a drop in the ocean. Everything around you and in you is the ocean. Breathe and imagine (don't force anything). Notice how as the drop you are part of the whole, belonging intimately to the whole, while at the same time a unique drop within the ocean. Breathe and imagine the physical sensation of this oceanic quality surrounding you and inside of you. This is what is meant to live life from your side. You are part of the whole but uniquely so. You can only contribute to the whole from your side, from your place in the ocean. (This agreement emphasizes from *your side, not* for *your side;* for *your side would be the antithesis of this principle.) I often use this brief meditation when I feel agitated by circumstances. I take a moment from the demands to breathe and imagine how I am this drop; how I am the ocean.*

Blessed by Choice

Behold this day. It is yours to make.

BLACK ELK, ELDER AND MEDICINE
MAN OF THE OGLALA LAKOTA

Each of us is always blessed with third options, with choices. If there is one thing the scientific approach to living life points to, it is that there is no end to our abilities to discover and make meaning. There are no absolutes or end points in our explorations and possibilities. The blessing comes in participating in our surroundings and consciously making meaning through our perceptions and choices. Everything is taken in as filled with blessing because no experience is exempt. We are always making meaning through our choices, but now we do so consciously, deliberately, and creatively while tapping into the universe's power to create our experiences. We are like gardeners (always) in the Garden of Eden, with even the most basic choices sometimes awakening us to our true nature—do I eat the apple? Every decision, as Joseph Campbell says, "is a destiny decision."

Sometimes our blessings are limited. There is a tangible poverty that surrounds us. We are not offered an obvious tapestry of choices. Still, even when the choices seem bleak—between a tiger's teeth or deadly fall—every moment offers up some third options (the true potentiality within the situation), and it is upon our choices (conscious or not) that a future harvest depends.

> *Epictetus said that people are disturbed not by the events but by the meanings they make of them. Stories contain the meaning we make of the events of our lives.*
>
> LEWIS MEHL-MADRONA, *COYOTE HEALING*

Even so, with a variety of choices available to us, research shows that we have a tendency to habitually respond in a patterned and limited way to our circumstances. Therefore we often remain blind to the variety of possibilities inherent in the situation. In these impoverished circumstances, blinded by our habitual view, when there is a strawberry or even more to reach for, we still don't see it. This is because our own perspective and history limit us. So we remain hanging on the limb for decades until our metaphorical arm gives out and we fall to our death.

Our past agreements and beliefs and our supporting assumptions based on our history prevent us from taking risks, reaching out, and making something remarkable happen. I refer to these as the pain stories we carry around with us. Up until now you may have been using much of your energy (consciously and unconsciously) to perpetuate your pain stories. In these stories, you carry around assumptions about why things are the way they are and why you need what you need, as well as your assumptions about everything and everyone. Our pain stories may have originated with acerbic events, but we are the playwright of our lives (and the director and actor). Therefore, the historical and conditional cause of any particular pain story holds no power in comparison to our ability to rewrite (remyth) and recreate our lives from the zero point.

We tend to relive our pain stories until we consciously name the patterns and *agreements* inherited with the pain. When in agreement with the past, we keep projecting the past onto the present. We live from the past, seeing and creating it over and over again. Many people ask, "Why does this keep happening to me?" when the questions would best be, "What do I do to contribute to this pattern again and again?" and "What can I do to interfere with this pattern and create a new story for myself?" One doesn't need a therapist to be free from the past. One needs the tools (sometimes afforded through therapy) that allow you to be aware of your pain story, along with a willingness to practice living life actively and ethically from your side.

In living as a meaning maker we cease to be so limited by our past and its memories because we bring a creative consciousness to our experiences. Quantum physicist David Bohm refers to this as creating "the movement in which there is the constant unfoldment of still more comprehensive meaning." We are saying that there is no limit to our ability to make meaning; to be in a creative and dynamic exchange with the world around us. By taking one hundred percent responsibility for our experience, we can fully free ourselves from our pain stories. And, of course, as we free ourselves from our pain stories, we influence and uplift our communities and natural environment. You make meaning with your life and the world makes its meaning through you (the drop in the ocean). And this is not some grandiose claim but knowledge based in a spiritual science, natural law, and (the best possible proof) your personal experience.

To give ourselves more possibilities we must retrain the mind and change what we perceive as possible in our circumstances. This book offers such techniques. We can release ourselves from our pain stories and from our habitual states. We can increase our awareness of the potentialities of any experience. We can give ourselves more to create from no matter what our circumstances. We can take hold of the wisdom presented to us through nature (natural law) and live as part of a dynamic system, not separate from it. All this we can do.

But you must know yourself as a meaning maker. This approach to life relies on a willingness to experiment with life (like a scientist or philosopher). Your personal future and the future of your family, communities, and our precious Earth depend upon it.

The question is how our own meanings are related to those of the universe as a whole. We could say that our action toward the whole universe is a result of what it means to be us.

DAVID BOHM, *THE ESSENTIAL DAVID BOHM*

Finding the Bodhi Tree

LIFE AS A MEANING MAKER

The power of a thing or an act is in the meaning and the understanding.

BLACK ELK

Nature, with its true voice undissembled, cries out to us: "Be as I am! I, the primordial ever-creating mother amidst the ceaseless flux of appearances, ever impelling into existence, eternally finding in these transformations satisfaction."

FRIEDRICH NIETZSCHE, *THE BIRTH OF TRAGEDY*

The Gift of Free Will: Use It or Lose It

The capacity to make meaning is a fundamental expression of our free will. Importantly, our free will is *relative* within the context of a whole—so we are not able to act entirely free. We are always part of the great ocean of life. Instead we act *within* this interdependent system of life. Everything is constantly changing and is influenced by so many causes and conditions that there can only be relative free will. Below I offer up an image from the 1993 movie *Free Willy* in which a boy helps free a captive killer whale. Consider freeing Willy from his holding tank as a way to remove what holds us back from our creative expressions as meaning makers. At the same time, Willy can be released into the ocean but not onto the land. His freedom, too, is limited. I appreciate the natural limits to our free will as they express a universal connection we have to all of life; some natural boundaries and laws that hold us altogether. We are, after all, in this together; this alone makes our free will relative.

Most importantly scientists, philosophers, and those in the field of psychology point to how an inner lack of freedom is far more restrictive than anything that occurs on the outside. Therefore our free will is made manifest through the conditions and transformation of our inner landscape.

We cannot just say "I am using my free will to . . ." and be done with it. So much from our inner landscape (based on our personal histories) holds us back. To continue to awaken to our full human and spiritual potential means to personally awaken to the interconnectedness of all of life, which is only achieved through direct experience as a result of using our free will and taking responsibility for our experiences. Spiritual awakening isn't about any type of perfection or achievement. Awakening isn't even a state of constant bliss. Awakening to our greatest potential (true nature) is a resounding knowing of our connectedness to all things. This too then awakens us to the potentialities within the situations themselves. This knowing comes first in blips of awareness and experience, then in longer moments, then in streaks, and then our full awakening is experienced as a constant wave upon the shore of our experiences. It may not help my credibility to share that I am still at the blip stage; but the blips are increasing. Yet, I gratefully participate and celebrate in these flashes of awakening. These blips of connectedness, of wakefulness, are wholly dependent upon my efforts to heal what separates me from the natural and spiritual world and are a direct result of my mind-training practices and my insistent use of my free will as a meaning maker.

Free Will-y

> *I have come to understand that life is composed of a series of coincidences. How we react to these—how we exercise what some refer to as free will—is everything; the choices we make within the boundaries of the twists of fate determine who we are.*
>
> JOHN PERKINS, *SHAPE SHIFTING: TECHNIQUES FOR GLOBAL AND PERSONAL TRANSFORMATION*

> *Rae: [Anxious about Willy's ability to clear the rocks in the marina]* You ever see him jump that high?
>
> *Randolf:* Things can happen.
>
> *FREE WILLY* MOVIE

Most assume we are using our free will when in fact we are not (at least not to its fullest capacity). So much of our histories and stories of our self and the world have been chosen for us. Our legacies of beliefs, genetics, religions, assumptions, traditions, cultures, agreements, and habits hinder our expressing our free will. To fully express ourselves, to reach our greatest potential, means to dismantle our pain stories, challenge our assumptions, and rewrite our personal and global myths.

Although we all experience limitations, far too many have their free will trapped in a holding tank. Our relative free will is released by first understanding that we are in fact being held back. We need to "free Willy" and jump over that which holds back our ability to live freely within the natural limits to which we were born. We want to exercise our free will deliberately and out in the open with others. Our free will makes meaning from our coincidences and spiritual experiences by acting upon our situations with as much awareness and knowledge as we can gain. And as part of the whole, our free will adds to the multitude of causes and conditions that go into the creation and manifestation of our circumstances. So free will, as well as feeling our freedom, is not a linear dynamic—we don't just express ourselves (jump the tank) and then expect a specific result. You will land on the other side, but you will arrive in an ocean of possibilities. I liken our limits to boundaries. Within the context of natural boundaries we can fulfill our greatest potential. The land is the boundary for the oceans, and the oceans keep the land and all of life alive.

Acknowledging What Keeps You Captive

Start with an acknowledgement of what may be keeping your free will captive, then "free Willy."

> *Believe nothing just because a so-called wise person said it. Believe nothing just because a belief is generally held. Believe nothing just because it is said in ancient books. Believe nothing just because it is said to be of divine origin. Believe nothing just because someone else believes it. Believe only what you yourself test and judge to be true.*
>
> THE BUDDHA

In David Bohm's discussions on free will in his 1986 essay "Freedom and the Value of the Individual," he points to how our beliefs, our alliances, and our assumptions limit what is possible for us: "If something is not considered a real possibility, there is no chance at all that it will appear among one's choices. . . . Too often those before us have decided already what the meaning of our life is, so our possibilities become thus trapped. A good place to start is to look and challenge what was given to you through another."

In the Zen practice they warn how great teachers and teachings can be a fierce and intimidating enemy for one on the spiritual path. Teachers and doctrine can often become a block to our exploring and discovering truth for ourselves. It takes away an opportunity we have to make meaning and truth for ourselves, from our side. If we simply plug into some religious program or blindly go the way that others have found worked for them, we will miss the genuine cultivation of our own true nature as meaning makers.

If we go about life living others' answers to the immediate and grander questions, we will find ourselves on some distant shore without proper navigational tools. We will be holding the tools (ideas, meaning, beliefs, assumptions) someone else presented to us.

If we just follow what we assume another is saying we should do (because "they know"), we won't feel the discomfort and pulse of our own life. We will feel the comfort of the tank but not the vastness of the ocean. We will make choices based on someone else's perspective. More likely we will then miss the opportunities that only this incarnation can give us. We can't, as Joseph Campbell says, follow someone else's hero path. We must pave our own paths through life. We can of course borrow from those who we discern have gone successfully before us, like Christ or Buddha, or poet and pacifist William Stafford, or author and environmentalist Aldo Leopold, who each paved their own way.

> *Sacred or secular, what is the difference? If every atom inside our bodies was once a star, then it is all sacred and all secular at the same time.*
>
> GRETEL EHRLICH, WRITER AND NATURALIST

> *When people lose their sense of awe,*
> *people turn to religion.*
> *When they no longer trust themselves,*
> *they begin to depend upon authority.*
>
> LAO-TZU, TAO TE CHING
> (AS TRANSLATED BY STEPHEN MITCHELL)

Creativity, inspiration, and all that goes into living a meaningful life come, too, from our ability to distance ourselves from all that limits the expression of our free will. Such moments of awakening arouse our creative nature. To give in to a mechanistic life of habits is to give up on the authentic, creative self and the possibility of truly benefiting others.

Any time we follow the dogma, rules, or ideas of others, without personal investigation, it is at the expense of our personal integrity and free will. When we don't question authority, don't challenge what is passed on to us, don't determine for ourselves (from our side) what works and what does not work, we forfeit our free will and further limit ourselves. And we must exercise our free will consistently and pervasively. Once we've jumped the wall, let's not create another with our own newly made assumptions and beliefs. Any time we are on automatic pilot or acting from our habitual states, or are caught up in thinking and projecting such habitual thoughts outward, we are not inviting direct experience or exercising our free will. When stuck in a closed way of perceiving and experiencing the world, we see and experience what we have been habituated or told to see and experience. We live by a set of known and unknown rules passed down through our families and culture. In relationships, we may habitually no longer see the other, but see some historical perception we have held on to. Within this habituated context we find no need to call on our free will or to make personal meaning from our experiences. We discover that our habits are often living our lives for us. We have forgotten how to look for the strawberry and lost sight of the myriad possibilities available to us. We are swimming in circles within a holding tank of beliefs, habits, and assumptions.

When our free will is confined by assumptions and habits, we experience an underlying disconnect so we respond by searching for this connection outside ourselves and come to depend on outside confirmation to make us feel better, or to numb us. Even these forms of confirmation become habituated and mechanistic, like in our own versions of cocktail hours, watching television, or hours spent on Facebook. When someone or something outside ourselves directs our choices and experiences, we are not living life from our side and we are held captive by this limitation. When limited by our perceived choices for a prolonged stint of time, we become uninspired. This lack of choices is a form of self-deception based on our pain stories; our beliefs and assumptions and the myths we agree to. An enduring lack of inspiration can lead to giving up, addiction, depression, hopelessness, and helplessness. We then get held back, too, by blaming others for our lack of happiness or success.

Blaming others without taking any responsibility for our own actions has almost become a socially acceptable behavior. . . . Such compulsive blaming is a form of entrapment that is not only self-perpetuating but that robs us of our power and free will.

TRALEG KYABGON,
THE PRACTICE OF LOJONG

Then, out of our depression or exhaustion we get a glimpse of something in our peripheral view. We sense that something else wants to and can happen here if we just allow it. But we can't see beyond the holding tank, even as we sense there is more available to us. This limited perspective is the real culprit, not the tank itself. Once we understand that there is an ocean to experience, we have to find the courage and trust to jump out of the holding tank. So it begins with self-understanding. We each reach a place in life when we have exhausted the limited ways of living a certain aspect of our life. Living automated to our habits and the wishes of others has not resulted in a truly satisfied life, but one drained of essence. Blaming others has not resulted in better outcomes. This exhaustion and disappointment often leads into a new way of being; we listen to the exhaustion (the depression, the anxiety, the disappointment, the illness) and gain a truer and wider perspective. Even when there is a physical tank (relationship, job, poverty, or depression, for example), one has to achieve a wider perspective of reality—the oceanic view. We must trust the possibilities beyond the holding tank and be willing to do what it takes to hold on to the view of the vast ocean in our reach. We begin to see that just over the interior wall of our limited perspective is an ocean of third options available to us.

Jumping the Holding Tank

In order to go beyond what confines us we must first see what restricts us. Any time and effort we put into self-investigation and transforming the inner landscape of the mind not only makes the vast ocean available to us—soon we will be living more freely in it. As a comparison, animals that have been caged, penned in, even domesticated over the centuries (like cows), and somehow escape, take off singularly or collectively to destinations beyond their captivity. They seek the adventure and edginess of the unknown terrain. We too can experience the freedom of the more vast openness. Some will find themselves outside of the tank only to find a way back in again, only to have to jump over the wall again—and sometimes again and again. This is our history lying to us; convincing us that being held captive is safer. Then at some point you will make that final leap into freedom and will swim so strong and fast you will have lost sight of what held you back for so long. I promise.

Take the time to name and investigate what keeps you trapped in a holding tank. This may be generalized to your life right now or more specific to a certain relationship or situation within the greater context of your life. We need to reflect on what we should eliminate from our lives so we can discover what is truly worth pursuing. As long as we remain bound to (or by) our history and the surrounding culture's beliefs, we remain behind a wall of ignorance; the ignorance of all that is truly possible.

Here are some questions you can use to pursue your own personal inquiry. You can simply contemplate them or write them out in your journal. (See "Making Meaning through Spiritual Journaling" on page 50.)

+ What are some of your strongest beliefs about life and how things work?
+ What do you view as holding you back?
+ What do you assume about how a present difficult situation is likely going to work out (or not work out)? What is your greatest fear around this difficult situation?
+ What do you want in comparison with what you are experiencing?
+ Are you blaming outside circumstances or others for holding you back?

As we have seen, we are primarily the present, which is the unknown.

DAVID BOHM, "FREEDOM AND THE VALUE OF
THE INDIVIDUAL" FROM *THE ESSENTIAL DAVID BOHM*

Keeping It Simple

The next step is to actively become more and more aware of yourself—what is really happening and what you really want in the moment. From this place of presence, the oceanic potentiality of each situation emerges and meaning can be made. Here's the thing—the problem may seem big and complex (and actually may be) but the solution should be quite simple.

Life as a meaning maker gives you the authority and ability to give up the past and its problems and to find simple solutions in the present moment. (See "Say Yes to the Big Idea" on page 181.) We learn to distinguish between what we think is going on and what are the real possibilities of what can happen. This brings to mind the pithy phrase that reappeared in the 2012 movie *The Best Exotic Marigold Hotel* when Sonny says, "Everything will be all right in the end . . . if it's not all right, then it's not yet the end." Experience reveals a similar truth in our responses to life situations: if the solution is complex and confusing, it isn't the right solution.

> *With thoughts you pave a path . . . so what are your thoughts?*
>
> GESHE TENZIN DORJE, TIBETAN BUDDHIST
> MONK AND TEACHER, DEER PARK BUDDHIST CENTER

An Exploration into Presence

Give yourself at least ten days to practice this exercise, which encourages you to become more aware of yourself, including your feelings (both emotionally and physically), your thoughts, and assumptions in any given moment. You start here with a simple investigation into your experiences and what you genuinely want. During the day, practice taking nice deep breaths. Use the breath to help bring you in to the present moment. And from this awareness ask these questions:

+ "What am I thinking right now?" Then take note of what is getting your attention. Just notice. Don't go on a search or extend the thought with a story line. Simply notice your prominent thoughts.

✦ "What am I feeling right now?" Notice the different feelings and sensations that are present at this moment. Start with your body. What sensations are noticeable in the body? Then notice your emotions. What emotions are present? Again don't investigate these, just notice. Also check in with any intuitive feelings. You may notice how any of these may relate to your thoughts at the given time.

✦ "What do I want?" Keep breathing and ask, "What do I want right now?" Breathe into the belly and create room around this question. You may carry a pocket journal with you as you practice creating more space for yourself, writing down what you notice as you do this exercise. Let this practice take you where it wants to take you. Initially you will likely gain some valuable insights. Later, with these insights, you may have awareness around thought patterns and feeling sensations that accompany certain experiences. Or it may become apparent that you don't really know what you want. This will prompt you to continue to determine what it is you do want. What you are in agreement with will also begin revealing itself through such inquiry. Your thoughts and emotional content reveal your agreements. This practice prepares you by setting the groundwork for living life from your side as a meaning maker.

The Art of Wanting

The word *wanting* can hold many meanings. In some new age and Buddhist thought "wanting" gets a bad rap. For some it means we are noticing what we lack, while for others it points to being attached. But it can also mean to want what you have. For me, it is okay to want. Wanting can create an opening to be present to our experiences. And many people have lost the skill of knowing what they want. So I begin many of my classes and trainings with students asking themselves: "What do I want?"

- Do I want to discover my purpose?
- Do I want to find the love of my life?

- Do I want to live life fully in my later years?
- Do I want to forgive? Forget?
- Do I want to get my book published?
- Do I want to be happy in my body?
- Do I want recognition?
- And, what do I want from this experience?

David Whyte, poet and teacher, in his talks on creativity points to how people often create their life works from what they want but do not have—like how Jane Austen wrote of romantic love but lacked it in her life. Many poets write about what they long for. This just points to another side of wanting.

So, just as an exercise, let go of one definition or meaning of "wanting" and then, *let yourself want*. From this you can invent, recharge, or update your intentions. (See "Create an Intention to Live By" on page 196.) To want can mean to open up to your heart's desire, to follow your bliss; it can mean you are focused on what you don't think you have, and it can point to what you are missing. It can mean all this and more. It's up to you. You are the meaning maker.

From a place of more awareness and curiosity you can wake up to more of life's offerings. This process of awakening the meaning maker acknowledges that you will find your own Bodhi tree,* discover truth for yourself, and awaken to your own potential. Invest, as the Buddha did or as I believe Eleanor Roosevelt did, sincerely and deliberately in your own personal awakening. When you do, remarkable things happen—you awaken to all the potential available to you and in you. Ideally you have at this point given up the search for meaning as the fundamental motivation to moving forward and are step-by-step becoming your own meaning maker. (That's the purpose of each technique in this book.) We are ending our search for meaning and becoming conscious meaning makers through our spiritual practices and creativity.

---

*The Bodhi tree is the sacred fig tree that the historical Buddha, Siddartha Gautama, sat under and achieved enlightenment.

Just so, when I offer practices or journaling prompts know that there is not a wrong way to make meaning with them. Where the practices and prompts in this book take you is where you allow or choose for them to take you. This makes life more interactive and conversational. This way we are open to new meaning or to understanding others' meanings while valuing our own.

Ideally we always put our own original twist on things.

But It's Complicated

> The centipede was happy, quite!
> Until a toad in fun asked,
> "Pray which leg goes after which?"
> This worked his mind to such a pitch
> He lay distracted in a ditch,
> Considering how to run.
>
> ZEN POEM (AUTHOR MEMORIZED FROM CHILDHOOD)

I want us to investigate how we get overwhelmed and can find it difficult to make meaning when life just gives us too many lemons to make lemonade with. It is so easy to think ourselves into distraction. We can gobble up a lot of energy trying to figure out the one "right" way to do things. We can forget what we know when we focus too much on which leg goes after which, and remain stuck in the ditch of our lives. We can keep asking, What *should* I do here? instead of just taking the next step.

As it is, we have numerous ways to work ourselves into a pitch. Besides, life *can* be complicated. It's what we do with the complexities and complications that will in large part determine the direction of our lives.

As an example, while engaged in writing a novel, I discovered the plot was getting more and more complex. I went in search of some help in how-to books and quickly felt like the centipede being stopped in the natural flow of my writing. Which word goes after which? The jargon for writers can be as dense and labyrinthine as I find in my Buddhist studies.

So what is a writer to do? What is the student of Buddhism or yoga, or any meaning maker to do when the seas get rough and the way to success seems complicated and maybe even beyond our reach? First take a deep long breath, one that allows for a nice sigh on the exhale. Then let go of the rules and "supposed to dos." Don't burn the sacred texts or writing books. Just set them aside and breathe. Now, move; *take the next step.* Walk if you are a centipede; let the wisdom of your body do what it knows to do. If you are a writer, write. If you are confused by some of your spiritual practices, wrestle with them through personal inquiry or go for a long walk. Let go of the rules of meditation, and meditate. Listen to your questions. Of course, we want to do things in a way that reaps the most benefits, so quality instruction can greatly assist us in our own personal investigation and journey. We can look to those who have gone before us and have succeeded. But too much instruction will work against you. Especially inhibitive are the instructions that come with a solid plan for you—a clear distinction between good and bad, right and wrong. Such distinctions we each must make for ourselves.

The spiritual journeyer and writer are meant to discover this world for themselves. This is the path of the meaning maker. When we are too focused on the rules of writing or the doctrine within our spiritual practices or what the instructions are, we lose our chance to discover our own writer's voice, or in the case of a spiritual life, to truly be present for this most amazing journey of discovery we are on.

I do rely on masters of writing and Buddhism. I study writing techniques and Buddhist philosophy nearly every day. I let the wisdom and information drop down into me like the rain into ready soil. Then I go about my day. When things get complicated in writing my novel or in my spiritual practice or in my life in general, I trust that the wisdom will bloom from my having nurtured the soil. When things get really complicated I rely on the basics of the writer's or Buddhist's life. In my novel everything returns to its theme, the core plot of my story. If what I am writing doesn't link directly back to my book's story, it can be cut out. In my spiritual practice I can always rely on meditation and living an intentional life. I don't get all stressed out and stopped by worrying about whether I am doing something right or wrong, or whether I am following the teachings exactly. I trust that the teachings are taking root in me and will develop in me as I continue to study, practice, and, just as importantly, explore and discover.

Rely on the naturalness of life. Let go of the "right and wrong," the dogma, or someone else's way (no matter how successful they were) and walk your own life. Write your own story. Paint in your own way. Everything you study and explore will take root and bloom in your life.

> *Out beyond ideas of right doing and wrong doing*
> *There is a field*
> *I will meet you there.*
>
> RUMI, THIRTEENTH-CENTURY PERSIAN POET

Be the First Responder

Whenever my husband, Bill (a wildlife biologist), found me distracted in the ditch, like the poor centipede, he asked me, "What did the first person who encountered this come up with?" There are guidelines, laws, jargon, rules, instructions, programs, and processes for every known pursuit. Someone had to come up with the original idea. Someone was the first responder. He suggested that I act like the first person that encountered this present challenge or idea. Now I pass this recommendation on to you when you find yourself doubting your abilities to move forward. Give yourself permission to explore the possibilities instead of relying on someone else's formula. Imagine yourself as being the first one to encounter this question or dynamic. Then go about responding to it.

Here's another analogy that works when you find yourself in some ditch: compare your creative life or spiritual practice to putting your pants on each morning. Most of us had help with the basics early on because we couldn't do it for ourselves. But we quickly picked up on how to dress ourselves. Once we figured it out we wanted to show how we could do it without help. It felt good to dress ourselves, even though we may have put our pants on backwards or worn plaid with polka dots. It felt good, and it didn't take much thought on our part to put our pants on. This can continue to be true. As you study the basics of your particular creative pursuit, you will be empowered by your natural ability to simply do the work. In your spiritual practices you will be rewarded through your resulting direct experiences with a spiritual concept you have studied. These uplifting experiences rely on you "putting on your pants" yourself and taking the next step without overthinking it.

Just do what comes naturally.

> *There is no place in this new kind of physics both for the field and matter, for the field is the only reality.*
>
> ALBERT EINSTEIN

Awakening to the *I Am That*

> *As long as we live in the misperception of being a separate entity, we encounter frustration, confusion, difficulties, and turmoil.*
>
> KEN MCLEOD, *WAKE UP TO YOUR LIFE*

Even with so many spiritual, philosophical, and scientific axioms pointing to our "belonging" we tend to operate primarily in the big lie that keeps us scared, doubtful, and lonely—the agreement that we are somehow separate from the rest of life, that we are outsiders or superior and do not intimately belong *mutually* within the web of existence. The original sin in the Garden of Eden story was when Adam and Eve bit the apple, which caused them to see themselves as separate from God. Prior to eating the apple, they had simply experienced the beauty and simplicity of belonging in the Garden of Eden. Once they bit into the apple, they became aware of feeling separate.

This is the paradox of consciousness—we become more aware and, with this awareness, our feelings of separation become known to us. However (and this is where the paradox lies), through the transformation of our consciousness the truth is revealed to us: we are not separate.

When Adam and Eve sensed their differences, they felt a need to cover up with fig leaves. When we experience ourselves as separate from natural phenomena, from each other, and from ourselves, we tend to "cover up" with the false self. The false self is made up of our pain stories and outdated myths and underlying assumptions, agreements, and beliefs that are linked to our past.

To help heal the separation, ask yourself, "Who or what do I feel separated from?" Take the time throughout the day to notice feelings of separation or isolation. Look into times when you feel lonely, anxious, worried, depressed, confused, defensive, misunderstood, and frustrated—there you will find a point of separation. Since our sense of separation is held in the mind through our perceptions, we hold the power to transform and heal all that separates us. Thought transformation is the central tool of the meaning maker.

When we recognize that everything is sacred, that *tat tvam asi* (a Sanskrit sentence that means "thou art that"), then we will always behave as if we are walking among the holy and on sacred ground. We make contact with our own holiness and recognize it as such. *Mitakuye oyasin* in Lakota is translated as "all my relations," pointing to how we are all related to and dependent on everything that is alive. We are all part of the Tao (unifying principle) and Brahman (ultimate reality). *Ehyeh* in Hebrew is a name for God and translates into "I am," or "I shall be." In the yogic tradition "I am that" is the *so ham* mantra, believed to be seven thousand years old and passed down from the historical Shiva. In Tibetan Buddhist practice the *hung* mantra, which is considered a seed syllable of wisdom, for me represents the wisdom of our oneness. Each of these mantras holds the vibrational message of belonging. And from this belonging so much more is possible than from a place of separation. My realization of *I am that* came to me before I knew anything about the "I am that" mantra—a story I share in depth in my book, *Wheel of Initiation*. This is important to share, because this type of personal spiritual insight and direct experience happens to us all. The reality of *I am that* is present in your life, right now.

Here is a simple meditation from one of my teachers, A'cha'rya Jina'neshvar (James Powell).

I Am More Than My Body

Close your eyes. Take a moment and notice your breath, the natural flow of the inhalation and exhalation. Now, from that place where you are witnessing your breath, notice the experience of your body—its sensations, its form. Appreciate for a few moments all that your body does for you. As you are aware of your body, silently say to yourself, "I have a body, but I am more than my body." Repeat this a number of times and really feel how your I is more than the body.

Now be aware of your emotional body, noticing how the range of your emotions colors your life. Appreciate the varieties of emotions you experience and what they do for you. And now say to yourself silently, "I have emotions, but I (and really feel the consciousness of I) am more than my emotions." Repeat this until you feel the meaning of the I as being more than the emotions.

Now be aware of your mental body, and appreciate its ability to solve problems and help you navigate your life. Now say to yourself, "I have a mind, but I am more than my mind." Again, repeat and experience the I as being deeper and greater than the thinking mind. Thoughts will come into your awareness, but just simply note them and return to feeling that I. You can even say to yourself, "I am more than these thoughts."

After some experience of this I feeling, affirm to yourself, "I am." Do this a few times and then affirm, "I am pure being." "I am that."

Stay with this for a while. Whenever you become aware of the mind drifting, gently pull it back to the pronouncement, remembering to experience the statement in your body. If you like, you can coordinate the declaration with your breath, such as I am on the inhalation and that on the exhalation. If you have a mantra, experience the vibration and consciousness of your mantra from this place of feeling I am. Continue until you are ready to come out of your inner being; then, after your eyes are open, look at the sacredness of that, which is all around you, with new eyes.

Ending this state of ignorance may then open a new possibility for the mind to be creative at its own level. When it does this, it is still participating in the universal creativity, but now it is realizing its proper potential.

DAVID BOHM, "FREEDOM AND THE VALUE OF THE INDIVIDUAL" FROM *THE ESSENTIAL DAVID BOHM*

I Am This and I Am That

When living life from our side, we understand *Thou art that* to mean "I am that." Whatever we say "I am that" to holds a strong influence on our experience. Too often we can *feel* apart from our creativity, our sense of purpose. Every day, we struggle because of our sense of separation and alienation. We tend to focus on our differences. This would be like the drop of water in the ocean saying "I am different from the ocean." Wherever we insist on pushing our differences on others we feel the separation. We name this separation resistance, laziness, loneliness, depression, anxiety, or some kind of lack in ourselves. Then we claim these as *who we are*—I am resistant, I am lazy, I am lonely, I am anxious, I am stupid, I am unappreciated, I am unworthy, I am alone, and so forth.

Meaning makers understand that everything and everyone is part of "the field," as Einstein states. We are always part of the ocean. We want to be conscious of what we say *I am that* to so we can experience this truth of belonging. The mind becomes our ally when we are conscious of what we say *I am that* to. When we consistently align our *I am*'s to something uplifting and meaningful this widens the field and expands our possibilities. Whatever we consistently say "I am that" to is expressed through our actions and becomes manifest. We become more receptive and open to others who once seemed less approachable to us. We discover how we fit everywhere rather than limiting ourselves to one group. Everyone and everything becomes part of our field to explore.

Personalizing the I Am

As meaning makers we claim our true inheritances through our personalized *I am*s. We participate in this ever-changing and dynamic world, knowing our past influences us while becoming more and more active within the present moment. We each in our own way make the whole possible. We can start from an oceanic perspective of knowing we are part of the whole and then give ourselves full permission to express our part within the whole. We open ourselves up to the awe and wonder of this universe where we *do* belong and where we know we belong because we see clearly how it is within us as well as without.

Each drop of water is inherently and equally valuable to the whole of the ocean. So your particular drop of water may carry the nutrient essential for a particular red coral to exist. We each belong and add to the whole that is unique but not remotely separate. Your unique and personalized version of the *I am* is how you claim your spiritual inheritance, which is within you at conception and belongs to the creative movement of the universe.

We claim our spiritual and creative inheritances in two ways—through meditation practices where we make contact with the universal *that* of our spiritual source and through the daily practice of identifying and expressing the personal *I am* in each context we find ourselves. In meditation practices we claim our natural inheritance through recitation of *I am that* mantras; such as, I am that greater, ideal self.

Guru Yoga (or Becoming "That")

Guru yoga has benefited practitioners for thousands of years and is a fundamental practice within Buddhist and yogic traditions, including the indigenous shamanic practices of Tibetan Bön. The Sufis say, "There are as many paths to god as there are breaths. Every path is an ideal, and everyone has an ideal." In guru yoga you identify with a spiritual or ethical ideal. This ideal gives you something to resonate with through meditation. The meditation brings your ideal into your mind's view. As a basic guru meditation you can visualize enlightened beings or teachers to which you hold an affinity. Guru yoga can be understood as an invocation. Here you invoke the image and ideals of an enlightened being or spiritual ally. You then "become one" with this energy or being through this meditation. If you hold no belief in a deity, this practice at its core is a great mind-training exercise that has you hold your attention on an ideal.

Becoming That

Begin with a few minutes of quieting yourself, closing your eyes and resting your attention on the physical sensation of your breath. Then from your heart invoke in front of you the embodiment or expression of an enlightened being. Trust that this being is in front of you and request from your heart that it help you. Ask this being to fill you up with its wisdom, love, and compassion, or any qualities that would benefit and uplift you. Understand this being as an embodiment of these qualities.

Next, merge with the energy of this being by imagining that it sends you light from its heart into yours, purifying any negativity. Once the light expels negativity it begins to fill you up with the enlightened energy of the being you have invoked. (Just breathe, imagine, and allow . . .) Begin to completely merge with the enlightened being so that you become one. There is now no separation between you and your being or ally, your ideal. Enjoy this energy by sitting in meditation for a while and focusing your attention on the breath, or repeating "I am that," tat tvam asi. Know that you are this enlightened being. You have bridged the illusion of separation. Touch your own inherent enlightened self.

In our daily lives we may make claim as an accomplished poet, a conscious parent, or a master gardener by aligning with the ideal of each. To make these claims real we need to first have an understanding of what they mean for us to "be that." What does it mean to be a poet? What is the ideal? What does it mean to be a conscious parent or master gardener? (See "Profound Awakening through Inquiry Meditation" on page 39.) Then we create intentions and take steps associated with these declarations. We don't just passively say, "I am a bodhisattva," or, "I am a parent. I am a spouse." We go about investigating, understanding, and living by what this means to us. (Refer to chapter 5.) The "I am" statement becomes "I am the one who . . . ."

In our becoming *that,* we emancipate ourselves from our fears and limitations because everything is material to work with as we consciously choose who we are in a given situation instead of relying on outside circumstances to determine our experience for us. We can always be investigating who we truly are or want to be in a given situation. We can make the claim of *I am that*. This inquiry and understanding of who we choose to be is then followed up with the self-determination to make meaning of either restrictive or beneficial situations.

We discover who we truly are in the *act* of making meaning.

Living the Answer

We can *live ourselves into the answer,* as Rainer Maria Rilke, Austrian poet and novelist, pointed out. He too mentions how we must give up the search for answers to have the answers. When living from the zero point we make meaning with this question of who am I every day, in all situations, consciously and deliberately. Not who was I, or who do others think I am, or who should I be, or even who have I become? Interestingly enough, this is not even the question of who do I feel I am? We live instead, who am I today, in this moment. The question becomes: *Who do I want to be?* The living answer is: *Who do I choose to be?* Asking the question and living the answer offers us the spiritual experience we desire, the door out or into the next room, a way to manifest our dreams.

We can wake each morning and realize that once again we have an opportunity to ask the questions: Who do I want to be this day? Who do I want to be with this person? Each day is also then an opportunity to live ourselves into the answer: Who do I *choose* to be today? Who do I *choose* to be in this situation? Living these questions gives us the ability to begin again at any point in our lives and to revitalize our relationships and communities.

Begin by bringing these questions to mind during the day and during times of reflection: Who do I want to be? Who do I choose to be? Become more aware of your experience by gently asking and living these questions. Such a daily practice loosens the grip of our negative or limiting perspectives and opens us up to our larger potential. We become less reactive and impulsive because we are living from this zero point and giving ourselves more opportunity. In each given moment there is an affirmative *I am* to awaken to and live.

Don't dissipate the energy of this inquiry of *who do I want to be and who do I choose to be?* Then your response will naturally be in the living of *I am that.* Too often we drain the energy out of such personal realizations by either putting it off somehow (this is who I am but I will get to it later), or we "talk the talk" and never put action to our words. Or we simply keep searching for meaning outside of ourselves. (Remember, living the question is not searching for the answer.) *In order to generate any desired change, there must be an action accompanying any realization.* I have found many spiritual seekers greatly disappointed following a powerful retreat where integration of what they learned was sorely lacking. They were truly inspired but had no valid action plan, no commitment to live life from their side once they returned to their daily lives. Evidence shows that we tend to bounce back to our habitual ways. And we all know how challenging it can be to transform our lives against the tide of others and our own habitual states.

We tend to keep our realizations captive when the outside circumstances don't seem to support our new insights or our intentions. Our inner desires are not matching our outer experiences because we have not crossed the bridge from insight to action. We tend to let a bad job or a depressed economy or the losses of our lives determine our next step (or stop us from taking action). So it is pertinent that we ask ourselves who am I in *this* job, who do I want to be in *this* circumstance. We want the ability to make meaning in times of lack as well as in times of plenty.

> *the truth includes all, and is compact just as much as space is compact,*
>
> . . . .
>
> *And henceforth I will go celebrate any thing I see or am,*
> *And sing and laugh and deny nothing.*
>
> WALT WHITMAN, EXCERPT FROM "ALL IS TRUTH"

Everyday Awareness to *This*

We often are told that we are what we do. However, more often than not we are doing one thing while thinking about something else, mired down by distractions. Try this simple awareness technique:

✦ Say to yourself "I am . . . driving the car." Then bring your attention to the physical sensations of holding on to the steering wheel, sitting in the seat, and gazing out the front window.

✦ Become conscious of the breath, and bring yourself fully into experiencing this activity, be it driving, eating, or gardening. Use the awareness of the breath as a leash into the present experience of driving, or eating or gardening. Practice this "everyday awareness," to further generate wakefulness in your routines.

To express an affirmative *I am that,* we want to be able to examine what is and isn't working in our lives. Confucius teaches us that the more "superior" person must do personal inquiry in order to cultivate such qualities as compassion, wisdom, and happiness. He reminds us that in order to experience happiness and contentment, we must know the makings of the internal landscape of such qualities and how we might be getting in our own way when not experiencing these qualities. Resonating with Confucius, the Chinese philosopher Mencius says,

> *If one loves others, and they do not respond in the same*
> *way,*
> *one should turn inward and examine one's own love.*
> *If one greets others politely, and they do not return*
> *politeness,*
> *one should turn inward and examine one's own*
> *politeness.*
> *When one does not realize what one desires,*
> *one must turn inward and examine oneself in every*
> *point.*

In this new age mind-set of manifestation, success, and abundance, we often lose sight of what actually results in lasting success and authentic satisfaction. Above, Mencius points to how when the outside world doesn't match up with our expectations we need to examine our side of the equation (as the zero point agreement encourages). Therefore, disappointing situations are an invitation to examine how we might improve a situation through inquiry into our selves. We are the ones planting seeds of either discontent or satisfaction.

Revitalizing the *I Am*

This simple exercise can transform a relationship or role you have in any environment or group. You can use it to consciously engage in a more dynamic relationship with your aspirations and your chosen role in a given environment.

✦ Consider any group or clan you are a part of, be it a family, a spiritual Sangha, or a community alliance. Give yourself some time to contemplate who you are and who you want to be in this context. Do the two statements match—is who you are who you want to be? How do others likely experience or see you in this clan?

✦ Begin by making a conscious choice of who you want to be in this group. Then, give yourself a title within this clan (be it a temporary one for a given project or a more solid one that has no known time limit). Have this title reflect your greatest self and all its aspirations. I am the . . . (fill in the rest). Hold this in your mind when in this particular group or setting. I recommend you use the adjective *the* rather than *a* in the proclamation. This holds a stronger intention. It is possible that there will be more than one person claiming to be the poet, the artist, the compassionate one. The intention is to make this denotation clear to yourself, so that you can live it from your side.

✦ To further explore who you are in a given dynamic use this journal writing exercise. Bring to mind the setting or relationship you are revitalizing. Then at the top of the page write, "I am the (bodhisattva, teacher, one) who . . . ." Repeat this phrase instead of stopping your pen. Don't take time to "think"; instead allow for your inner wisdom to emerge. Fill up at least one page.

✦ Once you have determined your *I am,* continue to hold it in your mind during all of your interactions with the group or within that given environment.

In family and relational systems there can be confusion and distractions about who we are to one another. Decades ago, when I worked with families of those with persistent mental illness (resulting in the

eight-stage healing process and book *Hidden Victims, Hidden Healers*)
I noticed how role confusion disrupted the relationships further. Many
siblings of those with mental illness often acted like their sibling's parent. Adult children of those with mental illness often became the parent of their parent early on. I recommended that they allow themselves
to be the child in the relationship where they were the child and the
sibling to their sibling.

Personally, I stopped being my older brother's "mother" and allowed
for us to be siblings. (One of my brothers has schizophrenia.) This was
far more respectful and enjoyable. The stress of mental illness may be
present, but our sibling relationship is still intact to this day. He is still
my older brother. So, in this relationship, "I am the younger sister."
After a couple of years of being *that*—the younger sister—I no longer
had to hold it in my mind. It became a natural expression of our relationship. Interestingly enough, there was societal and family pressure to
remain being his "parent," or "social worker," but I found I could help
him better as a sister. You will find this true for you too. As you consciously choose from your side who and what you are in the world, to
others, it may shake things up for others, but it will strengthen relationships. Some will want you to remain in your old identification. Some
will be afraid of what this might mean for them. Now, these choices are
not necessarily announced to others (typically not). More important is
that you live by who and what you choose to be.

"Angie" revitalized herself and a significant relationship through
this practice. In her own words: "I felt shrunken and dumb in this one
friendship. It got so old I really wasn't sure if it was me or her. Julie suggested I use the zero point agreement and do what I could from my side.
I started with what I really wanted from this friendship. Did I even want
the friendship? I wanted to give it a try so I practiced naming who I am
in the relationship. I realized that up to then I had been a twelve-year-old
girl in a woman's body; a dumb twelve years old at that. Not just in this
relationship but at work too. I felt dumb most of the time. So, I decided
'I am the Ph.D.' (I actually do have a Ph.D.) I am the Ph.D. of friends. I
am the Ph.D. of knowledge. I am the Ph.D. of compassion. I wrote pages
in my journal of how I am the Ph. D. Well, it worked. Not overnight or

anything, but I kept with it because I found out that saying to myself I am a dumb twelve-year-old wasn't working for me. It took some time on my part to really feel myself as the doctor of compassion and wisdom, to be the Ph.D. My friend didn't seem to notice much change in me at first anyway. Julie warned me that it can take years for some people to experience you differently. As she said, 'we tend to hold each other captive in our minds.' But my friend did finally seem to notice a change in me. At first she commented several times on my losing weight (I hadn't) but then said, 'I just love your view of things, Angie, you are so brilliant.' I did experience some changes at work too, and the best part is how much more energy I have now. I also came to understand that others are living life from their side and I can't make anyone think or feel a certain way about me."

Done collectively within a group setting, "Revitalizing the *I Am*" can identify what each member is to the group and go about honoring each title within the context of the group. For example, a woman who attended my Spiritual Journaling class came in with a history of neglect and abuse within the smaller context of her family and the larger one of the community. She came into the class at the age of sixty-five. She was an unrecognized Native American elder. In identifying and establishing herself in this tribe (of the class), her *I am* was, "I am the Native American Elder." This gave her a strong sense of purpose and role within this clan and allowed others to respect and honor this in her as well. She went on to announce, "I am the elder who shares her stories." This can be done in an organizational setting where each person claims some authority in their announcements of, "I am the . . . who . . ." Each group member can consider what this means for the individual and what the titles mean for each other in relationship to the others and the group.

Innovation in organizations is being seen as more and more necessary. We want to generate more energy, integrity, and creativity in all of our institutions. I have worked with several organizations where this was one of the exercises used to revitalize the creative energy within the system. Again, this appreciation of the individual makes for a healthy and dynamic collective.

As we revitalize the *I am* in our many circles by claiming our place among others we then come to more fully participate in the revitalization of the world.

Buddha and the Bodhi Tree

The Buddha found his Bodhi tree through personal discovery. He incorporated and practiced what he was offered by other teachers, coming to the realization that awakening can only be accomplished personally, from our own side. While sitting under a fig tree he reached a state of *bodhi,* which means "wakefulness." For each of us to awaken we must rely on our own journey and sit under our own Bodhi tree.

Your Journey to the Bodhi Tree

The journey to the Bodhi tree, to your own personal mountaintop, or to the creation of your own *Mona Lisa* can be achieved by engaging in these four practices.

+ Listening (taking in teachings, holding intimate conversations with life and the natural world)
+ Contemplating spiritual, ethical, and creative teachings and principles
+ Acquiring some personal understanding of what we are studying
+ Meditating (both calm abiding and analytical)

The mountain or Bodhi tree is there, but it's up to us to make the journey. This is about claiming our own wisdom and creativity by not accepting any teachings or instructions at face value; we should thoroughly analyze what is presented to us as a teaching on how to live our lives. To do this we must use our investigative powers in our daily lives and in our meditation practices. This is living life as the scientist investigating truth for ourselves. These four practices of listening, contemplation, understanding, and meditation bring forth our creative and spiritual inheritances and are presented in the various techniques throughout this book.

Profound Awakening
through Inquiry Meditation

These two capacities—to analyze and to remain focused—
are essential to seeing yourself as you really are.

His Holiness the Dalai Lama,
How to See Yourself as You Really Are

Inquiry practice is your way to sit under the Bodhi tree of awakening. The Dalai Lama often writes about and advocates for analytic meditation. What he calls analytic meditation is what I refer to as *inquiry meditation*. "In analytic meditation, one brings about inner change through systematic investigation and analysis. In this way we can properly use our human intelligence, our capacity for reason and analysis, to contribute to our happiness and satisfaction." Dalai Lama, *Stages of Meditation*. This may sound complicated—all this analysis, which is the reason I like to call it inquiry meditation or practice. This type of meditation not only brings illumination to spiritual truths but also can unlock the doors to creative and scientific truths.

Einstein is often quoted when it comes to analytical meditation because this type of concentration led to his theory of relativity. His investigation and discovery of relativity (through his meditation) further revealed to him the fundamental truth of how everything is connected to everything else. Inquiry meditation has the potentiality of transforming our minds and lives in truly profound and lasting ways. This is a core practice of the meaning maker as it helps you discover truth and meaning for yourself while still borrowing from the wisdom of ancient and contemporary teachers.

Generally speaking, Buddhist meditation is of two types—analytical and concentrative. In analytical meditation, we use our powers of meaning making to examine teachings, assumptions, beliefs, and practices to determine for ourselves whether or not they are true, to eradicate uncertainty, and to come to an unshakable connection to our creative spirit and the creative pulse of the world. In concentrative (mindfulness) meditation we learn to focus single-mindedly on a mental object until our mind can rest effortlessly on that object for longer and longer periods of time.

Among the many benefits of inquiry meditation is improving your thinking (just focusing on the breath alone doesn't result in a better state of mind). But you must be able to stay focused on a concept or idea long enough to harvest some real insight, so being able to concentrate is essential. You first tame the mind and then train the mind. We tame the mind through mindfulness and train the mind through inquiry meditation and other cognitive techniques. So before you begin your inquiry meditation you will want to have the foundation of a mindfulness practice, which is also called calm abiding. The main objective of mindfulness is to develop single-pointed concentration. This gives you the ability to place your attention on an object during meditation and tames the mind to be attentive outside of the meditation practice as well.

The Thread of Attention

> The essence of the Buddha's teaching is to turn our undisciplined mind into a disciplined mind.
>
> His Holiness the fourteenth Dalai Lama,
> "Je Tsongkhapa's Experiential Teachings"
> (lecture, Madison, Wisconsin, May 2–4, 2007)

The Dalai Lama went on to point out in this teaching how the undisciplined mind is the root of all suffering. He speaks of spirituality as being about thought transformation, or "freedom found through the discipline of the mind." In all the teachings of his that I have attended, he focuses on the supreme vehicle, which is mindfulness. The Bible points to this supreme vehicle as well: "Be still and know that I am God." We can understand this to mean to be still and know *I am that.*

> Quantum physics suggests that by redirecting our focus—where we place our attention—we bring a new course of events into focus while at the same time releasing an existing course of events that may no longer serve you.
>
> Sol Luckman, Conscious Healing:
> Book One on the Regenetics Method

An undisciplined mind, an inability to stay focused, makes you vulnerable to internal and external distractions. These distractions can ultimately lead you away from your creative and spiritual intentions. Calm abiding gives you the ability to place your energy and attention where you choose. This is what you must pursue. Nothing else in your spiritual or creative life compares with your ability to place your heart and mind where you desire. Cultivating attention is really about letting go. Instead of holding on to the past, or the negative thought pattern, or the outside drama, we can let it go. This teaches us to be the cause rather than the effect of our lives. We are not so bounced around by outer conditions. We are then able to transform our thoughts and the world around us because of our ability to place our attention where we choose. This helps us make conscious choices that result in more favorable outcomes, because whatever we give our attention to *becomes*. Mindfulness practices are powerful antidotes to any flavor of resistance that we experience in our creative and spiritual pursuits. Many who seek consultation with me want to know their calling or know how to follow a calling when they already know what it is. Many ask, "What stops me from following my heart and doing what I love?" Every time I receive a flyer or read an ad in a magazine on an upcoming conference, there is typically a workshop on finding your purpose.

How is it we don't know our calling? How is it we don't get down to following our bliss, as Joseph Campbell would say? How much of our money, time, and thought goes into trying to figure out what our purpose in life is? Everyone knows their calling—it boils down to listening to the call and following it, rather than getting lost in all the distractions. Meditation will make it possible to fulfill your promises to self, to others, and to your vocation because it makes "showing up" easier.

Evidence on the benefits of meditation is abundant and well established. Being able to focus your attention, to rest your awareness in the breath, brings you all sorts of rewards. Because there are many methods of cultivating attention, developing mindfulness, and transforming the mind through meditation, use these research-based parameters as a way to establish your own personalized practice.

1. You must be actively cultivating attention while meditating, not just reciting a mantra or simply sitting on the cushion and breathing.
2. The sitting practice includes an observation of impermanence. For example, you meditate on the breath, letting each one go. You let go of thoughts and return to the breath or the mantra. (In your inquiry meditation below, you may further meditate on the aspects of impermanence.)
3. You sit through the rising and falling of different emotional, psychological, and physical states as you return your attention to the object of your meditation (the mantra or the breath); thus learning not to be so easily distracted.
4. The calm abiding meditation is understood as a means to tame the mind; to still the mind and prepare it for mind transformation (mind training). You can't train a wild animal until you have quieted it down enough. (It's hard to catch a flying bird.)
5. There are no preferences or attachments to certain states, such as bliss, clarity, or insightfulness. Such forcing or attachment to these states actually interferes with experiencing them.

When I was introduced and initiated into my first meditation practice at the age of sixteen (transcendental meditation), I would say it saved my life. When I began meditating with a mantra, I mostly meditated by myself. What I sought was inner and outer peace. Later in life, when I was trained in vipassana meditation, my teacher at the time, Shinzen Young, would remind us, "Don't prefer. No preference, just presence." What a wonderful tool to take with me in the world—the ability to let go of preferences! When we are attached to preferences and how things *should* be, we are no longer in calm abiding. This does not mean I don't have preferences and wants. What it means is that I have an expanded capacity to let go of what I think should be happening and embrace what is actually taking place. This allows me to work with what I actually have in the moment rather than what I wish was going on.

Be aware that all your internal issues are likely to arise on your meditation cushion and that this is also a place of transformation as you meditate "holding your seat," sitting still and being attentive—practicing attention no matter what arises. So, for example, any impatience you feel during your sitting meditation is an opportunity to practice calm abiding with this particular emotional state. This state then may not come up as often off the cushion, or if it does you have the ability not to let it distract you from your creative process.

Establishing a Practice

To make meaning from your life, to live the *I am*, you must put everything else aside to give time to a meditation practice. Learn to focus and calm the mind and contemplate, and the rest of your life will come into alignment with your creative intentions (no matter what the circumstances). A teacher once shared this story of a Tibetan monk who was imprisoned around the time the Dalai Lama was exiled to India. This monk spent most of his adult life in prison, undergoing abuse and torture by the Chinese government. On his release, he met up with his friend the Dalai Lama.

"Each day I was quite afraid," he said.

The Dalai Lama listened.

"I was not afraid for my life. Every day I feared that I would lose my compassion for the Chinese."

Any time you are feeling disconnected, defeated, afraid, or anxious, find the thread back to the moment and be willing to do whatever it takes to keep hold of your compassion, your humanity. Just for now. Just for this moment.

Only through various practices of cultivating attention *and* transforming our thoughts can true, lasting freedom and happiness abide. Only then can we give ourselves over to our creative lives. With the ability to focus we have an essential inner navigational tool that allows us to participate in our life regardless of the outward circumstances. Such meditation practices fulfill the promise to self, so then we can fulfill the promises to others and to our vocations. (See "Fulfillment of the Three Original Promises" on page 172.)

The transformative results of a mindfulness meditation are profound and lasting because you apply key practices for lasting happiness just by sitting still for fifteen minutes a day. In the practice you first focus on the breath, thus learning to tame your mind. Then you find that your mind wanders (which it often does), and you bring your awareness to this point of distraction. This gives you the ability to bring your awareness to everything (even your distractions) because everything becomes part of your meditation practice. Then, you experience the profound wisdom of letting go as you let go of the distraction and do not follow a story line around it. You gently and lovingly return to the breath as your focus point. This has you cultivating equanimity with yourself and strengthens your willingness and enthusiasm to return to something (in this case the breath). There is so much that is achieved when meditating in this way!

> *By knowing how to succeed in tranquil repose,*
> *one is able to obtain careful deliberation.*
> *By knowing how to obtain careful deliberation,*
> *one is able to harvest what he really wants to pursue.*
> SHANTIDEVA, EIGHTH-CENTURY BUDDHIST SCHOLAR

Calm Abiding Meditation

Simply begin with a fifteen-minute morning meditation of sitting and watching the breath. If you already engage in regular morning meditation, consider adding five minutes to your already existing time. Begin with fifteen minutes until you can calmly abide for up to thirty minutes each morning. The point is to establish a routine of daily meditation; the most challenging part will be actually showing up and taking the time to sit and meditate.

Choose a specific time each morning for meditation. Commit to show up at this time and place even if you don't believe you have time to meditate. What you will find is that once you show up and are ready, you will make the time.

+ Sit like a mountain, erect but naturally alert, not rigid. Your spine should be upright and not resting fully on the back of a chair. Neither should you slouch if you are on a cushion. If you can, sit on a zafu (a meditation cushion) or stool, whatever allows for an alert spine.
+ Relax your shoulders and take a couple of deep breaths into the belly. If

you like, release a few purification breaths—ahhs—on the exhalation.

+ Bring your awareness to your body, *sitting*. Bring your attention to the physical sensations of the body. Relax your awareness in the body. Notice any sensations, without judgments, that may be rising and falling in the body. Just notice.

+ As you continue to breathe naturally, choose a place in the body where you can bring your attention to the breath (either the rise and fall of the belly or, more commonly, the in-and-out of the breath through the nostrils). Let this be where your attention returns to the breath. Let the breath breathe by itself. Make no effort; just breathe. Then rest your awareness in the physical sensation of breathing. Rest your awareness there as best you can. Rest in the sensations of your body sitting, your body breathing. Then give your attention to just being— have a sense of your own presence. *Just sit, breathe, and be.* Let go of thought and expectations, just rest in the breath and the body sitting, rest in the moment of being.

+ If you find your mind wanders off, which it routinely will, first let your awareness flash on the distraction. Then gently and lovingly return your attention to your breathing. Just sitting, just breathing, just being—the three points of calm abiding. Flashing on where your mind has wandered gives you the ability to even use your distractions as a point of awareness. When you return your awareness to the physical sensations of breath, do so lovingly and compassionately. Try not to add to the thinking mind by judging your abilities or getting down on yourself if your mind wanders off. I spend much of my time in my sitting meditation *returning* my attention to my breath.

+ Use the leash of awareness to bring yourself back to just sitting, just breathing, just being. Practice compassionate action on the spot with yourself by letting go of all the mental constructions, and just rest your awareness in sitting, breathing, and being.

+ When you find yourself caught up in thoughts, you can label them by saying silently to yourself, "thinking, thinking," and bring your awareness for a moment to that point of distraction, then gently and lovingly return to the breath. When we flash our awareness on the distraction it becomes part of the meditation! And, labeling thoughts can help you realize more fully that thought is just that—thought. Otherwise you find yourself building on these thoughts and losing your experience of calm abiding. This tames and disciplines the mind, which is a strong aspiration for the meaning maker. This also prepares your mind for any of your creative pursuits.

Compassionate response to yourself as you sit in meditation greatly benefits you as you learn to be kinder with whatever arises. Do your best not to become impatient and annoyed with yourself if and when you are distracted by your thoughts. You may also get upset with yourself about being upset, and on and on the judgment goes—until you bring compassion and equanimity to it. Then, in that instant of bringing compassion to the judgmental streamline, all the layers of negative thoughts and feelings in the moment dissolve. Notice that!

You generate a lot of freedom and bring forth the inherent qualities of presence, wisdom, and love when you meditate consistently enough.

Inquiry Meditation: The Meaning Maker's Meditation

> Gain as much explanation and teaching as possible, then go cultivate the wisdom mind through analytical meditation.
>
> GESHE TENZIN DORJE

The foundation of inquiry meditation is the study and understanding of spiritual and ethical principles, but it can be used to investigate scientific, social, and creative concepts as well. As an example, I have studied and consulted the I Ching for over forty years. (See chapter 6 on the I Ching.) When I consult the I Ching, I typically contemplate one of its themes during my meditation. I investigate the concept of humility or patience, for example. The value of receiving teachings from qualified teachers cannot be overemphasized. These teachers can be in the spiritual, creative, or scientific fields. (In my book, *Wheel of Initiation* there is an appendix: "The Tao of Not Following." In it I offer a template to use when choosing a teacher or group.) We tend to suffer unnecessarily because we don't have the concentration to focus on concepts, such as on our intentions or the quality of compassion. We remain distractible from our creative and spiritual intentions because we have not tamed or trained our mind in meditation. To create a *Mona Lisa* or to awaken under the Bodhi tree, we must be able to be absorbed in the activity itself—be it meditation or painting.

> *In our meditation practice we empower our ability to stay focused on an object of wisdom.*
>
> GESHE TENZIN DORJE

You will get the most from an inquiry practice when you hold a strong effort during the meditation. If we don't meditate upon a certain subject we won't really come to understand it in a personal and authentic way. When we make meaning through such inquiry we experience personal freedom from suffering because the more we focus on such principles as compassion, creative concepts, forgiveness, or unity, for example, the more we and others benefit. Engage your mind in a particular concept and watch that concept come to life!

> *Too often we are like a frozen leaf in the ground that shakes by the wind. We can be like that leaf, not able to evolve spiritually because we are unable to focus. We are stuck in our afflictive emotions, blown about by distractions.*
>
> GESHE TENZIN DORJE

The Basics of Inquiry Meditation

We must be able to relate to what we are conducting inquiry around. If, for example, I believe that compassion is the most powerful energy available to us, how is this so? What does this mean? How does this energy look? Investigate the meaning and reasons of this particular concept. You must have some understanding of compassion or whatever concept you are investigating beforehand. Choose a topic that you have been reading about and studying over the years.

Such analytical meditation makes meaning by engaging the mind with a particular concept. In our creative and spiritual lives this helps us become familiarized to a positive concept, so choose a concept that you appreciate. The meditation may take one of many forms. It could be a simple question regarding day-to-day affairs like, what would it mean to apply forgiveness to this problem that faces me? Or, it could concern itself with a profound metaphysical query such as, what is the meaning of sacrifice? Or, it may simply involve silent deliberation on a principle such as, love your neighbor as yourself. A good inquiry to consider might be one based on your spiritual intention (see "Create an Intention to Live By" on page 196). What is the meaning behind your intention?

+ Give yourself at least fifteen minutes in a quiet place. Take a few minutes to sit in calm abiding by resting your awareness in the breath and the body sitting.
+ Then drop the particular question in your consciousness—for example: What is the meaning of dependent co-arising, or what does it mean to be generous, or to live life from your side?
+ Keep your focus on this inquiry and investigate this topic. Hold your mind to this one topic of meditation without wavering.
+ Imagine looking at the focus of your inquiry from many angles. Any time your attention may wander, bring it back to the point of inquiry.
+ You can ask more questions, as well as bring in what you have come to understand about this particular quality. If you are investigating some spiritual or philosophical concept, you may ask: What does it mean to me to accept this idea as mine?
+ Attempt to arrive at a certain feeling state, an emotional or energetic state of understanding, as you connect more with the meaning of this concept. Breathe naturally and investigate the topic as thoroughly as you can.

Just Like Einstein

This practice brings out the creative genius in each of us as we discern meaning for ourselves based on our interests of inquiry. Use this analytical practice, as Einstein did, to open up to other possibilities in your creative, scientific, or vocational pursuits. Ask yourself in meditation: What do I mean by . . . or what is meant by . . . My understanding is that Einstein started with the topic of gravity in his analytical meditation and arrived at the theory of relativity and interdependence of life. You can start with any topic and see where it leads you. And it will lead you somewhere.

Through such investigation, inquiry meditation allows us to "search for meaning" while we are *making* meaning. While you ask and investigate, *what does this mean?* you are making your own meaning. You are pulling together all the wisdom teachings and experiences you've had so far into something useful, creative, and meaningful. Most importantly, through this personal investigation you then hold a dynamic conversation with some valuable concept or practice. Such meditation practices offer you direct experiences with spiritual and philosophical concepts. Whenever you come up with meaning for yourself, there is a much deeper appreciation and understanding than if someone else came up with it for you, or if you unquestioningly accepted someone else's version. This profound practice gives us personal realizations. Recently I was doing inquiry around the quality of ethical generosity.* What makes generosity ethical? In my investigation I realized how ethical generosity diminishes my self-absorption. Now, this wisdom around ethical generosity is surely known and written about by a multitude of masters over thousands of years, but in my putting it together myself, with my own experience and teachings as a foundation, it became real. The concept of generosity became authentic and tangible.

You are developing positive states of mind through this meditation technique, but don't expect expedient results because we tend to bring to our meditation practice a long history of obstructions and distractions. When we don't get what we want soon enough we may lose the effort. Stay with this practice and you will find yourself sitting under your own Bodhi tree.

> *Under the Bodhi Tree*
> *reading*
> *about the bodhi tree*
> *last night*

---

*Ethical generosity comes from the six perfections of Buddhism, which are generosity, ethical discipline, patience, enthusiastic effort, concentration, and wisdom.

a ginko leaf
fell into my mouth dream
agape
and drooling on the pillow

a man wondered
what voices he heard
from the branches
if the monks heard them too
but no one asked
they all walked away
dust on their pants.

MOKASIYA ALAN, "BODHI TREE"

Waking Up Post-meditation

There are many ways to use inquiry practice following your sitting meditation and to use the activities in your daily life to awaken.

Among post-meditation practices, spiritual journaling can be one of the more profound and simple tools for spiritual inquiry and can be used with the other practices throughout this book.

Making Meaning through Spiritual Journaling

Writing, above all, is seeing clearly.
PETER MATTHIESSEN, *ZEN AND THE WRITING LIFE*

Spiritual journaling consists of methods for using journaling and personal inquiry to investigate our life circumstances, deepen our spiritual practices, increase our awareness, and open up to our creativity. Self-inquiry through journaling is a method used for thousands of years and is recommended as part of the treatment for depression, anxiety, eating disorders, and self-abuse (cutting). Many remarkable books, such as *A Sand County Almanac* by Aldo Leopold, come from a journal. Journaling accesses the inner teacher as well as opening us to all the creative wisdom we hold within. Journals are our field notes where we can jot down insights and observations from our day. I have been facilitating spiritual journaling classes for over twenty years and wrote a book for young adults on the topic: *Spiritual Journaling: Writing Your Way to Independence.*

Consider your journal as an outer temple, a place where you can engage the techniques and practices offered here and also document any insights and meaning you have made. Writing exercises can be practiced to increase insight and your ability to stay focused. Spiritual journaling is a universal means to access your meaning maker and a method to give yourself personal insights without the direct guidance of a group or teacher. You can investigate and ignite creative ideas through your journal entries. Take the inquiries I offer and write about them, and also carry them in your consciousness as questions. Maintain a curiosity with these questions rather than searching for answers. In other words, *live* the questions. Start with the particular writing prompt or inquiry, then let it take you where it will. The experience will be personal to each of us. And that is the point—to engage in practices that bring forth our personal insights and unique creative ideas.

When journaling, date and title each entry. That way you can find the piece in your journal that relates to what is being discussed in this book, and doing this makes it easy to find later, too.

Making Meaning through Dissension

> *Make your own Bible. Select and collect all the words and sentences that in all your readings have been to you like the blast of a trumpet.*
>
> RALPH WALDO EMERSON

We tend to hold on to our ideas while using a familiar approach to figuring things out. We tend to hang out with the same crowd, go to the same church or temple where we hear familiar and shared views. As Werner Heisenberg, a German theoretical physicist who founded quantum mechanics and the uncertainty principle, points out, don't just hang out with those who agree with you: "in the history of human thinking the most fruitful developments frequently take place at those points where two different lines of thought meet. These lines may have their roots in quite different cultural environments or different religious traditions: hence if they actually meet, that is, if they are at least so much related to each other that a real interaction can take place, then one may hope that new and interesting developments may follow."

The idea of meeting with others of different backgrounds and expertise has been used in generating innovation and enthusiasm in the corporate and business world. We also find this true at university campuses across the globe—the coming together of different disciplines results in more useful discoveries. This points to another post-meditation technique used in Tibetan Buddhist practice and in other creative settings—debating with others (especially those who hold different viewpoints). Debate for the monks and nuns of Tibet is not pure academics but allows for exploration of the meaning of spiritual concepts that have been handed down through the ages. Spiritual truth then is *personally experienced* through a process that includes debate. You can also engage in post-meditation practices by willingly exploring opposing or new ideas on your own. You can attend lectures by teachers with opposing views; or, you can take a class that teaches oil painting if you have only worked with colored pencils. Work with different ideas and mediums and discover new frontiers within your own mind, as well as the ability to develop new ideas in the world.

Finally, test out whatever is presented to you. For instance, if you find yourself questioning the validity of any of these claims and techniques I offer to you, *test them out*. Even though there is an extensive bibliography to check out, first take these ideas to the street. Ultimately each of us decides for ourselves what practices are beneficial or not by trying them out. I would give any of the techniques in this book (or elsewhere) a solid ten days of practice to adequately discern what works for you. I would also recommend that you use inquiry meditation as a tool to investigate the meaning of any principles and techniques offered in this book or elsewhere.

Baptized as a Meaning Maker

This process of beginning with our own experience and using it to verify the teachings and the teachers is quite important; one could say, in fact, that this is the only way to open us.

His Holiness the fourteenth Dalai Lama,
Essence of the Heart Sutra

I chose to be baptized at the age of thirteen, more than forty years ago. I did this with a progressive Lutheran minister as my teacher. (He is the same one I mentioned earlier who shared the story of the monk on the cliff, and who later left the ministry.) He instructed me to read and study the New Testament on my own and then asked me questions about it at our meetings. He knew I wanted to be baptized since this was not offered to me through my family, and I admit that at the time I had some concern about the afterlife if I was not baptized.

After several months of study, the minister and I got together one Saturday for my baptism. I sat in the room as he shared a few prayers and some doctrine with me. Then he got up to retrieve the holy water that I would be baptized with.

I sat in anticipation. I felt ready!

He reentered the room carrying a little bowl of water. When he saw the eager, expectant look on my face, he said to me, "It's only tap water, Julie." And then he said a few prayers over me and baptized me.

Only tap water.

Somehow, for me, this "only tap water" generated a more meaningful entrance into a new way of being than if it had been sanctified water. The threshold I passed through inside my heart was profound—I began to understand how it is all just tap water. I started to become my own meaning maker. I would stumble quite a bit along the way, but here I began with a larger map of the world, a map that showed me that we sanctify water or other objects with the meaning we consign to them.

All water can be holy water.

There is nothing but water in the holy pools. I know,
I have been swimming in them.
All the gods sculpted of wood or ivory can't say a word.
I know, I have been crying out to them.
The Sacred Books of the East are nothing but words.
I looked through their covers one day sideways.
What Kabir talks of is only what he has lived through.
If you have not lived through something, it is not true.

KABIR, INDIAN POET AND MYSTIC

2

Don't Believe
Everything You Think

THE LURE OF THE FALSE GODS

In choosing your god, you choose
your way of looking at the universe.
There are plenty of gods.
Choose yours.

The god you worship
Is the god you deserve.

JOSEPH CAMPBELL,
A JOSEPH CAMPBELL COMPANION

This is how it works:

We carry a pain story shaped by past experiences.
We then build and establish beliefs and assumptions around this
    pain story.
We become habituated to repeat the past.
We encounter something or someone.
We respond habitually to events with our pain stories and support-
    ing beliefs.
We lose confidence and we suffer.

Suffering always points to a pain story and its sustaining assumptions and beliefs.

Suffering and pain is not the same thing.

Pain may be physical, emotional, or mental.

Suffering is the added story lines, beliefs, and assumptions we add to the difficulty.

Our mind is the key player in our suffering and our freedom from suffering.

Difficulty (of any kind) without the added suffering is more workable.

We can be free of our suffering.

We can be free of our pain stories and sustaining beliefs.

We have the means to personal freedom by living life from our side as meaning makers.

But first we must name and kill off the false gods.

> *The strangest and most fantastic fact about negative emotions is that people actually worship them.*
>
> P. D. OUSPENSKY,
> RUSSIAN MYSTIC AND PHILOSOPHER

Beliefs; habitual emotional states such as disappointment, blame, and shame; our need of fame, gain, and praise; as well as our fears of loss all become godlike when they rule our experiences. When we believe in a smaller version of ourselves, or the world, the god of settling shrinks us down to a suitable size. These gods often claim to be our protectors but what they do instead is steal from us like thieves. Unfortunately, we tend to worship these states as gods through the continual sacrifices of our creative aspirations.

To Catch a Thief

> *Until you make the unconscious conscious, it will direct your life, and you will call it fate.*
>
> CARL JUNG

Once we attend to our underlying problems and issues (the thieves or false gods) we can then bring our lives more fully into alignment with our spiritual and creative intentions. I liken this to a bank where a bank teller is stealing money. The bank is losing money to a thief that works right within the walls of the bank. If the bank were to simply deposit more money into its vault, this would only give the thief more to steal and would not take care of the underlying issue. How can we expect our minds to be free when we leave a thief as teller at one (or several) of our booths? Our false gods, certain beliefs that hold a seat of power in our lives, are robbing us of our abilities to live actively and creatively. We need to identify them first, make the unconscious conscious and not jump ahead to make more deposits (of goals, projects). We must clean our inner sanctuary of false gods and make room for the creative.

Although it is necessary to first find and then name the false gods, once identified, your energy and attention would best be directed toward the antidotes. It would just be giving over more of your life to what is draining you if you were to keep your focus on the problem. Therefore, following the presentation of the various false gods, I offer up antidotes for your consideration.

A universal antidote, the foundation to all the others, is to see the thieves, each false god, as *the path*. Whatever arises in our lives can be used to awaken us further to all that is possible. Wherever you find yourself, you're always at the zero point. Everything that arises then is workable. Every situation and person who comes into your life brings along with them opportunities. This antidote gives you permission to understand that whatever comes to you is there for you to make meaning with. Whatever you have brought with you, too, is all part of the path. Life's calling is to use whatever we have been given to wake us up to our creativity and capacities as meaning makers.

The False God of Belief

If these gods have a hierarchy, the god of belief would be like Zeus. This god comes before and holds authority over all the other gods.

As Ghandi points out, our beliefs become our destiny.

Your beliefs become your thoughts,
your thoughts become your words,
your words become your actions,
your actions become your habits,
your habits become your values,
your values become your destiny.

MAHATMA GANDHI

Numerous covert beliefs that reside underground in our psyche guide us. We live by our beliefs—and what we hear and experience is filtered through our beliefs. Most of our beliefs are hidden from our ordinary, routine awareness. We don't realize (or we forget) that we are constantly responding to a belief system (made up of assumptions, agreements, and thoughts). We often fool ourselves into assuming we are in the moment, when in truth we are reacting from a set belief system that was established in the past (often in response to difficulty). Consequently, we take on a mind-set that prevents us from experiencing our own personal transformation and spiritual aptitude. This further thwarts our ability to live life from our side. The Buddhists, Toltec, Sufis, yogis, and philosophers for thousands of years have given us tools to transform our lives through our ability to change what we believe. Living life from our side will always be dependent on using our minds creatively.

Reality exists independent of human minds, but our understanding of it depends on the beliefs we hold at any given time.

MICHAEL SHERMER, *THE BELIEVING BRAIN*

In reality there are a multitude of reasons and conditions that establish what comes into our lives, what happens to us. There are a multitude of people and variables, seen and unseen, that are involved in any given result. We can't possibly hang our reasons on one cause or assumption. Life cannot come down to one cause or one condition. Take a look for yourself—what did it take for you to experience your breakfast this morning? A menagerie of causes and conditions are involved in creating any given situation, no matter how small. This *complexity of reality* is a reason many grasp for a core belief to hold to as an explanation to "all that is." This gives them a set way to respond to life. Knowingly or unknowingly they are choosing to be habitual. But such a core belief (and we all have them) ultimately diminishes and limits us. Beliefs, like the teller in the bank, can rob us of our present experiences and the possibilities inherent in each moment.

Since beliefs drive our experience and influence events, when we hold such a solid one, it colors everything. Everything we experience is strongly influenced by what we believe in that given moment. As a result we unknowingly shut ourselves off from other possibilities and experiences. Furthermore, when something happens to us that triggers a negative memory, our habitual self gets activated, and along with it a core belief. We are not consciously choosing our responses, but our entire psychophysical system has been triggered into a habitual, robotic reaction. (Typically some fight-or-flight pattern is activated. We either want to run away or grab on.) We are actually responding to a belief that is rooted in some negative experience in our past. Then we find ourselves repeating the past, sometimes oblivious to the reality of the present situation.

It's important to know that all these negative habits or wounds are not rooted in some character flaw but are simply the result of becoming habitual in our ways. Parker J. Palmer, author of *Healing the Heart of Democracy* and founder of the Center for Courage & Renewal, once said to me, "How we are wounded does not make us right or wrong, only human." Most of our habitual beliefs and agreements are linked to an original belief and behavior that helped us interpret or survive a difficult situation.

It is also most helpful to know that studies reveal that our state of mind is self-reinforcing. Whatever we prime our minds with—becomes. The brain is understood as a recursive system with our state of mind as the reinforcer with its beliefs, assumptions, and habitual reactions. What this says is that in our mind training, the transforming of our beliefs, we also change the brain's hardwiring. We are removing the thief from the bank. This emphasizes how valuable it is for us to pay attention to our state of mind—to invest in becoming more and more aware of our thoughts and beliefs.

But, It's Not Your Fault

On one of my vipassana meditation retreats, the teacher's theme was— it's not your fault. He referred mostly to the negative patterns we have acquired. He would give an example of a destructive pattern and then say, "It's not their fault." Depressed? It's not your fault. Chronically disappointed? Not your fault. This was a surprising concept in Buddhism and is so here with the zero point agreement as well, because we are encouraged in both to take responsibility for our lives. In Buddhist practices we hold ourselves accountable for how we respond to our circumstances. Following the retreat, I found myself working with this life paradox of how we are responsible for our lives, while at the same time understanding how our habitual patterns are not our fault. Both are true. Both can help us transform our negative habitual patterns into skillful responses and favorable experiences. This comes back to how these reactive patterns or emotional states got established in the first place. It's not our fault that we were neglected, or abused, or somehow put down. There is no benefit in shaming ourselves for what we have come to believe. However, and fortunately, we now have the ability to catch the thieves that rob us of our present happiness. We can dethrone the false gods.

> The greatest challenge to increased self-awareness is to remember the difference between unconscious reflexes and conscious consideration.
>
> P. D. OUSPENSKY, THE PSYCHOLOGY
> OF MAN'S POSSIBLE EVOLUTION

All negative habits originate from some intention to take care of ourselves. If we have trauma, neglect, or other difficulties in childhood, our brains and bodies learn how to react and protect us. Research in neuroscience and human behavior demonstrates that our brains and our neuropathways "remember" the pain, and it is this memory that gets triggered. When this negative memory gets triggered, some psychophysical reaction kicks in. We are, after all, mammals that hold in our neuropathways the protective response of fight-or-flight. Basically, our negative habitual patterns are hardwired into us. So when we find ourselves reacting in the same old way—it is an *entire system* kicking in; the brain, as well as the body and mind, knows the routine and (based on our history) "thinks" it knows how to help us. So, it really isn't our fault. And we will keep repeating the old patterns of behavior if we continue to live by the beliefs and agreements set in response to past events.

Fortunately, studies in behavioral change demonstrate that we can "rewire" what has become hardwired in us. (Science has simply caught up with what the Buddhists, philosophers, secular humanists, and the Toltec have known for thousands of years.) But it doesn't take a neuroscientist or physicist to tell us that we can change our behaviors. I too have witnessed this transformational propensity in my work with people over the past thirty-five years—we can move beyond the pain stories of our past. We can take responsibility for our lives and transform our negative habitual responses to uplift our lives. There are practices and meditations that will transform these habitual responses and allow us to respond competently to our circumstances, rather than react habitually. It does take a regular commitment to rewire our reactive and habitual traits. Further good news is that we don't actually have to know the event or events that took place to wire us in this way. Most of us have some awareness of the original causes of some of our pain stories, but we don't have to know them or go over them to transform them. We simply have to use our present situations and awareness to let go of the past and live in the present.

> *If personal history is the principal obstacle to change, then the power to erase it represents the doorway to freedom.*
> VICTOR SANCHEZ, *THE TEACHINGS OF DON CARLOS*

Living the zero point agreement impacts our psychophysical system and rewires us to experience more satisfaction and happiness.

Through the strategies offered here we diminish the fight-or-flight reaction to circumstances. Fear and anger get triggered less and less. The mind learns to open up more and more to the possibilities inherent in each situation (recall the monk reaching for the strawberry) and the psychophysical system becomes rewired to retrieve positive memories and responses.

Furthermore, it's not our fault if our psychophysical system is reacting to *implicit* memories. There are two basic systems of memories—explicit and implicit. With explicit memories we are aware that a memory is being triggered, or we are consciously retrieving a memory from the past. Implicit memories, and all that goes with them (emotions, physiological reactions, protective strategies), are triggered without our knowledge. This means that we think we are responding to the present situation when in fact a great part of our reaction may be to a past event! This way, too, the past keeps repeating itself because we have an established way to react to such situations.

As shown in recent books such as Daniel Siegel's *The Mindful Brain* and Michael Shermer's *The Believing Brain,* mind training and meditation practices, as well as yoga, purposeful rituals, and techniques that challenge our psychosomatic reactions, are able to help change the hardwiring in our brains. The practices of attention and intention, both of which tame and train the mind, are known to gradually free us from our negative and reactive states, change how we see and experience our world, and increase our sense of belonging.

Whether it is the brain or mind (or both) that tends to reach for the negative memory—we are all hardwired to retrieve what we need to do when we sense danger. (And most of us instinctively sense danger when we feel vulnerable or are dealing with an unknown.) So the softer, more loving memories take a backseat as it were so that we can be better prepared to protect ourselves from anticipated danger. This protection mode really gets in the way of taking risks, experimenting, and enjoying ourselves. I hear pain story after pain story about how negative encounters in the past set that person to avoid certain circumstances or somehow put them in a defensive-protective posture. I always have a couple of students in my spiritual journaling classes who are afraid to write in their journals because their privacy was invaded or their writing negated earlier on.

Here is a simple but powerful meditation that helps unravel our habitual reactive posture and, instead, "hardwires us to love." It only takes a few minutes a day. This trains your mind while imprinting the memory of love on the psychophysical level. This meditation helps us to retrieve a positive memory when life's circumstances trigger a pain story and accelerates undoing the belief systems that are hardwired into us. For me this is a form of loving kindness (metta) meditation offered up in Buddhism. At the very least, it helps set the mental tone of love and compassion. This then directs the mind toward love.

Hardwired to Love

Sit with both feet on the floor resting your back in a chair. Close your eyes. Take some time to rest your awareness on your breath, noticing how it rises and falls in the body. Place your right hand on your heart chakra (in the middle of your chest). Notice how this feels good—that sensation of a touch. Take a couple of deep breaths and bring your awareness to the sensation of breath and hand on heart center. Bring your attention to the rise and fall of the breath and your hand on your chest. After a few moments, bring to mind a favorable memory. A time you felt loved, appreciated, and safe. This could be with a loved one, a pet, or even a time in nature—though a memory with a person is preferable. Sit in this memory as you keep your hand on your heart center and breathe. Do your best to stay in this one memory. Repeat the loving scene if it is a brief one. With a more lengthy memory, enjoy the details. After a couple of minutes, take several deep breaths and bring to mind simple and recent things you are thankful for. Keep these simple, like your cup of tea this morning or the easy traffic into work or how your clothes feel or the beauty of the sunrise. Then take a couple of more deep breaths and open your eyes.

This meditation is inspired by the works of Terry Fralich, author of *Cultivating Lasting Happiness*. For more go to www.mindfulnesscenter.org.

The past may be hardwired into us, but we are creating the conditions for our future right now. I recommend that you do this practice every day, at least once.

> *It's never too late for a happy childhood.*
> A POPULAR BUMPER STICKER

Freedom from the Bondage of Belief

We need the ability to break through our beliefs and their related habitual states into the mystery and potentiality of the present. To experience freedom we need to experience our moments more consciously. I often ask my students, "Are you or your habits living your life?" We can, through the transformation of our beliefs, be free of our habitual ways that keep us tethered to the past.

> *Reexamine all you have been told at school or church or in any book, dismiss whatever insults your own soul, and your very flesh shall be a great poem.*
> WALT WHITMAN, PREFACE TO *LEAVES OF GRASS*

● Transforming Experiences through What We Believe

Here are several practices that you can use to become aware of your beliefs. Once you are more aware of the beliefs that underlie your thoughts and behaviors, you can live more consciously and creatively. You can reject, change, or transform your beliefs.

✦ Try this out for a day: ask yourself, What am I believing at this moment? You can check in on the hour or choose another method to check in with your beliefs. For example, you could have your watch beep every hour or your computer send you a reminder—"What are you believing right now?" Simply take note of your beliefs. This time you listen to the beliefs that are under the surface of your thoughts, feelings, and experiences. Since beliefs direct our experience, becoming aware of them can be a simple but transformational exercise. At the end of the day, journal around what you discovered about yourself and your beliefs.

+ You may also want to use this awareness exercise in situations where there seems to be a lot of emotional intentisty for you. What are the beliefs underlying this experience for you? In the moment simply ask, without forcing a response. Allow for an awareness of the underlying beliefs by asking yourself, "What beliefs do I have around this?" Making the unconscious conscious in this way will begin to uplift you as you name the thieves in your bank.

+ Next, try this: Recognize a daily routine that you have, up to now, related to habitually. It could be something as simple as always having to have a cup of coffee before you have breakfast. Or you eat in the car on the way to work. Change it somehow and relate to it freshly. Altering one small habit is a great way to challenge our beliefs and assumptions.

+ Here's a journaling prompt: Write about something you *don't* believe. Repeat the line, "I don't believe . . ." without stopping to think. Keep writing nonstop until you fill up at least one page. Then, review what you wrote. What we discover is how our strongly held beliefs often are dependent upon or point to what we *don't* believe. If you don't believe in hope, God, the president, universal health care . . . then you believe in . . .

+ Finally, apply inquiry meditation to explore what you believe. (See "Profound Awakening through Inquiry Meditation," page 39.) When you have brought an unconscious belief to the surface, such as "I believe people can't be trusted," investigate this further through inquiry. Investigate the concept of trust. What does it mean to trust? What does it mean to trust people? How does this belief of not trusting serve you?

Most of us are reluctant to become conscious of our beliefs, let alone challenge them, because they offer us a sense of false security. We tend to be afraid of what we don't understand. This resistance to consciously look at what we believe (and don't believe) sets us up to be motivated by fear.

There is no security in life, only opportunity.

Mark Twain

The Fear Factor

Fear works. Fear motivates. Scare people enough and they will follow you, or vote for you. Over the years (starting in my teen years), I've encountered paths and teachers who rely on fear to motivate people to either follow them or their precepts. At the age of sixteen I was condemned to hell by a Baptist minister who claimed to have a direct line to God. I've been warned and encouraged to follow certain paths, "truths," and techniques if I want to avoid hell, be happy, or be born into a higher realm. I am always disappointed to witness respected spiritual teachers and students use fear as a motivator to practice. Dogma can be found anywhere—and where there is dogma, there is the fear factor. I could not embrace fear as a motivation to do meditation or yoga, or to practice my principles. Furthermore, I have not and will not use fear as a tool with my clients or students, or recommend it as a therapeutic or motivational tool. As we go deeper into living our life from the zero point, we free ourselves from this old myth of needing fear to motivate us.

But fear does work.

Relying on Personal Experience

> *Where to begin? Do we measure the relaxing of the feet? The moment when the eye glimpses the hawk, when instinct functions? For in this pure action, this pure moving of the bird, there is no time, no space, but only the free doing-being of this very moment—now!*
>
> PETER MATTHIESSEN

Instead of fear we can base our choices on the *science of personal experience*. True science is evidence-based claims. Buddhist philosophy encourages trying all the teachings out for yourself. Don't take anybody's word for it! There are times it will be like a free fall; where you let go of all that you've been told and walk the walk by yourself.

With a recent encounter with dogma and fear, I hit a wall within my own spiritual practice and had to find a way to embrace my journey without throwing the baby out with the bath water. The sad truth is we often cannot return to the church or the temple when feeling we have to accept it all. Many "recovered" Catholics speak to how they are in search of a church that allows them to explore their faith, rather than accept the doctrine without question. Many in the Buddhist faith encounter a similar paradox. How can we select from the teachings without getting into spiritual trouble when it's suggested we are misinterpreting doctrine?

Bottom line is we each have to trust our experiences, argue with the teachers and the doctrine, and try the teachings out for ourselves. We cannot awaken by following step-by-step the path of others. And to a great degree, to evolve we must rely on our inner navigational forces that got us this far. Something—maybe very basic, but something—is already working for you. Even early on in our spiritual explorations we have to trust ourselves enough to contemplate and study what we are being told. We have to be willing to do inquiry and contemplate what is presented to us throughout our lives. The focus of your personal path must be on the practice and on inquiry of the concepts, not on following the instructions. When we are just following instructions or reacting habitually, fear is likely at work. We follow because we are afraid someone else holds the key to the kingdom; we don't trust ourselves.

Instead of being fearful, you can remember and trust that what got you this far in your life is the navigational force within that you use when challenges arise on your path. This doesn't mean you won't be confused or make mistakes. However, during difficult and confusing times it has been and will be that inner guide who will continue to assist you. You can listen or study spiritual teachings, let them stir you up, get you wondering about what is real and what isn't, then you decide; you make the meaning.

> *The entire heavenly realm*
> *is within us, but to find it*
> *we have to relate to what's outside.*
> JOSEPH CAMPBELL, *A JOSEPH CAMPBELL COMPANION*

The Mastery of Returning

I told my fourteen-year-old daughter that I hadn't written a word in my novel for a week. Her response was, "That can be a good thing, Mom."

I did return to my writing on another day only to have thousands of words pour out of me onto the empty page. A few days later I was one chapter nearer the completion of my novel. I am glad I returned and did not get caught up in reprimanding myself. Now I am happily into the third writing of my novel.

The thing is, I spend a great deal of effort returning to the page just as I do returning to the breath in my meditation practice. I realize that there are writers out there that are with the page consistently every day; Stephen King, for instance. And there are meditators who likely rest in the breath without wandering off to other places, and having to remind themselves to return to the breath. His Holiness the fourteenth Dalai Lama comes to mind. My creative and spiritual paths are more often in a state of returning to the empty page or meditation practice than actually being engaged in writing or meditation.

The truth is that in meditation we spend a great deal of our time returning to the breath. Our practice is to rest in the breath, have our attention on the breath; but, oh, how our mind wants to wander to and fro! Such, too, is the life of the writer, the artist, and the spiritual practitioner. The page or canvas calls to us, relying on our ability to give our ideas our full attention. But our attention is often elsewhere. Life interrupts the best of our plans. As Joseph Campbell phrased it, "Be willing to give up the life you planned, to have the one that is waiting for you."

Then something remarkable happens—we realize that we are off the breath, which itself is a moment of awareness, and so we then return to the breath. This happens again and again, if we are truly practicing. This returning is *an integral part* of the meditation practice. Now, into my forty-some years as a writer and meditator, I can trust that I will at the very least return to the page, return to my meditation, return to the breath. I will never wander off so far that I cannot find a way back.

The way back to the breath or the page or the canvas, or to whatever creative promise you have made, is in becoming aware *in the moment* of where you are, and then, where you want to be. Since returning is an essential part of our spiritual and creative life, even when we are not creating or meditating we can be living the creative or spiritual life. It just so happens that the creative and spiritual path is a spiral that always circles back to our creative aspirations or our spiritual principles and commitments. *What matters is that we give ourselves something to return to*—and that we do so when we find ourselves wandering too far out beyond the boundaries of our creative and spiritual life. Remember the exercise "An Exploration into Presence" on page 20. When we ask ourselves what is it I want—*really* want, this gives us something to return to. I frame it like this: It's not so much that I should stop eating so much sugar, but that I want to return to a healthier diet. Focus on what you want to return to. We are getting more conscious of our thoughts, our beliefs, our habits, and what we want; so we can more easily name what it is we want to return to.

> *The paradox seems to be, as Socrates demonstrated long ago, that the truly free individual is free only to the extent of his own self-mastery.*
>
> STEVEN PRESSFIELD, *THE WAR OF ART*

Navigating Your Life

Each of us has practices we use and activities we engage in that have gotten us this far in life. We can rely on those! We can return to those! No judgment if you keep falling off the wagon—as long as you return. These are part of your ground zero—your zero point. These navigational references bring you back to yourself, to what's important to you, and to the source of your inspiration.

✦ Write a list of navigational sources from your internal and external landscape that got you here. For example, trusting my experience above all else got me here; I can rely on that; I can return to that. What else? I trust my intuition, consulting and studying the I Ching, writing, walking, nature, keeping a journal, ending relationships, the Lojong practice, friends, and so on. I recommend choosing one navigational source within each aspect of your life (personal, spiritual, vocational, relational). This list will be unique and personally relevant to you.

✦ Next, look over your list of navigational sources and take two or three as your *core* practice for ten days. See yourself as *returning* to these, now and on a daily basis. Write them in your journal:

I return to meditation.
I return to walking.
I return to . . .

+ Take some time now to script how this will look, feel, and be in your life for these upcoming ten days. (See "Scripting Scenes for Your Creative Life" on page 203.) If you don't give yourself the time to script these practices, then close your eyes and imagine for a few minutes fulfilling these commitments. Let yourself enjoy the imagined results of returning to a practice you know works for you.

+ The spiritual questions we engage in (and do not let ourselves be distracted from) expand the mind and open us up to personal experiences. It is in asking and living the questions that we come to the brink of illumination. In order to evolve spiritually, live within the paradox of finding personal truth within your tradition by trusting the navigational sources that got you this far. Simply put, you got this far by doing something right. To use the metaphor of thieves in the bank— you have a lot of cash already saved up.

Relying on a Spiritual Science

What I have discovered is that within the various spiritual and religious traditions of the world is a vibrant science. It is the science behind the rituals and practices that makes it work. It is not the specific deity or doctrine or religion that makes it work but the science behind the techniques that makes it effective. For example, the science behind meditation includes how it quiets the mind, helps remedy worry and anxiety, and results in a mind that can keep focused on a task. This is all proven. The proof includes our personal experiences with our practices. If it weren't for some scientific grounds to our rituals and practices, they wouldn't work. When we have a powerful spiritual experience, whether in a temple or nature, something very real takes place in our entire psychophysical system.

This science of spirituality is universally applicable and can be relied upon. The science behind meditation is presently being studied at our very own University of Wisconsin–Madison. There is a cognitive-behavioral science behind the benefits of purposeful ritual, setting intentions, and visualization. Research points to the benefits of prayer (more for the individual than the one being prayed for). I attended a conference in Minneapolis on the science of compassion. Something actually happens within us and in our environment when we practice compassion and have a resulting spiritual experience. Of course many people mistakenly attribute the spiritual experience to the teacher or to stringently following certain practices. The problem then comes when someone says, "All my happiness is because I believe in John 16:3" or "I am happy because I prostrate correctly to the Buddha." As I pointed out earlier, some debate or even struggle with what we are presented with will produce authentic spiritual and creative breakthroughs.

When we try to follow the path of Christ or the Buddha exactly (or believe what others say this path should be), we lose our chance to experience what Christ or the Buddha did in their pilgrimages for themselves. Both were heuristic. How did the Buddha wake up? He left the comfort of his home. He tried many paths. He made mistakes. He explored. He challenged himself. He kept returning to meditation. He kept trying to understand the meaning of life. He practiced. *He found his own way.*

> *Rest at ease in the infinite vast expanse, and don't rely on the hardships of hundreds of paths.*
> NYOSHUL KHENPO RINPOCHE, TIBETAN LAMA

Breaking the Rules as Another Antidote to the False God of Belief

Oftentimes to gain momentum in life, to express our greatest good, we have to break a few rules along the way.

> *You must kill your god.*
> *If you are to advance, all fixed ideas must go.*
> JOSEPH CAMPBELL, *A JOSEPH CAMPBELL COMPANION*

When my daughter was in middle school I attended a public-school gathering where the Pledge of Allegiance set the stage for the day. I overheard a mother direct her child of eight years, "Keep your eyes on the flag. Keep your eyes on the flag!" Of course, many of the adults around this child seemed to follow this rule and appeared to have their eyes on the flag as well. Apparently it was the right thing to do, without question.

Teaching a child (as well as employees, a congregation, or students) to follow rules and traditions without question generates a passive attitude to life. It teaches us to *follow* rather than listen. One doesn't have to question the way things are because one follows, automatically, in the established dogma. And it often appears as if everyone else is following the same rules. Rules help to some degree if we are to function as a community. The danger is when we cut off our ability to hear our intuitive wisdom. While we follow the prevailing rules and dogma, our intuition may be saying, "This isn't right!"

This is particularly troublesome, if not downright dangerous, in psychological, creative, and spiritual settings. The teacher or the doctrine may suggest that there is something wrong with you (not the situation) when you feel ashamed, afraid, or threatened. You may put expectations on yourself to assume the prevailing belief system. This pressure may be particularly strong in a group where most of the people present agree with and conform to a particular mind-set.

Being able to question authority and its attendant doctrine and rules is necessary for personal spiritual and creative awakening. Remove yourself from routines and accustomed surroundings so you will have to question how things are. This helps bring forth a transformation in your consciousness. Any setting you choose to enhance your creativity or spirituality must be able to help you shift your perspective "from the flag" and onto other phenomena. The group or teacher should not insist that your eyes be upon their flag. Instead, the group or process should lead you to inner doors; doors you will move through in your own way.

Some are afraid of the responsibility that goes along with such independence. They want the backup of set rules, or dogma, rather than taking the continued journey inward to discover and bring forth their own inherent qualities. Indeed, a healthy group (like the truth circles described in Parker J. Palmer's book *A Hidden Wholeness*) can be quite helpful to one's transformative process. But too many of us have been trained since childhood to follow, mimic, fit in, and do whatever we can to be part of a group. Many people just want to feel part of something and to know they are appreciated.

When we set ourselves up to follow rules in this way, we never have to deal with the discomfort of the unknown or answer the difficult questions for ourselves. But alas, we also cut ourselves off from the beauty and mystery of personal spiritual experience. The real impetus of making meaning is that we take our own direction instead of going in the direction of the crowd. When this happens, some religious fundamentalists will say that we are heathens. Some of our friends or family may say we are being imprudent, and those who are somehow attached to us not taking a new direction or a direction that differs from theirs may call us ridiculous.

> *Follow your bliss.*
> JOSEPH CAMPBELL, *A JOSEPH CAMPBELL COMPANION*

> *Follow your heart.*
> ED MCGAA (EAGLE MAN), OGLALA SIOUX AUTHOR

> *I find myself wanting to do something stupid and lovely.*
> DAVID WHYTE, FROM HIS POEM "FOUR HORSES"

Holding On and Letting Go

> *The psychologist Paul Rozin, an expert on disgust, observed that a single cockroach will completely wreck the appeal of a bowl of cherries, but a cherry will do nothing at all for a bowl of cockroaches.*
> DANIEL KAHNEMAN, *THINKING, FAST AND SLOW*

A lot of people carry old, outdated stories about themselves and the world, as I've already shown. Once a belief is established we have difficulty letting it go. We then build entire stories around what we believe. If you are unhappy in your life, you may want to take a look at the stories you hold around happiness and success. You can begin with investigating a belief you hold around success, for example. From here, you can become aware of the "full story" you hold that supports this belief and way of life. You may quickly find yourself, as I did, in a paradox of discovery—my old story is what got me here; *and* it was time to let go of the old story. Of course the old story helped me get to this new frontier. At the very least, the old story is part of the foundation to this new story. I have mentioned how our pain stories are repeated if we don't challenge their underlying beliefs, agreements, and assumptions. However, all our stories are not pain stories; nevertheless, they may be outdated. The story of me as an advocate for the mentally ill is no longer the story of me. Old stories include our identity. Since our old stories of ourselves are familiar we tend to hold on to them (knowingly and unknowingly) as a way to resist stepping through the door into our new frontier, a new experience and story of ourselves. We hesitate because what lies ahead is a lot of unknown. I spent a decade working in the field of advocacy and mental health. During this time I wrote my first book and traveled around the world to train others on the eight-stage healing process. This story held a lot of purpose and identity for me. But there came a time for me to let it go so I could discover and explore the new, emerging story of myself.

Taking the step toward our new story means we are letting go of the known for the unknown. And the unknown can appear like that bowl of cherries with a harmless cockroach sitting on top.

> *I think, at a child's birth, if a mother could ask a fairy godmother to endow it with the most useful gift, that gift would be curiosity.*
>
> ELEANOR ROOSEVELT

We must awaken our curiosity by seeing beyond our doubts and fears, but it's hard to get beyond the cockroach sitting on our bowl of cherries. A simple wondering will do. Curiosity (once again) can help when we find ourselves on the edge of a new frontier. Both feet may be in the old story, but our eyes are gazing out into the world of new possibilities. Instead of trying to fill in the unknown with the past or with false guarantees (such as, if I do this first, I will be happy), simply allow yourself to be curious about your future possibilities. This willingness to be curious helps to loosen the hold the old story has on you and take your mind off the cockroach (if there is one). Einstein would be pleased by this willingness: "I have no special talents," he once declared. "I am only passionately curious." For me the cockroach was no guarantee of income. Could I risk the known consistency of my salary and the accompanying identity to leap into the unknown of my next dream? This cockroach had the potential of stopping me. But I became more curious of what lay ahead than attached to what I was leaving behind.

> *Constant development is the law of life, and a man who always tries to maintain his dogmas in order to appear consistent drives himself into a false position.*
>
> GANDHI

Unleashing the Dogma of Comfort at Any Price
To really see the new story that may be offering itself up to you (or that is calling to you!), you have to release old stories about how things are supposed to be or look. Unleash yourself from the dogma that keeps your stories chained to some outdated perception of how life is supposed to continue to be for you.

> *The modern dogma is comfort at any cost.*
> ALDO LEOPOLD, *A SAND COUNTY ALMANAC*

It's not so much whether something is dogmatic in its offering, but whether or not we are dogmatic in our application. The old story always includes an exaggeration as well as assumptions. This is so because we build on our stories until they become solidified and dogmatic in our mind. Or we take on someone else's version of "how it should be" because we don't know how equipped we are or what the benefits will be to forging our own way.

To leave the old story behind means to release your own personalized dogmatic beliefs and resulting responses about your life. It's about being less dogmatic in what you believe and how you act. Loosen your grip on how you think things should go. These old stories can be in any area of your life—your vocational, spiritual, or relational pursuits. Letting go of comfort allows for more joy in your relationships because it invites you to let go of the little dogmas you hold of how things should be. Who says the dishes belong in the dishwasher in that way? What makes you certain that if you follow how someone else meditates exactly you will have the same results? Who says you need the security of that job?

Sometimes remaining in the old story of our life comes in the form of settling.

The False God of Settling: Spoiler Alert!

There is no passion to be found playing small—in settling for a life that is less than the one you are capable of living.

NELSON MANDELA

In order to discover the lives we are capable of, we have to take a look at places we have settled. Too quickly the places we settle become a pattern established in our lives. We have somehow convinced ourselves that "this is enough," or "I can't expect more of myself, or life." Or we spin some pitch that puts the brakes on any chance of exploring our possibilities. Here is the spoiler alert: *If you always do what you always did, you will always get what you always got.* So, there's no need to hang around for the rest of the movie when you know how it's going to end. Our lives can easily become a stream of spoilers.

I think about a boy I knew in high school whose father died of alcoholism long after abandoning him. This boy followed in his father's footsteps. He too abandoned a son, and to this day he can be found in the same local bar he favored all through his young adult years. I suppose they will name a barstool after him. I am certain he feels hardwired to his life as an alcoholic. He may wonder what would be the point to change course now, if it were even possible to do so.

Many take the well-worn, familiar path because every time we even consider getting up from our bar stool with the hope to never return, resistance rises up and we settle. We settle for the comfort in the routine, for what feels familiar, for what we know. Sometimes we settle for what someone else wants for us. Every time we want to create something new, leave behind some old way of being, or challenge ourselves to try something different—resistance arises and we find ourselves on this slippery slope of settling.

We all have dreams for ourselves. We often hold in the secret chamber of the heart a dream that constantly calls to us, even wakes us at 3:00 a.m. Or we sense an urgency and envy when witnessing someone else activate or achieve their dream. We feel a dissatisfaction brewing deep within us. Our envy and dissatisfaction are the result of our own lack of movement and settling (See "The Hungry Ghost of Dissatisfaction" on page 92.) If you are not moving toward your dream, you are settling. So if you claim that nothing out of the ordinary calls to you—you are probably settling.

Most of us have settled. Maybe not entirely, but in part we have given our time and resources to something or someone that is less than what we want or, more importantly, what we are capable of. We lie to ourselves and say that "this is enough" or, "I need to give this more time" (kicking a dead horse comes to mind). We trick ourselves constantly with, "This is all I am really capable of." We convince ourselves we don't even know what we want! Or we remain in a state of codependency; blaming our circumstances or others for our lack of success. We may not think these thoughts too loudly, for they tend to be assumptions kept under the radar of our full consciousness. Have you noticed the popularity of zombie movies these days with young adults? I wonder if the youth see us adults as turning into a nation of the living dead. Are we not settling for less than pristine water? Are we not settling for jobs that are killing us so we can have the insurance? Are we not settling when it comes to climate change? Carl Jung refers to the adult who is not really living an active life as the biggest threat to their children's future.

We settle for less in ourselves and then in others and miss the fulfillment of a vision. These visions have often taken seed in us at a very young age, but the lack of a fertile soil prevents them from sprouting and seeking the light. To live life from your side is to fertilize the soil of an active life.

We settle into our old stories of ourselves; believing the limits and agreements of these stories. We settle for far less than what our creative visions pointed to. This not only applies to settling for a lesser image of the big picture we hold for our lives and environment but also to the small settlings throughout our day—settling for less meditation or creative time than we deserve or settling for less of ourselves. These smaller settlings are what make it possible for us to settle in bigger ways. In each small way we settle we limit ourselves in larger ways. Since we can only discover our capacity through experience, we must step outside our comfort zone and challenge our habit of settling. We can do this first by daring to give ourselves more time to be creative; or we can dare ourselves to do something larger like change vocations.

What you are comes to you.

RALPH WALDO EMERSON

The Antidote to Settling: Truth or Dare

I played truth or dare with my daughter and our foreign exchange student (both of whom were fifteen at the time). They shared that neither of them ever chose *dare*. This seems to be a common theme among teen girls in this game—to not choose a dare. The irony came with one of the *truth* questions: What is your biggest regret? Both responded with regrets of not taking a particular risk. Even in their "game of life" you could say they chose a certain version of personal truth over a dare only to later regret playing it safe.

We all hold a lot of beliefs about ourselves and the world that are accepted as personal truths. Just like the teens here, adults, too, tend to choose personal truths over dares. After all, we tend to be comfortable and set in our truths, our stories about ourselves.

Many adults come to me seeking ways to enthuse their lives with creativity and meaning. Some have a list of regrets they carry with them like a slogan. Others anticipate future regrets because they fear they may not dare enough to fulfill their dreams. I find that all regrets include not having taken a dare, a risk over some personalized version of what we tell ourselves is truth. Too many personal truths keep us captive, such as our "I should or shouldn't do that," "I can't, don't, or won't." A popular personal truth is "I will get to that sometime." Many hold on to the security of some personal belief, not trusting the outcome of taking a risk. This choice then gives them a way to settle in the known rather than risking the unknown.

> *There is no security*
> *in following the call to adventure.*
> *Nothing is exciting*
> *if you know what the outcome is going to be.*
> JOSEPH CAMPBELL, *A JOSEPH CAMPBELL COMPANION*

> *If a man gives way to all his desires, or panders to them, there will be no inner struggle in him, no friction, no fire. But if, for the sake of attaining a definite aim, he struggles with the desires that hinder him, he will then create a fire which will gradually transform his inner world into a single whole.*
> P. D. OUSPENSKY

This Time Choose Dare

Fortunately, experience shows us that inherent in each risk is the possibility of even more than you imagined from the present vantage point. At the very least, the risk leads to an experience that naturally generates more possibilities and movement in your life.

If the meaning of life were to get down to one kernel, one absolute, this would be—choose more dares.

Choose the dare.
Then do it.
Participate fully.
Savor the moments.

Enjoy the aftereffects of having *been, done,* and *experienced* the results of your dare.

> *It takes courage*
> *to do what you want.*
> *Other people have a lot of plans for you.*
> JOSEPH CAMPBELL, *A JOSEPH CAMPBELL COMPANION*

In one version of the truth or dare game, if you don't complete the dare, you will be faced with an even more challenging dare. This too mirrors life. If you postpone your adventures and risks long enough, if you keep settling, it is likely to get more and more challenging to fulfill your dreams.

Then there's the "double dare ya." So, I double dare *you.* I am living my dream as a fiction writer (within the context of all my other intentions and commitments). I double dare you to live your dream. Now you double dare your partners and friends. You go ahead and choose a dare, take a risk, and invite others to dare along with you (to take their own version of a risk). This is how my Spiritual Journaling classes and my Initiation Courses work—we constantly double dare each other simply through our continued risk taking and adventures in the presence of each other. The energy in these circles is doubled when we witness others taking risks and positively transforming their lives. This also happens in other group environments such as corporations, educational institutions, and small businesses. Risk taking is contagious.

As it turns out the happiest among us are those of us who take risks and are loyal to our spiritual (ethical) and creative commitments no matter the results. We will each discover for ourselves just how much more we get when we choose the dare over some personalized version of the truth. Even if I write garbage on the empty page during my fiction writing time, at the very least I am given the satisfaction of having written, of having risked.

Sometimes, though, the difficulties or resistance seems unmovable. There are times that the settling can turn into depression.

The False God of Depression

When things fall apart, heartbreak happens.

PARKER J. PALMER,
REFERRING TO A RECENT ENCOUNTER WITH DEPRESSION,
HEALING THE HEART OF DEMOCRACY

So you are moving along in your life and then something happens that stops everything. You find yourself unable to get out of bed or off the couch. What once was easy is now riddled with anxiety and difficulty. Panic or depression sets in and takes over the mind, body, and spirit.

I refer to depression as a false god because it does not deserve to be the sole force in anyone's life. Remember the first and primary antidote: everything is part of the path; everything is workable. Some people, like Parker J. Palmer, share that they are predisposed to depression. Yet this predisposition has not kept Palmer from living an active, fulfilling, and purposeful life. He shares in several of his books and teachings how he has worked with his depression. In my eyes he holds up a bright light of proof that everything is workable. Even in times of depression and heartbreak we can lead meaningful lives. Abraham Lincoln was another exemplar of working with depression. He suffered from depression but also held on to the meaning of his life, which was to be of public service. Several biographies on Lincoln reveal how he made meaning with his depression (called melancholy at the time), working with it instead of giving into it.

Clearly a lot of people experience various degrees of depression and anxiety. Even in good times, an average of sixteen million new cases of depression occur in the United States every year, leading me to ask, What is really going on here? There are numerous ads announcing the latest drug treatment. A friend told me recently that one such television ad announces that "if none of your other medications work for depression, tell your doctor about this one!" An implication here is that this drug may be your last chance. There are no last chances until you are dead. And even then it may be that our karma continues, as might our chances.

Antidotes for depression are presented below. I have found that the best antidotes for depression include continued awareness of the makings of our hearts and minds as well as participation in the world around us.

An Antidote to Depression: Listening to the Pain

Just as the African proverb suggests: "The treatment is right next to the wound." Some of the antidotes to depression can be found right next to the problems. It begins with listening to the pain, the depression, and not separating yourself from it. In my years of offering counseling, I have found that the answers are often hidden within the questions and in the experience itself. Each person carries within themselves the answers they need. Don't kill the messenger, as they say; the messenger in this case being the depression.

Depression is a part of a whole life, not something one can separate out and label as strictly chemical, biological, or biographical. Even so, in those situations where biology may be a primary factor (as in Abraham Lincoln's case), to leave out the rest of the human experience (emotional, mental, spiritual, social, and environmental) would be a failure in treatment. In fact, when you experience an onset of depression your life is talking to you. Some part of you is sending out an SOS: "Something is not working here!" To only rely on medication would be to cover up the discomfort of the message and in so doing kill the messenger. To be free of depression and anxiety or to at least not be run down by them, you must be able to listen to the voice of the antagonist. So even in the situation where medications help, be mindful to take enough to help but not so much as to kill the messenger before you can hear and understand the message of your depression.

What Wants to Die?

If the message seems to be to kill yourself, here too I want you to listen to this intense pain by asking yourself instead; what in me wants to die? I have worked with people who are suicidal and others who obsess about death. Some have come to me with repeated dreams of death. They want help. And I rely on the wisdom borrowed from Carl Jung when I ask them, "What in you needs to die?" Their soul calls out for a death. Not an end to life, but an end to whatever prevents them from living fully and from moving on. They need to let something die. They may even need to kill another false god.

So, what wants to die? Notice I don't ask what are you *willing* to let die but what *wants* to die. The depression (at least in part) is holding on and pointing to what needs to go. First ask yourself: "What wants to die?" and then check in with your willingness and commitment to do whatever it takes to fulfill your intention to live a vision (from chapter 1). Again I will offer up both Parker J. Palmer and Abraham Lincoln as examples. Parker speaks often about the wisdom of his depression and how it continues to teach him compassion and the need to live life actively in community. Abraham Lincoln's depression, at the very least, made him wiser to the sufferings of others, and he worked hard toward unity among people with different views. In this way, depression can offer up a bigger and stronger vision of what is possible.

So, what needs to die in your life to make room for your vision? What beliefs may need to die? What relationship is dead? What old story needs to die and be buried? What are you giving your life-force to? If your job is killing you, why not kill your job? Is an addiction to alcohol ruining your life and your relationships? Let it die. If the depression is strong, chances are that something false, something that no longer is true for you, has to die. I once killed my television. Another time in my life I killed off my expectation of what success was supposed to look like. At the very least kill any isolation that may be keeping you from healing and exploring your options.

> *Western psychotherapists say that you can learn a person's reasons for experiencing depression if you look into their biographical or biological history. From the Buddhist point of view, though, the fundamental understanding is that depression is based on our interpretations of our life situations, our circumstances, our self-conceptions. We get depressed for not being the person we want to be. We get depressed when we think we have not been able to achieve the things that we want to achieve in life.*
> TRALEG KYABGON, "DEPRESSION'S TRUTH"

Stop the Bleeding First

When we become ill there is a need for us to become attentive to ourselves. For example, if we are hit in the head with a brick we need to clean the wound and bandage our head. We would need to stop the bleeding. What tends to happen, though, with depression and anxiety is we may get too caught up in the whole experience and confusion of it all. Everything becomes about our depression and anxiety. As soon as possible we have to agree that this dis-ease, this depression, *is not just about you*. It affects everyone around you, including your larger community. Self-absorption is not a cure and will result in an even greater sense of isolation. Take care of the bleeding and then get on with the transformational healing that wants to take place. Hold a conversation with your depression within the context of your larger life—how might you use the experience of your depression to help the larger needs of the world around you? Make your depression transformational. Choose to have your depression be part of your creative and spiritual path as best you can. Don't wait until you are feeling better to be creative or to attend to your spiritual life. Come as you are.

A New Map of the World

If you are feeling overwhelmed or stuck in a long bout of depression, you can't afford to keep looking out into the world in the same way. Some views you hold of the world will need to change. This is part of the inner work I mentioned above. For a change in perspective to take place you will need some process of thought transformation. Such practices can be found in Buddhism (Lojong practices, meditation), cognitive-behavioral and didactic therapies, awareness techniques, and all therapies that include ways to investigate and transform your thoughts.

Paradoxically, depression and anxiety can be brought on by one's internal paradigm shifting. Life has brought to your doorstep some big changes, but you keep holding on to the old paradigm. You keep insisting on responding to your life in the same way. Depression and anxiety then are a call to change your view, to transform yourself. For example, perhaps in the past everything came easily, you didn't have much to worry about; then you lost your job or a loved one or some other

---

The Lojong Slogans

Lojong is translated literally as "mind training" and comes from the Mahayana school of Tibetan Buddhism and is my central spiritual practice. The principles that Lojong practice is based on are thousands of years old. They are attributed to the great Indian Buddhist teacher Atisha Dipankara Shrijnana, who was born in 982 CE. Atisha studied and practiced under a renowned teacher Dharmakirti. For a long time, these principles (first called the Atisha slogans) were kept secret and revealed only to select disciples. They have since been transmitted in several forms (by various adept teachers), and for the last couple of centuries they have been available to us. These and other established principles can be relied upon to guide us.

---

outward circumstance triggered a big change. Now you need a new map of the world since the world around you has changed. If you keep trying to take the old road to the new place you will remain lost (and depressed). Other times it may be that the life you thought would bring you happiness isn't. So the paradigm wants to shift but you may not know how to go about this internal transformation. Simply put, life is constantly in motion and changing, and when we hold on to an old story that is no longer even possible, depression can take root.

Most folks are as happy as they make up their minds to be.

ABRAHAM LINCOLN

A Spiritual Antidote to Depression

Your antidote to depression needs to include a spiritual component. This spiritual component means to bring forth (out into the world) such inner qualities as love, forgiveness, creativity, compassion, and awareness. Some spiritual step toward a new way of looking at and responding to your life must be part of the antidote. This is a willingness to make meaning of the depression.

Many times someone has come to me depressed and angry and it doesn't take a long exploration to find out that they are leaving a large part of their life unlived. Their antidote is simple (but not easy): They need to activate their creative life—take that class, bring out the guitar, write that book, advocate for legislation that protects the environment, move to the country and raise organic chickens, or hold more conversations and take more trips. They need to commit to the active creative life and do so in the open. And where the depression is persistent or recurring they need to commit again and again to the conversational life—the creative life that is lived in the presence of others.

If you don't fulfill your creative calling, we all lose.

Spirituality also means that we come to deeply understand that we are all connected somehow, that each person's life and what they do with it (or do not do with it) touches everything and everyone. Your life matters and it matters in a big way.

More Antidotes to Depression

Because depression is so pervasive and disabling, I offer up a few more antidotes for you to explore.

+ Spend time outside in a natural environment. Allow the natural beat of nature to soothe you. Breathe in some outdoor air, notice where the moon or sun is in the sky, get at least fifteen minutes of natural light a day. A fifteen-minute walk can cure just about anything.

+ Watch *Off the Map,* a 2003 movie about a family living "off the map." What do you think uplifted the husband and the visitor from their depressions? Consider how the entire movie is a metaphor for life's journey and the different choices we are presented with. How does each person represent different parts of you? Notice how the characters in the movie influence one another. This movie also struggles with the question of medication in the treatment of depression.

+ Don't isolate. No one can heal in isolation. Engage yourself in relationships with others such as your family, friends, and community. Do one small act a day that takes you outside of yourself and into conversation with another human being.

America will never be destroyed from the outside. If we falter and lose our freedoms, it will be because we destroyed ourselves.

ABRAHAM LINCOLN

The False God of Indifference

Have you ever relied on indifference to navigate a challenging encounter? Have others bumped up against this wall, this god of indifference in you? Or have you hit an interior place of indifference with a creative or spiritual commitment because it just doesn't seem to be going your way? Indifference is a powerful god with the power to build or destroy worlds. I also find that some confuse the meaning of *nonattachment* (found in Buddhist philosophy) with indifference. In the Buddhist philosophy being nonattached means you are not so self-absorbed. You are not attached to outcomes, or how others perceive you, for examples. You are not attached to getting things your way or having others be in agreement with you. This practice of nonattachment, however, does not invite us to put up a front of indifference.

A casual, dispassionate response to life's circumstances becomes, even if unwittingly, a defense from having direct experiences. Indifference used as a method of protection inhibits us from fully participating in life's conversations; conversations, not only with people, but also with the offerings of each experience and encounter. Furthermore, this indifference can show up in relationship to ourselves and to our choices. We may claim that this choice doesn't matter, but in reality every choice counts in that every choice plays a significant part in future conditions and experiences.

Indifference turns us away from situations that are innately intimate and often uncomfortable. We may choose indifference because we somehow want to shut out people or experiences from getting into our hearts and minds. I learned in my youth to use indifference as a way to protect and defend myself. In my indifference I could walk away without having risked anything. While it may have protected me in some past lethal situations, to have this as a habitual response only holds me back from true intimacy. Indifference prevents me from truly exploring places and people, and even the internal landscape of my own heart and mind. It makes me less vulnerable and available.

An Antidote to Indifference

The antidote to indifference is vulnerability—a vulnerable curiosity. Develop an appreciation for the other, whether the other is an individual or a situation.

Instead of bringing in our assumptions and projections, which cause us all sorts of problems, we bring in a vulnerability through our curiosity and appreciation. When we are reactively defensive and indifferent we close ourselves off from the other and all that the moment may truly be able to offer us. This vulnerable curiosity, which is a state of appreciation, can be defined by a willingness to learn and to be influenced by others. Curiosity allows us to explore the possibilities inherent in the given dynamic.

Instead of going into a situation with a mind set on protecting ourselves, we enter each conversation with a question mark. What wants to happen here? What is happening here? We keep an open heart to discover, listen, and participate in all that arises in each interaction. We become more and more curious and open in our interactions with others and in our different surroundings. Curiosity then is appreciative. When we are open, undefended, and curious we will naturally find ourselves in a state of appreciation. And from this comes a natural state of nonattachment to outcome because our energy and attention is going into appreciating the other, where a mutual exchange is taking place. We then don't hide behind a wall of indifference.

We remain curious about our choices, too. This does not mean we won't say no or decide not to participate in a relationship. What it means is that even in our rejections and disillusionments we can maintain vulnerability, a sacred curiosity to the other and to self.

Each of us has various titles and personas we can remain behind to keep us distanced from the vulnerability of an open heart. We can use our titles of professional, spiritual, teacher, author, counselor, or minister as a way to maintain a false separation from the other, an indifference that does indeed keep us from intimacy. We can feed a grandiose sense of self in rigidly holding on to certain beliefs we have of ourselves or the world. Such rigidity, a black and white stance to life, is a disguised form of indifference. Attitudes such as "I don't have to care because that is not important to me and my beliefs," or "I don't believe that," both give permission to shut oneself off from others.

I looked up the definitions and synonyms of the word *vulnerable,* and it does hold mostly negative references, such as "exposed to the possibility of being attacked or harmed." This mind-set of being prepared for the possibility of being attacked or harmed sets us up to be in a constant state of defensiveness and secrecy. I prefer to take *vulnerable* to be undefended and wide open to all that is possible in any given situation. I consider myself better prepared for the negative and positive when I hold a vulnerable curiosity. I view vulnerability as an open door and indifference as a locked door where the keys have gone missing.

In Buddhism it is recommended that your spiritual and creative pursuits be done in the nature of generosity through the motivation to experience the benefits of the act itself; that the practice be your goal, not what you will get from it. There is a great generosity of spirit and ethical discipline when we pursue beneficial acts for their own sake. I help someone across the street because she needs the help, not to feel good or to show off my spiritual integrity. When we write or paint simply for the sake of doing so, then the results will be beautiful and beneficial. This also alleviates a great deal of suffering because it gives us permission to let go of results, perfectionism, worry about or focus on outcome, or dependence on the response of others to our actions.

What both these qualities point to is nonattachment. We are nonattached to outcome, to how we appear to others, to praise and blame, to getting it just right. We generously shed our skins of attachment so we are then ethically sound in our states of generosity. We can only be generous when we are nonattached. So nonattachment is beneficial to you and others, while indifference can cause suffering to both.

And as far as our creative life, an attitude of nonattachment results in more movement, more ideas, and more room for what wants in next.

> *Ten thousand flowers in spring, the moon in autumn,*
> *a cool breeze in summer, snow in winter.*
> *If your mind isn't clouded by unnecessary things,*
> *this is the best season of your life.*
>
> WU-MEN HUI-K'AI,
> CHINESE ZEN MASTER

Further Tools of Exploration

✦ Contemplate and journal around these questions: What methods of protection have you used to keep yourself less vulnerable? Where are opportunities to cultivate a vulnerability through curiosity?

✦ Attend something that you would normally be closed off to and cultivate a vulnerable curiosity. Hold at least one conversation with someone else in this situation. Come away with an understanding of this "other." Write about how the other influenced you.

✦ Write about a childhood experience that trained you to be defensive, protective, or secretive. Once written, set it aside for a while, then come back to it and rewrite it. In the fictionalized rewrite have the story show a positive side to curiosity—how it may even "save the day."

✦ Explore and write about something you don't know anything about.

There Are Always Do-Overs

To the boy I knew in high school I say, "It is never too late for a do-over." I have a simple exercise with my daughter that helps undo negativity and generate positive karma on the spot. Sometimes I make a mistake with her. I get impatient or make a rude remark or assume incorrectly and act on this assumption. When this happens (and I catch myself or my daughter catches me), we have a do-over. I stop myself as soon as I become aware and say, "Do-over." Then I do it over with more patience and integrity. Maybe we even throw in a little humor. This helps purify the previous negative actions, and we get to create from this more generous and loving place. We can do this in any area of our lives. Anyone who has ever dieted knows the importance of being able to start over after indulging in a bit too much pie. Better to start over than to live one more day intoxicated by suffering and alcohol; better to start over with a healthy breakfast than give up on the wholesome diet. Better to keep taking the next step, and then the next. Any day can be a do-over. I have known the use of do-overs to save a few relationships.

Inevitably we can get to a place in life where a do-over is not possible. I can imagine how hard it is to do a major do-over after a lifetime of drinking or putting things off. I worked with a woman who lived with her mother up to the age of fifty-five. This was not so much to care for her mother but was her part in perpetuating a codependent relationship. She sat before me and said, "I never lived my life, I lived my mother's." Before you are incapacitated, too old to move, or brought down by a disease or death—take that next step toward something that calls to you—take the path of intention.

> *There is no reality except the one contained within us. That is why so many people live such an unreal life. They take the images outside them for reality and never allow the world within to assert itself.*
>
> HERMAN HESSE, *DEMIAN*

Reshaping your life at midpoint can be particularly challenging, but maybe more necessary. Routine, habit, and comfort play a big role in life by midpoint and beyond. We become accustomed to certain states and experiences. Yet, something keeps calling out to us. Something inside keeps nudging us to explore something yet uncharted. And all of us know stories of people recovering after decades of alcoholism, creating something beautiful in their nineties, or starting up a business or project in their retirement years. I have a friend who is accomplishing his dream of writing a book; he just turned seventy.

The Hungry Ghost of Dissatisfaction

I can't get no satisfaction
but I try . . .

MICK JAGGER AND KEITH RICHARDS

Dissatisfaction is a hungry ghost. And, Dissatisfaction is a protective deity.

As a hungry ghost, dissatisfaction can keep us in a chronic state of hunger, discontent, and perfectionism. This flavor of dissatisfaction often arises when we have our attention on the results of our efforts rather than the activity itself. We don't enjoy the journey there because it is all about *getting there*. This focus on the end result is a huge diversion—when is something actually complete? Where in nature, or in your life, is something truly done? Every living thing is part of a life-death-life cycle. Even dead doesn't necessarily mean done. In my writing life there are so many stages of completion, making writing more like walking a spiral than a linear path. Even when I have finished writing a book, my relationship with it isn't over.

On the spiritual path, the hungry ghost of dissatisfaction arises from being told what a spiritual experience or practice "should" look like. Instead of enjoying the moments of meditation, encounters in nature, or studying spiritual text, we remain dissatisfied when we haven't achieved some predetermined state. It's not enough to just enjoy the benefits of a practice; we have to experience something specific that is already set for us. This hungry ghost can rob us of any happiness with ourselves because we never get *it* quite right. Or when we do get it, the experience doesn't last. Some religious enterprises require that we remain dissatisfied with ourselves, thus we always have to perfect ourselves if we want to obtain some heavenly state or to avoid hell. (And this fills up the pews, as we are in constant need of guidance.) A spiritual tradition that doesn't allow for satisfaction is a good one to abandon.

Letting go of perfection and expectation is an antidote to chronic dissatisfaction. Harvest the joy from each moment of working with whatever is in front of you and let go of expectations of how it "should" be. This allows for surprises—then as you let go of perfection and expectations something bigger and better emerges. In spiritual practice, letting go of expectations makes room for direct spiritual experience in the moment because we are in attendance to the here and now. In creative life, letting go of expectations and perfection allows for more play, along with the enjoyment that inventiveness brings.

As a protective deity, dissatisfaction holds up a mirror for us. Sometimes dissatisfaction points to a place, endeavor, or relationship that can't be fixed and is better off abandoned. Sometimes it is correct to let go, move on, or give up. Dissatisfaction as a protective deity lets us know that something is off. As a protective deity it taps us on the shoulder and asks: "Are you doing your best?" "Is everything really okay?" "What would bring more lasting satisfaction?" This deity acts as the sand in the oyster shell with the grittiness of discontent resulting in a pearl.

Lasting satisfaction comes in our discernment of what flavor of dissatisfaction we are experiencing—a hungry ghost that can only be transformed from within, or a protective deity that points to an external situation that needs transformation? Even with the latter, most of the transformative process will be an internal one. To leave a bad marriage, abandon a worn-out commitment, or ditch a dead-end job first depends on a shift in the internal landscape of one's mindset and self-perception.

In both cases chronic dissatisfaction can lead to depression, hopelessness, negative habitual states, and, fundamentally, a wasted life. It is essential that we hold a conversation with our dissatisfaction. Where does the dissatisfaction truly arise, from within or without? What can you do with the situation from your side of the equation? Through actively living life from our side we discover that everything, and I mean absolutely everything, is workable. Again, this points to the zero point antidote—everything that shows up in our life is workable. No one can take your place as the meaning maker in your life; no one is in the position to transform your life but you. You hold the best seat in the house. Always have. Always will.

+ Take a personal inventory of your own life. Where does dissatisfaction persistently arise? Is this the hungry ghost of dissatisfaction or the protective deity of dissatisfaction?
+ Write about when enough wasn't enough.
+ Write about contentment from a migrating bird's perspective using the following words: exodus, sea, arbor, guest, song, and advantage.

I love Jesus, who said to us:
heaven and earth will pass away.
When heaven and earth have passed away,
my word will still remain.
What was your word, Jesus?
Love? Forgiveness? Affection?
All your words were one word: Wakeup.

ANTONIO MACHADO,
FROM "PROVERBS AND TINY SONGS"

The False Gods of Blame and Shame

The following excerpt was written by a client, "Steven," about our discussion of his mother's response to his decision to avoid certain family situations detrimental to his recovery from alcoholism: "My mother keeps telling me I hurt her. I have been in recovery for fifteen years, straight and getting happier by the day. It still takes some effort to fight the addict but I find life getting easier and easier. My mother says I am hurting her when I don't show up for some of the family get-togethers, which are a time of overeating, overdrinking, and doing drugs behind closed doors. There are usually fights. Julie said, 'You *are* hurting her.'"

Steven is hurting his mother because she chooses to be captive of a victim mentality where her son's well-being disrupts her plans and what she believes. When one is "hurt" there is a belief of blame that goes with it. She blames him for her unhappiness or disappointment in this case. He is seen as the cause of her hurt feelings. In her view, he is to blame. She will not be able to transform the negativity in any way because she is feeling hurt. She is being a victim. If on the other hand she were able to live life from her zero point, from her side, she could feel the transformative *pain* of disappointment and choose what to do about it. She might then wake up to another way of being in the world that was unavailable to her through her previous beliefs and assumptions.

Feeling hurt and blaming others will not bring about any positive change. Whereas, in feeling the transformational sting of pain and taking responsibility to confront what inside us is likely contributing to this painful state, positive change is then a given. Take the time to differentiate between the states of "being hurt" and experiencing pain. Allow yourself to feel the transformative power of pain, recognizing what is contributing to it and the relative antidotes.

This entire book, with the premise of the zero point agreement, gives antidotes to blaming others for our experiences.

The False God of Shame

It finally came—that knock on my door. I knew it would. I was found out. Caught. It was a Saturday morning (back in the early 1990s), and the mailman brought a note to me that said the post office had a certified letter for me, but I would have to go sign for it. I had to wait until Monday morning to read its contents. The unexpected knock itself triggered shame (who besides an unhappy visitor with bad news would be knocking on my door?), which the unknown contents of the certified letter only strengthened. I was in some big trouble for something. Only, I couldn't pinpoint what caused these feelings. Where did this feeling of shame come from? What would cause me to hold a negative assumption about an unexpected knock at the door? I couldn't connect it to anything I had actually recalled doing, ever.

This is the face of shame—a feeling there is something fundamentally wrong with us, even though we can't always join it to something. What is the meaning of those dreams we have that we didn't actually take enough college credits to get our diploma and that they would soon hunt us down and get their credentials back? What makes us feel bad about ourselves when we are actually doing well? The false god of shame is jealous, possessive, and deceitful. She will ruin your life if you let her.

I would not waste a moment on trying to figure out why you feel this shame—suffice it to say it derives from some past experience. Do not confuse shame with guilt. Guilt takes on the flavor of feeling accountable about something you did or experienced like accidentally hitting an animal with your car (you may have been driving too fast) or getting angry with your child (you may have been having a bad day). Similar to the difference between hurt and pain, guilt (like pain) results in some transformative effort on your part while shame (like feeling hurt) mires you down. Instead of getting caught up in the *why* of it all, work with the energy of shame itself. Understand that you have come to personalize a negative past experience. If there are no words or explanation for your feelings of shame, the incidences may have occurred before you could speak (so there are no words for it). And, understand that both children and adults tend to personalize abuse. When this happens, the shame tends to go underground and surfaces to interfere with the naturalness and joy of future situations.

This knock on my door, which occurred more than twenty years ago, helped me become aware of the shame I carried within me and how easily it was triggered. I took this as the entryway into my true inheritance of happiness and freedom and began to release the bonds of shame. Fortunately, we don't need to know the specifics of the original causes to heal or transform the shame. Instead of holding shameful thoughts and acting from this place, we can name shame for what it is—a false god. What really pointed to the pressure of shame for me was when I discovered what the letter actually contained. The bank was letting me know that my security box payment was due. Ha!

Relying on these false gods only strengthens the habitual patterns that cause you to suffer and to lose the trust you have for yourself, for others, and for the spiritual qualities, such as compassion, that unify us all. Wherever you lack trust (which can only be had from your side) is also where you will find you lack the ability to move forward. Faith (or trust) is a major lubricant in our spiritual and creative life. We cannot take the next step if we don't trust our own abilities, trust in what's possible, and trust a bit in the unknown. We can't take the next step or see what is possible if we don't have some faith in others and in the process of life.

The Antidote of Faith

> *There is infinite space in your garden;*
> *all men, all women are welcome here;*
> *all they need do is enter.*
>
> THE ODES OF SOLOMON

She hasn't budged from her nest. The snow now covers her entirely, making her look more like a snowy muskrat den than a sandhill crane. And it is April. This is her third attempt to nest her eggs to life. Last spring a local raccoon or coyote got her eggs, the year before that the pair was too immature to succeed. Now, the cold and snow threaten her chances of fruition. Watching her helps me understand the natural power of faith. It takes faith to try something—to consider a spiritual or ethical path. It takes again more trust to get through the rough spots of your chosen spiritual practice. Finally, it takes continued faith to practice every day. But with this faith to practice comes the fruition of practice—genuine spiritual experiences.

Early on in my spiritual search and adventures (in my teen years) I desperately wanted to feel the faith so many around me claimed. I wanted to feel "the love of Jesus in my heart" as the Southern Baptist minister and his followers said I could (and should). But I felt nothing. I never could blindly follow any teacher or doctrine. I have a history of arguing with teachers and challenging doctrine. This has mostly been good, but even now I covet the *instinctual confidence* of the sandhill crane—I want that kind of faith. What it must be like to just know and trust that at some point such effort leads to something worth the effort.

From the start of our spiritual journey to the end, we must have real faith; real confidence, a trust that our efforts will give us results. To even "build the nest" of a spiritual or creative practice we have to have just enough confidence to give it a try. Investigate the territory. Lay the foundation. It takes faith to even explore a possible path (nesting ground). At this initial stage, you require just enough confidence to be willing to try a practice or idea on for size. One size does not fit all when it comes to a spiritual practice or a creative endeavor. Trying one on to see how it fits gives you some experience on which to base your decision whether or not to choose this as your spiritual path or creative pursuit.

When a teacher or doctrine wants you to build your nest and lay your eggs without any discernment on your part, or the teacher discounts any of your concerns, they are recruiting you and creating the experience of a counterfeit faith. Most often such means to recruit followers results in more suffering on the part of the practitioner and certainly cuts off opening up to greater possibilities. Again, this also applies to the creative path where the teacher insists that all trees be painted in her image of a tree. Blind faith doesn't allow for any genuine development of character or advancement of the practitioner or artist. In this case you just swallow someone else's truth without investigation or true understanding. You then progress along someone else's path and not one you have forged for yourself. In the spiritual world, you learn to regurgitate texts and doctrine; in the creative life, you learn how to draw by numbers. Obviously, authentic faith is not blind faith in doctrine, technique, or a given teacher.

Faith that results in an authentic and meaningful spiritual experience is faith that arises from within. Faith is authentic when it springs from reason, infused in the reality of personal experience. Give yourself just enough confidence to explore and find a spot in the diverse prairie of the spiritual traditions offered us. Listen then to the teachings and to your intuition as you forge your own path, using the wisdom from your chosen teachings. Or, as in the creative life, explore the medium for yourself. Based on hearing, studying, and practicing your chosen spiritual principles, you begin to experience the benefits from these efforts directly.

Faith increases through personal experiences, which were a direct result of your having enough faith to even give it a try. The beautiful truth about such confidence is that it generates more possibilities. Losing faith leaves us with less, not more. True faith can get us through the worst of scenarios. Like the snow-covered crane incubating her clutch, we can tap into our inherent confidence to endure the obstacle and transform our difficulty into an opportunity. Given a little faith at each step and turn, we can take the next step and turn. Each of us can come to realize our ability to increase our faith through our own efforts. We, too, can be like the sandhill crane who has chosen her spot to nest despite any present hardship.

The real beauty of faith is revealed to us through our daily efforts. Every time we meditate, our faith in its benefits increases because we experience its returns. We study and rehearse our spiritual and ethical principles and notice our hearts opening more and more. Our faith increases and deepens with each experience. We create a poem or a sketch and experience the exuberance of such acts. It feels good. *Faith begets faith.*

As I write this I look out through the spotting scope and can see the neck of the sandhill crane standing out like a sentinel, the thin red strip of her crest a signal—*I am still here,* she declares to me. Her body is an epic of snow and ice. She sits and does what she knows works; what has worked for eons. She waits faithfully. And in my watching, my faith deepens too. I will keep watch as we both move closer and closer to the realization of our intentions.

When Giving Up Is the Best Antidote

The longer I live, the more beautiful life becomes.

FRANK LLOYD WRIGHT

I continued to watch as the sandhill crane sat on her eggs in our prairie on the border of the pond; by this time she had been incubating them for more than forty days. She sat through the spring snowstorm, a cold and wet month, and several thunderstorms. The incubation period for a crane is around thirty days. By now, she sat on eggs that were not viable. Dead. I watched the entire process through our spotting scope. I watched the pair do their mating dance. I saw her sit for days covered in snow, which had previously inspired me to persevere. I watched her turn the eggs and attend the nest. I kept looking for that small, downy head to appear from the prairie. This was her third attempt at nesting in as many years.

Where her tenacity in the past gave me evidence of the power of faith, her inability to give up mirrors to me the suffering caused in not letting go. Sometimes we hold on just because it feels impossible to give up on something that we have invested so much time (and perhaps money and attention) in. Or, we simply don't know that what we are sitting on has lost its vitality.

What is the point where we say to ourselves, this egg is dead? I realized that depression and disappointment are more about sitting on a dead egg than it is about the egg being dead. The longer you sit on something that is long past its due date, the more depressed or unhappy you are likely to get. So the question is, what needs letting go of? What do you need to give up on so your energy and attention can be put into something viable, something alive? If you spend most of your days and nights incubating something that is dead you will lose sight of what else is possible. At this point we often feel as if the potentiality of the situation is holding on to us. But the possibilities live elsewhere. There is a quote in the Bible that comes to mind, "I will not release you till you bless me." Bless your efforts and willingness to sit through the cold nights, and then say good-bye. It's time to move on.

Eventually the sandhill crane did let go and fly off. (It was too late in the year to attempt another nesting.) I am told that if all the birds that laid eggs were to succeed the sky would be stuffed with birds. Sometimes we give birth to an idea that is not going to have its chance for flight. But I trust she will try again next spring, ready to succeed.*

> *The creative act is not*
> *hanging on, but yielding*
> *to new creative movement.*
>
> JOSEPH CAMPBELL,
> *A JOSEPH CAMPBELL COMPANION*

---

*Dear reader, the following year, the year this book goes to print, the crane pair succeeded in hatching two colts.

3

Here, Take This Gift

REVITALIZING THE WORLD
ONE RELATIONSHIP AT A TIME

Here, take this gift,
I was reserving it for some hero, speaker, or general,
One who should serve the good old cause, the great idea,
the progress and freedom of the race,
Some brave confronter of despots, some daring rebel;
But I see that what I was reserving belongs to you just as
much as to any.

WALT WHITMAN, "TO A CERTAIN CANTATRICE"

The promise of the other—to experience and engage in intimate and dynamic relationships—is something wholly in our hands. To bring ourselves fully out into the open with who we are, as best we can, is the gift we offer each other. "Here, take this gift of me," you say to the other. We reserve nothing for a better time or for later. We offer the gift of self in our relationships *now*. We transform the world; heal the ecological and economic wounds through our relationships, one relationship at a time. As the I Ching points out in its five-thousand-year-old philosophy and David Bohm shows in his research in relationships and quantum mechanics, we start with the individual, then go out to our intimate relationships, then to our communities, and then the world. It always starts here with you, at the zero point, transforming the world by what you do and bring to the relationships close to you, always starting with yourself. (You will find that we tend to want to go transform the world while ignoring the more intimate relationships in our lives.)

To heal the world's pain stories we need a willingness to cultivate a fearless heart—a heart that will keep opening to life and to the others.

Letting Go of Holding Back

Revitalizing our lives, our relationships, and the planet is all about letting go of holding back.

This makes me think of the woman who buys bananas but waits too long to enjoy them so they go bad before she eats them. It's that part of us that saves the best for last, or that saves and saves to the point of hoarding. We may have a lot of stuff or even be in relationships, but without a true interaction with these, one is holding back. There are so many ways we hold back, pull away, hide out, and don't show ourselves. And then our sweet opportunity in this relationship or in this lifetime is gone. It is in relationship with others that we really encounter our edges of vulnerability, intimacy, and creativity.

Through our more intimate relationships we really take the hero's journey—the pilgrimage to the holy site. In our relationships we will consistently bump up against that place where we hold ourselves back and where we are invited to open ourselves up to the other (and to ourselves). Again because of our personal histories, assumptions, and beliefs we enter these relationships, and instead of opening ourselves up to the other there is a tendency toward protecting ourselves from what we anticipate may hurt us. And if we ever get to the point where we get exhausted by our holding back (because it takes energy), the banana may have already gone bad so all we can do is throw it out. This *not holding back* doesn't mean to eat all the bananas at once either. It doesn't mean that we have to share all of ourselves, all the time. In John Gottman's research* on marriages they discovered that we don't have to air it all

---

*See Gottman's book, *Why Marriages Succeed or Fail: And How You Can Make Yours Last*.

out, all the time to consider our relationships intimate and healthy.

When we are in a marriage or other long-term relationship we create *patterns of agreement*. We come to assume certain things about ourselves and the other and create patterns around these. Everyone does it. When someone in the relationship is seen as overly emotional or needy, for example, the relationship begins to form itself around this story. This makes it very challenging to transform this perception and get beyond it. Too often our view of others is quite narrow and limited, as if we are peeking through a crack in the door. The small view limits what we can actually perceive. We hold a false perspective of others. Ironically it takes quite a bit of energy to hold that view—imagine bending down and always looking at the other through a narrow opening, eyes squinting. When we watch another through a narrow view, the other becomes narrow. Every one of us does things (unconsciously and consciously) to fulfill certain patterns of agreement, living by our assumptions, until we decide (from our side) not to.

Fortunately, all our relationships respond and align to the efforts made on our side of the relationship. We can create a more spacious attitude toward others and let in all the potentiality that our relationships bring to us. We need to stop seeing others through such a small crack in the door.

This is how it works—you show up for your part of the conversation, take one hundred percent responsibility for your issues, and transform the world (one relationship at a time). This is the good news that comes with confronting our own issues and their sustaining assumptions; we are also breaking with the global pain stories and all the culturally endorsed assumptions that sustain them. Every time you are suffering, know that there are others experiencing something similar. With every dynamic we transform through our personal efforts, we transform this energy and dynamic in the world as well. Our personal and collective problems are all rooted in the assumptions we hold of ourselves, others, and the world. And although we hold many *personal* assumptions that keep a pain story active, we also are in agreement with *culturally endorsed* pain stories and assumptions. (Some of the collective assumptions we hold are presented in

Wheel of Initiation as the "culturally endorsed agreements" we live by.)

Many of our collective assumptions give us a posture of competitiveness over cooperation; a way to divide us and keep us divided and often at odds with each other. Unknowingly we become habitual and even dependent upon our assumptions (many of which are under the radar of our awareness). This makes it easier to blame our circumstances as the culprit for our unhappiness when all along we hold the means to create a truly rich and purposeful life. There is actually less energy and effort taken up by living more consciously and responsibly.

> *They would rather be dependent in a hostile environment and combat it every day than manage their own lives. In this way they avoid having to confront their own anxieties and discomfort about activating and asserting their real selves.*
>
> JAMES F. MASTERSON,
> *THE SEARCH FOR THE REAL SELF*

Assume This!

> *It is the nature of the mind to become addicted to certain ways of seeing things.*
>
> LAMA ZOPA RINPOCHE,
> *TRANSFORMING PROBLEMS INTO HAPPINESS*

> *Creativity, in almost every area of life, is blocked by a wide range of rigidly held assumptions that are taken for granted by society as a whole.*
>
> DAVID BOHM, "DIALOGUE AS A NEW CREATIVE ORDER"
> FROM *THE ESSENTIAL DAVID BOHM*

Assumptions underlie every thought, every interaction, and every experience. Somehow all of our suffering can be melted down to the assumptions we hold individually and collectively.

Assumptions predispose us to experience others and situations a certain way. There are countless assumptions built into our unconscious from our past, family, and cultural heritage. If we are part of some organized religion, we are in agreement with some rather significant assumptions. For those who are part of a group, especially where there is emphasis on those who belong to the group and those who do not—there are likely unspoken assumptions that keep you part of the "in group." Assumptions are so consistent, historic, and pervasive we can't expect to free ourselves of them with a simple affirmation.

What we all need to do to experience more joy and freedom in our relationships is *assume we are making assumptions*. When you do the "Being the Witness" exercise on page 123, just witnessing yourself in certain social interactions, you can add to this exercise by noticing what assumptions are (or may be) operating within and about you. By assuming we are all operating under assumptions, we will walk more consciously and gently among each other. Assume a posture of consciousness. What a gift to bring such consciousness to your relationships with the knowledge that you are always holding assumptions.

Transform the Assumptions

+ Routinely *assume you are making assumptions*. Go into encounters with a willingness to check in on what these assumptions may be or to simply be kinder to yourself and others knowing assumptions are in operation.

+ Look at it this way: you will have a choice to make assumptions or make meaning from your encounters. This is another opportunity to consciously practice the zero point agreement, *to live life from your side*.

+ You then focus your attention on your end of the conversation or experience, transforming the assumptions into a receptivity to the other. You transform them at first simply by becoming aware that you are making assumptions. After a while you become aware of specific assumptions underlying this interaction.

Since assumptions are typically made about the "other," when we act on our assumptions we are breaking with our agreement to live life from our side. Our focus then becomes about the other and not so much about what we can do to uplift the situation. The more we cross over into the other person's issues the further we make assumptions and lose touch with what is really going on. And more importantly we shut ourselves off from what else can happen within this dynamic. Our assumptions are restrictive; acknowledging them loosens the assumption's hidden grip on us. To live life from your side means to assume you are caught up in some assumptions about yourself, the situation, and anyone else involved in the predicament. Take time to make some inquiry into your own assumptions.

Consider which assumptions may be operating when you find yourself in a difficult or challenging situation, and do your best to live life from your side. You may also do this at unfettered times; this way you can learn to identify your assumptions without the pressure of a difficulty. This is where practice and realization become the same—while we practice more presence and openness in our interactions we experience personal realizations. We realize more of our own true nature and what is really going on rather than reacting to our assumptions. Bohm, in his work as a scientist, noted that true science is always challenging assumptions, even those made in the face of evidence of something solid and remarkable. We may discover something solid about the other; for example, that they have a master's degree in biology, but here too there are built-in assumptions about what this means, and how it came about. To be in dynamic relationships with each other and our surroundings, Bohm speaks of a "creative order" that at least attempts to break through assumptions.

> *It should be clear by now that the major barriers to such [a creative] order are not technical; rather they lie in the rigid and fragmentary nature of our basic assumptions. These keep us from changing in response to the actual situations and from being able to move together from commonly shared meanings.*
>
> DAVID BOHM, "ON DIALOGUE AND ITS APPLICATION"
> FROM *THE ESSENTIAL DAVID BOHM*

When we first accept that we hold assumptions, we are able to view and respond to new ideas, to see the many other possibilities inherent in the situation because we have gotten beyond an assumptive posture. Then in more challenging encounters you can become aware that the reasons for someone else's behavior, choices, and emotional reactions are not fully known to you. This way, you can offer up some equanimity and compassion when another's choices and behaviors are upsetting or confusing, instead of adding to the negativity with your assumptions.

Because we are always assuming *something,* using ethical or spiritual principles can help challenge underlying principles and direct our experience in a more compassionate and awakened way. This makes room for a more creative interaction between you and all others.

Here, Take this Principle

Nothing can bring you peace but yourself. Nothing can bring you peace but the triumph of principles.

RALPH WALDO EMERSON

Principles help us continue to break hindering patterns and live a truly inspired life. It is important to remember that our *principles* are chosen by us after we have given them much thought and consideration, whereas *beliefs* are based on our pain stories and assumptions we may not even realize we hold. When a habit arises, which is always based on some assumption, and we want to change it, a "destiny decision" is being presented to us (as Joseph Campbell would say). We can decide to do the habitual thing or call forth our inherent wisdom through the application of our principles. Principles are like oars in a boat or reins on a horse; they help move us in the right direction. Principles that are in alignment with our spiritual practices and creative ideals are capable of transforming our lives on the spot. They give us the means to navigate life and our relationships with integrity.

They give you a way to live a more inspired life in the world and a way to fulfill your creative and spiritual intentions and to open up more to what is truly possible. When you encounter difficulty, you don't have to engage with the problem or the drama. Furthermore, when you find yourself stuck or in resistance, assumptions are the culprit and principles can be the lubricant. We experience and see what we are habituated to. When we go into an encounter loaded with assumptions about the other and predict a certain result, we usually get what we expect. You don't have to do the same old thing based on your assumptions. We can do something differently and when we do something differently, we get something different.

His Holiness the Dalai Lama usually begins his teachings with an introduction that emphasizes applying ourselves and studying the dharma, spiritual principles. And he concludes with a reminder to access wisdom through reading and studying. He reminds us how the Buddha discouraged people from simply following him and instead emphasized the importance of everyone generating a mind and heart of compassion.

His Holiness talks about our ability to differentiate right from wrong, and how our choices and actions need to come from compassionate wisdom and moral principles. Every arena of our lives should be rooted in ethical principles. So we have to ask ourselves—What are my spiritual principles? What ethics do I live by and apply on a daily basis?

Earlier in the book I pointed to the value of understanding the motives behind our spiritual practices. What actually inspires us to commit to a more creative or ethical life? For many Buddhists, we are motivated to live a principled life due to our faith and understanding of karma—the law of causality. For Christians and others it may be a faith and understanding of "ultimate truth," or a concept of God. For those who come from a more secular or humanist tradition, they may have confidence that an ethical and compassionate person is more calm, happy, and beneficial to others and these are a great motivation to live a principled life. It is worthwhile for each of us to contemplate what underlies our motivation to live a principled life. For me, the resulting benefits are enough, but my added understanding of karma too influences my motivation to live a life guided by principles.

A disturbed mind makes mistakes and doesn't know or see reality.

His Holiness the fourteenth Dalai Lama

In order for us to see beyond our assumptions and negative projections, we need to rely on a set of ethical and spiritual principles. Rather than get caught up in your perception of a situation, bring forth a principle and apply it. Even in those times when you may forget your principles or cannot bring one to mind, your curiosity about which principle to employ may help you with the particular predicament you find yourself in. This will enlighten your perceptions and your actions. It's hard to be personally caught up in a difficulty or operate unconsciously by assumptions when you focus instead on the compassionate action you could take. Your curiosity alone will help you be unprejudiced about the situation and ethically find a creative way through it.

While investigating principles from diverse philosophies, practices, and traditions, I found that they share common elements. I present them here to help you identify or strengthen your own principles.

- Authentic principles offer an altruistic and ethical means to interact in the world.
- Authentic principles are simple to understand and can be used on the spot.
- A natural process of creativity is activated when using a principle: you are being active rather than reactive, and this allows for a more creative dynamic.
- You take one hundred percent personal responsibility for your life and use your principles to help you do so. They promote the zero point agreement, helping you to live life from your side.
- Authentic principles reflect and support the reality that everything in life is dependent upon everything else (dependent arising/Heart Sutra). Therefore, your principles positively affect others too.
- Authentic principles provide you with the means to be less self-absorbed.
- Authentic principles help you realize the preciousness of life and teach you not to waste it. I watched a wonderful docudrama, *The Cave of the Yellow Dog,* which took place in Mongolia. It depicted nomadic life in this century. An elder was teaching a young child how precious life is. She gave the child a needle and some rice, then asked the child to drop a kernel of rice on top of the needle. After many attempts, the

child was unsuccessful. The elder then said, "This is how easy it is to be born as a human being." This life is certainly a rare opportunity. Don't waste it!

- Authentic principles allow you to release habitual patterns and transform the mind.
- Authentic principles strengthen your trust in yourself and others because they bring out the best in you.
- Authentic principles instill and strengthen your patience and perseverance on the ethical and creative path.
- Authentic principles bring forth equanimity.
- Authentic principles are life-enhancing agreements that sustain and promote your creative intentions.
- Authentic principles are in alignment with spiritual and humanitarian traditions and wisdom that has been tried and tested throughout the centuries. They have some roots in our spiritual heritage. Sacred texts can be referred to for insight when applying your principles.
- Authentic principles will transform habitual thought patterns, clearing the way for your true nature. All principles should have the capacity to transform the mind, bringing it into a more enhanced state of awakening.

The Lojong teachings offer the practitioner seven points that have within them fifty-nine principles. Each principle (often referred to as a slogan—see "The Lojong Slogans" on page 85) gives us the ability to completely transform our attitude overall as well as on the spot. Fifty-nine may sound like a lot, too many to be truly accessible. I have memorized approximately a dozen of them and work with these twelve on a regular basis. I continue to study the others and apply them. After you have identified your core principles, a great way to complement your practice is to choose texts or books that help you understand your principles more fully. You can then do inquiry meditation around them (see "Profound Awakening through Inquiry Meditation," page 39).

Start with any principles you may already have or you can borrow from the Lojong principles or identify some others from your own spiritual tradition. Our spiritual principles, whether they come from a more secular humanist, spiritual, or philosophical tradition, are a strong expression of what we are in agreement with. When I practice a principle, I am stating to the world and to myself what I am in agreement with and what I am not in agreement with. Fundamentally I am also stating that I am not letting my life be dictated by known and unknown assumptions.

Here are a few of my favorites. But I encourage you to choose principles that both challenge your assumptive posturing and that direct your thoughts and behaviors in creative ways. And watch how these transform and uplift your relationships. A great resource for the Lojong principles is Traleg Kyabgon's book *The Practice of Lojong: Cultivating Compassion through Training the Mind.*

Always Maintain a Joyful Mind

We can practice a joyful approach to life's circumstances because we know every situation can be used to open our hearts even more and to discipline and transform our minds. I love this because then nothing can take us away from our principles and our creative and spiritual path. When we see those who cause us troubles as an opportunity to practice our principles, to open our hearts even wider, we are grateful to them. Everything holds the potential to bring us joy. We become more and more able to turn difficult situations into a place to make meaning. As a writer, I find too that challenges I meet on my path can be used in my work, both fiction and nonfiction. This helps create a joyful mind because everything is material, all grist for the mill of the spiritual traveler or writer.

This of course doesn't mean never feeling sad, disappointed, or even angry; rather, it is an opportunity for transforming our experiences through our attitudes. The real potential of a situation is revealed when we are able to simultaneously have such feelings while still maintaining an uplifting attitude. Our personal potential to live more fully and consciously in our relationships emerges from this practice. *Always maintain a joyful mind* is a motto I hold strong in my mind with my teenage daughter. It helps me to frame all my conversations with her in a positive way.

Don't Be Swayed by External Circumstances

> *A difficult and challenging time must be taken as an opportunity to express in the outer world our highest inner principles.*
>
> BRIAN BROWNE WALKER,
THE I CHING OR BOOK OF CHANGES

This is also phrased as "Don't depend on external conditions." Certainly this is at the crux of this book's message! If we wait on certain conditions, or hold off on enjoying the banana until it goes bad, our happiness will be taken from us. And this holding off or waiting on certain external conditions will become more and more habitual. Then outward conditions will always dictate how we feel about ourselves and others and will further determine our experiences. Even those who believe in fate, or determinism, can still choose *how* to make meaning from their fate. To say, "this is fate," and not do anything with it is truly passive.

We will continually meet with favorable and unfavorable circumstances. Since external conditions are outside of our control (not influence), we are better served by learning how to be content and creative *within* the diverse circumstances we are likely to encounter. Every situation can be an opportunity to develop living less habitually and more creatively. We need only to stop waiting on or withdrawing from the potential available to us in each moment.

Don't Bring Things to a Painful Point

This one is my favorite when it comes to dismantling aggression or difficulty with someone. This is reflected in this popular Zen story.

✦✦✦

Two monks were traveling by foot back to the monastery after a day of working in the village. As they approached a creek, they saw a beautiful woman standing next to it. Their vows included not gazing upon or touching a woman. When they arrived at the creek, they saw that she could not cross it, as it was deep and her dress long and heavy. The younger of the two monks nodded at the woman as he crossed the creek.

The elder monk, however, offered to carry the young, beautiful woman across the water and did so without any trouble. He set her down on the other side, and he and the other monk walked on. About a mile down the road, the younger monk, who was getting more and more agitated, asked the elder monk, "How could you carry that woman across the creek? We are not even to gaze upon or touch a woman!"

The elder monk smiled and said, "I left her at the creek, while you are still carrying her."

✦✦✦

Have you ever done this—carried around something that upset you, building on it and then bringing it to a painful point? This principle asks us not to humiliate other people or ourselves. This principle reminds us that when we bring things to a painful point we are building on and generating more negativity. Also, we are certainly strengthening some negative assumptions we already hold.

Instead of getting caught up in our own intense emotions, habitual responses, or attachments we can apply this principle. When our emotions are triggered it is quite a challenge to not follow them to their conclusion by lashing out at others. A willingness to walk away until you have diminished the negativity around it will allow you to apply a principle and not be caught up in your assumptions or negative reactions. When you find yourself bringing things to a painful point you can ask yourself, what am I assuming here?

Start with the awareness of how when you feel bad you tend to want to bring things to a "shared" painful point. (Misery loves company becomes manifest.) Let go of the drama and worst case scenario. Choose not to make things worse by adding to an already painful situation. Notice how you may be taking something personally, and bring some compassion to yourself and the situation. When you apply an antidote (such as a principle or some other remedy) your energy then goes into something positive. Instead of bringing things to a painful point through witnessing someone doing wrong, catch others doing well.

Some refer to this principle as "not making insincere comments" or "not acting with a twist." We often bring things to a painful point by making some remark to another or pointing out someone's mistakes (like the monk above). Or we speak with a twist—sounding nice but really delivering a dig.

Also, holding a grudge and any negative attitude toward another is false protection. We think this barrier keeps the other out (and it might) but it keeps a lot of pollution trapped inside us. Like the younger monk, the one carrying the transgression in their mind is the one who suffers the most. Much like a valley holds on to the pollutants, our holding a grudge ultimately makes us sick.

Through the cultivation of our principles we exhaust the negative habits and find ourselves being like the practiced elder monk—free from the bondages of assumptions and negativity.

Be Grateful to Everyone

When someone else bothers you it is because it connects with something you assume. Therefore we can be grateful to everyone, particularly our troublemakers, because they show us where we are caught up in our own assumptions. What bothers you doesn't in fact bother everyone. I've discovered that what bothers us can be ridiculously personal and something often no one else even notices. Others will always mirror to us where we are most stuck. They unknowingly shake up our assumptions by not being in agreement with the same ones. Others will say or do things that bring up our personal issues and make us want to hold back. Be grateful because it is within these relationships that we see how we are suffering and can do something about it. Without others triggering us we may not take the time to challenge our habitual and painful states. Be grateful for that!

This principle also applies to larger issues of valid disagreement—like where we might disagree with someone around a fundamental opinion, such as the value of recycling or the validity of climate change. Even here we can be grateful that they are offering us an opportunity to hear their story or express our opinion. Bringing forth an "attitude of gratitude" can generate spaciousness around what might otherwise be a tense situation.

Traleg Kyabgon echoes this principle when he says, "Meditate on the great kindness of everyone." This reminds us that our lives are built on the efforts and the compost of others. (And this often includes the troublemakers in our lives.) Nothing came to us on its own, without the participation of countless others. Instead of getting all caught up in how others bother or offend us, remember how your meals, your heating, all the comforts you experience are wholly dependent on a multitude of others. I realize everything I leave behind after I take the big journey to the beyond is potential compost for someone else's life. My books, my creative ideas, even my gardens and home may become compost for someone else's intentions and creations. Make rich compost.

Making Compost

Acknowledge the compost of your life. Ask yourself these questions:

✦ In the knowledge that everything I have now put out there may still be there when I am gone, how nutrient rich are my life and actions?

✦ Do I have creations in my life that are like plastic; biologically inert and a hazard to future generations?* Plastics are used because they are convenient and cheap. Am I doing something simply because it is easy and "cheap"? Am I cheap with my words or am I impeccable with my word? What in my life acts like plastic?

✦ Remember the false god of settling mentioned in the previous chapter? How might settling be making for nutrient deprived soil in your life? What would it mean to make your entire life suitable for the future generation's compost? Assess all levels with this question. Just what am I leaving behind? Let me make sure everything is rich with the potential to be used by generations to come.

Use of our principles in situations that are difficult reminds me of a Zen story about something that took place when the Japanese were overrunning Korea in the 1930s. Japanese soldiers entered a Korean Zen monastery and found most of the monks gone. But the abbot remained,

---

*Every year, around 500 billion plastic bags are used worldwide. This means every man, woman, and child on the planet uses eighty-three plastic bags every year. That's one bag per person every four and a half days. Of those 500 billion bags, 100 billion are used in the United States alone.

sitting like an iron lotus in the zendo. The officer in charge drew his sword, walked up to the abbot, and said, "I could run you through without blinking an eye!" The abbot roared back, "I can be run through without blinking an eye!" The soldiers left the abbot alone. I imagine that really happened. Our principles are often our best protection when we are in upsetting situations, as this story points out.

Avoid Misunderstandings—Don't Misinterpret

Don't misinterpret is ostensibly a simple slogan, but there is more to it. This is true of any chosen spiritual principle, such as the Lojong slogans, the four agreements, or the beatitudes.* They may be pithy one-liners that point to a principle, such as, *happy are the merciful; for they shall be shown mercy* or *be grateful to everyone* or *don't take anything personally,* but there is more text available to study to fully understand and carry them out. The beatitudes, for example, are followed by commentary in the version set forth in the Gospel of Matthew. Beyond the Bible or the original text where such principles are presented are countless other commentaries to study. A great book to accompany the beatitudes would be Neil Douglas-Klotz's *Prayers of the Cosmos: Meditations on the Aramaic Words of Jesus.*

The *don't misinterpret* principle is mostly about not misinterpreting spiritual teachings. Be careful *not to assume* what a teaching means. Or even once you decide, be willing to continue investigating its meaning for you rather than holding on to it like a weapon. Find out through an established teacher, read and study the text, and continue to learn more and more about a teaching and its meaning through inquiry practices as detailed in the "Basics of Inquiry Meditation" on page 47. It is not uncommon for people to take a spiritual teaching and twist it around to meet some self-absorbed posturing rather than use it to help them awaken (or in the case of some religious or cult leaders, use it to manipulate others). People recruit all sorts of "proof" to back up their assumptions.

Another way to misinterpret principles is to apply them only

---

*The term *beatitude* comes from the Latin adjective *beatus,* which means happy, fortunate, or blissful.

when it benefits you—for example, "I won't make assumptions about those who don't make assumptions about me." The Lojong teachings refer to six specific teachings that might typically be misinterpreted, and they all get down to how our misinterpretations are a means to benefit ourselves and promote more self-absorption rather than helping others.

This is a great slogan to carry with you into your relationships, guiding you to be less caught up in your own assumptions and desires.

> *Compost our inner, stolen fruit as we forgive others the spoils of their trespassing.*
>
> NEIL DOUGLAS-KLOTZ,
> *PRAYERS OF THE COSMOS*

Don't Carry Another's Shadow

Don't waste your precious time thinking about another's faults or wrongdoings. When we carry another's shadow we carry within us what we feel others *should* be doing to be better or to feel better. This of course is built on our assumptions about the other. "He shouldn't do that." Carrying another's shadow is not to be confused with compassion. Compassion is the ability to do our internal work so we can be present for someone else's suffering. In my Buddhist practice, carrying another's shadow is an example of mistaken compassion. You mistakenly assume that your "concern" for the other is correct when it is actually pondering their weaknesses. You carry this judgment and feedback within you as a weight—but what is the other up to? They are going on with life, making their own choices. Your carrying around their shadow does not help them.

I often suggest that people who are engaged in this internal gossip of what the other should or should not be doing might say to themselves, "This is none of my business." This is the principle within the Lojong teachings to *not ponder others*—not to ponder their faults. When we carry their shadow by thinking what they should and should not be doing, we are actually pondering their faults.

Once someone has offended or harmed you and you have decided to forgive them, do you find yourself reminding yourself of the offense when this person rises up in your thoughts? Why carry the shadow of the past? What happens to *you* when you ponder others' faults? Let these go by saying something like, "I let this one go" or "This is done." You can even respond with, "I no longer agree to carry this."

Practice checking in with your thoughts to notice how much you may be pondering others' faults or going over their wrongdoings in your mind. If you're feeling depressed, angry, or unhappy, notice how much of these emotional states relate to other people, how much of your accompanying thoughts are of others.

For me this also means not to compare ourselves with others. When we do this, we tend to believe ourselves to be better or worse, creating an unnecessary separation between the other person or persons and ourselves. This comparison is a seed of separation that has a tendency to grow into pathological assumptions about ourselves or others.

What you are likely noticing by now is that principles are pointers to what we are in agreement with and what we are not in agreement with. I often frame my principles in terms of what I am in agreement with (*I agree to maintain a joyful mind*), or what I am not in agreement with (*I don't agree to ponder others' faults*). Strong in our principles, we are able to see out into the world in a more sacred and creative way.

> *A sign of success in mind training is feeling more at ease with something that we once found difficult.*
>
> TRALEG KYABGON,
> *THE PRACTICE OF LOJONG*

The Transformative Power of Story

Another means to dismantle assumptions about a particular person is to hear their story. Through my decades of listening to others' life stories I have come to hold a wider view of the human experience. You will too. We all have a lifetime of stories. No one is ever just made up of what you see before you now (good or bad). And through the sharing of our life stories our assumptions about others get weakened in the face of their humanity. We witness more the reasons, the diverse causes and conditions that led this person to be this way. Sharing one's life story is an intricate part of the initiatory process I offer in my book *Wheel of Initiation* and in my initiation circles. You will find the process of storytelling in other places too, where narrative therapy is understood as a profound part of any healing process. Lewis Mehl-Madrona's work and books offer the sharing of story as wholly antidotal. You hear how others have made meaning of their lives when you listen to their stories.

It's good to start at the zero point—with our own stories first.

Listening for the Meaning in Your Life Story

When you write and listen to your own story, you hear the meaning you have made of your life up until now.

✦ Start with your own life story. In the writing and telling of your own life story, you discover personal truth and meaning. Begin with a journal and start wherever you like. Don't feel you have to write every detail or chapter of your life. You can even write lists of turning points and then write about various times that stand out. As you remember and write, you may find yourself stuck at certain times of your life. Acknowledge these moments and keep writing.

✦ Find at least one trusted friend, loved one, spiritual advisor, or transpersonal counselor you can tell your life story to.* Ask that they simply mirror your story and not give any suggestions or feedback. This is true for yourself as well—become your own mirror. Listen to your story and witness all your emotions, agreements, and beauty without trying to change anything or figure anything out. In the listening, the story itself will show you what you need to know—your agreements to the past, what needs releasing, what you have lost your energy to. It will also reveal some of your authentic story, your personal strengths.

✦ After writing and sharing your life story with others, you can do further inquiry using the following points:

---

*If you are going to read your life story to a circle of friends, please first read chapter 9, "Teachers and Groups," in *Wheel of Initiation* to help make this a safe and dynamic experience.

What are the assumptions that keep the pain story repeating? If you don't have any negative patterns (psychological, physical, financial, relational, spiritual) that seem to repeat over and over in your life, you are free of your pain stories and accompanying assumptions and are living the fully creative, engaged life. This is not to say that you will not have trials, however, for an awakened person is still human and must consciously keep their feet on the path. Through my work as a counselor and facilitator of transformation groups, I always discover the medicine next to the wound—within the stories we live and tell.

What are the times your view of yourself or the world have changed? This is sometimes where you moved from believing and expressing one assumption into another. Where once you were in agreement that you were an awesome example of creation, you began to feel small and devalued. Where in your story do you experience a shift in awareness or experience? The *why* is not important, but the *what* holds meaning for you here—what happened to cause you to shift your agreements and assumptions? What were the assumptions, and what did they become?

Every experience you have now is tied to an assumption you hold with yourself or the world. It becomes abundantly clear that it is not the event or person "out there" that keeps you in your pain, it is the *agreements and assumptions* connected with a person or an event that causes the continued suffering. So we take our focus off of how others are doing us wrong, how the other is causing us so much grief, and we name the assumptions within this dynamic. At this point, it doesn't matter whether you believe you can change the assumptions or not. Just begin here by naming the assumptions within your life story.

Ideally you can exchange life stories with others in a safe circle of trust or with a friend or loved one. The transformative power of sharing our life stories is beyond measure and worth the time and effort you put into it. As a therapist I've witnessed this experience result in profound healing and transformation of both the storyteller and the witness.

Everybody walks in the street, more or less straight down the middle, and if a car comes while somebody's having a good conversation or telling a good story, the car has to wait till the story finishes before people will move out of the way. Stories are important here, and cars aren't.

ANN CAMERON,
THE MOST BEAUTIFUL PLACE IN THE WORLD

It's the stories we tell and the conversations we hold and how we hold them that determine our experiences of each other. In each conversation you hold with someone, there is a story being told. After opening up to your own life story, you are more prepared to listen to others' stories.

Talk to Me: Sacred Dialogue

What is essential here is the presence of the spirit of dialogue, which is, in short, the ability to hold many points of view in suspension, along with a primary interest in the creation of common meaning.

DAVID BOHM AND F. DAVID PEAT, *SCIENCE, ORDER, AND CREATIVITY*

David Bohm, perhaps one of the most quoted physicists, became increasingly aware of how the ecological crisis can be addressed through personal transformation in how we engage in relationship to one another. He developed a personal and social transformational tool he called *dialogue*. In dialogue we each listen to the views and stories of the other while renouncing our attempt to convert each other. We don't attempt to override each other's free will but appreciate and participate as a team or, in the case of groups, as a whole. So participating in a conversation with another takes precedence over taking care of our own emotions (which he understood to be our habitual and cognitive reactions based on our personal history). In true conversation, or dialogue, he points out that the intention is not to solve a problem or to even find a compromise between conflicting and different views. When we do this we tend to perpetuate the underlying problem. Much like I pointed out earlier, taking our focus off the problem generates more possibilities. The purpose of dialogue is to be a witness. The purpose of dialogue is to hear the other's story. First we want to learn to witness our own internal dynamics (such as we did in the previous chapter); our habitual and emotional responses. We come to the conversation with some understanding of what we are habitually reacting to in regard to the other. Then we witness and listen to the other. Bringing more of a witnessing presence to the full internal and outward conversation permits a deeper creative level of shared consciousness, which brings about a genuinely common and natural appreciation for self and other. The conversation is experienced as an exchange of stories rather than an attempt to change someone's viewpoint or influence someone in some way. In the sharing of stories we don't interrupt or disagree, we listen attentively until the story is finished. (Remember, even someone's strong opinion on something that you may disagree with is simply a story they have.)

In relationships that carry a lot of painful history, weighing down the dynamic with emotions and expectations, try the following experiment. For example, this exercise in witnessing can be used the next time you go to a difficult family gathering.

Being the Witness

A simple but persuasive experiment is to go into a situation as the witness.

+ In your conversations, have the main intention be to notice and keep an account of what happens in the internal and external landscape. For example, when Aunt Sally says a certain thing, you notice yourself feeling . . . you notice yourself thinking and reacting in this way . . . And when your brother comes into the room you notice others and yourself reacting in this way . . .
+ Don't put any particular spin on it, just notice. Notice that when "that" occurs in the outside landscape, "this" is what goes on inside of you. When someone acts in "that" way, others react in "this" way.
+ Record any insights in your journal or field notebook for later reference. (I always carry around a small pocket journal so I can jot down insights or take notes "in the field" of my life.)

Documenting these times of witnessing can add to your present and future happiness. All that you notice, including the assumptions you make about these encounters, will reveal to you the origins of your experiences. You can harvest from this witnessing presence insights that can be the groundwork for a more dynamic future relationship. We show up for the other by our own willingness to work with our own false gods, our own discomfort and unhappiness. Then with this increase in awareness of your inner landscaping you can better navigate the outer world of relationships.

Going to the Hardware Store for Fruit Salad

If you find yourself in relationships where you are wholly and consistently dissatisfied and unhappy, perhaps you are barking up the wrong tree. Let's say it is with your father. You discovered that each time you went to visit him you hoped to get some recognition or love, but there was none. You find yourself playing out this pain story over and over again with him. You keep trying to find that one thing, that one act that will finally get the attention and love you so deserve. (And you do, of course.) But it is not there. I liken this to going to the hardware store for fruit salad. No matter how often you go, even with the money to pay, you won't find what you are looking for there. Nothing you can do from your side can change what the other has to offer you. Therefore, you either have to accept that you will only find certain goods at a hardware store and stop causing yourself unnecessary suffering by asking for something that the other simply doesn't have to give, or you can decide to put your energy and resources into locating the local grocery store. Or both. You can let go of trying to get the love and recognition from someone who historically hasn't had it to offer you and you can find those who will show up and appreciate you in a relationship. This is living from the zero point.

Our ability to influence how others relate to us is limited. We have no control over how others will behave toward us. We can never be certain how relationships will unfold. The great unknown is always dancing along with us on the floor as we move with our partners. All sorts of circumstances do and will unfold within our relationships. Even though we have no control over outside circumstances, we can have complete determination of our experiences. Divorce is often seen as the only way to break the habitual way a couple has come to relate to each other. The term *in a rut* often comes up in couples' sessions. I recommend that couples first consider changing the dance, from their individual sides, before giving up on the relationship.

As we transform our relationships by challenging our patterns and assumptions, we are also breaking with the global pain stories and the culturally endorsed assumptions that sustain them. The pull to remain habitual, unconscious, and caught up in our pain stories is very pervasive. Therefore, any effort in changing shame to self-confidence, blame to accountability, and fear to freedom is not only improving your life but helping revitalize the whole world.

> *A human being is part of the whole, called by us the universe; a part limited by time and space. He experiences himself, his thoughts, and feelings as something separated from the rest, a kind of optical illusion of consciousness. This delusion is a kind of prison for us, restricting us to our personal desires and to affection for a few persons nearest us. Our task is to free ourselves from this prison.*
>
> ALBERT EINSTEIN

You can also have meaningful and transformative conversations with yourself around areas where you suffer. Where there is suffering, there is a belief about yourself that is built on your assumptions. You may want to hold a conversation with shame ("Shame makes me think I should do this when I otherwise would not"). Or, hold a conversation with a particular pain story ("I may be an alcoholic" or "I always fail"). Have a good, long conversation with your fear. Come face to face with your alcohol abuse and its underlying causes. Keep a dialogue going with the hindering belief until it is transformed and you are revitalized. Take one hundred percent responsibly for your own issues (your assumptions, your beliefs, and your choices) and witness a personal inner and outer revolution that takes place as a result. Even in these conversations with yourself, listen attentively to the story of your shame or your alcoholism.

● What's Your Theme Story?

You can, as I have, write out the story around a certain theme in your life. You can then share this story with another as you did with your life story. I call these our "theme stories."

✦ Take time to identify a place in your life where you have difficulty or recognize a desire for transformation. For example, I took several weeks to journal around the theme of friendship because I was suffering in this area of my life. After I wrote out all the scenes and stories of friendship I had my "friendship story." I first reviewed it myself and later shared it with a friend. She listened and mirrored my story to me. (Refer to "Mirroring" offered on page 239.) I discovered some patterns in myself and in my friendships. I was also mirrored the ways in which I make a good friend. Up to that point I didn't realize how generous a friend I was. Again, the transformational effect in this experience took all my relationships and friendships to a higher level.

Thomas Paine had it correct: "We have it in our power to begin the world again"—one person, one relationship, one conversation at a time. We can transform the world by first challenging our own personally held assumptions and projections.

It is error only, and not truth, that shrinks from inquiry.

THOMAS PAINE

Owning Our Projections
Our projections are made up of our assumptions.

We modern humans live as prisoners in a reality constructed for us by our thoughts, thoughts that are

predetermined for us by the tonal of the times and by our
personal history.
    VICTOR SANCHEZ, *THE TEACHINGS OF DON CARLOS*

Both in psychological and in Buddhist studies we find the concept of projection. Briefly explained, it is our ability to not see things as they are but to see things as we are. Much like a movie projector sends out its images onto the screen, we send out our beliefs, histories, assumptions, desires, and emotions onto the "screen" of our lives, and onto others. Basically, what we see is ourselves.

Many psychological and spiritual practices offer ways to break through the delusions made by our projections and conceptualizations (beliefs and assumptions) so that we can experience reality. Delusions are those persistent beliefs and assumptions that are put out by our pain stories (our false self). The practices throughout this book facilitate such personal breakthroughs. The reason meditation teachers have you sit with all that arises is so that you can move through the duality of "me and other"—the delusion (projection) of separation—to experience oneness. But when we are too busy and caught up in outer distractions or inner habitual states, we miss the opportunity to be familiar with reality—with the true nature of mind and of life, which is intimacy. Instead we remain caught up in our projections.

Whatever we don't claim as our own, we project onto others. The more we project our assumptions outward, the more we experience difficulty with people and situations because we keep encountering our own projections. And it can get more complicated since what we tend to do then is recruit proof for our own projections. We come to conclusions about the other or the world around us and then we go about seeking evidence to back up our assumptions. We can lose all perspective.

Our assumptions and projections then undermine any chance of real conversations. And in conversation I don't just mean with another human being but also with the world around us at any given moment. Instead of having the intimacy of being engaged in a real conversation, we are busy living our own little prejudices, dreaming up a world that fits our mind-set, beliefs, and assumptions.

When we do not truly perceive people or situations, but actually see and respond to what our thoughts (beliefs and assumptions) dictate to us—which we are habitually projecting onto the world around us—then freedom from projections can only come from an ability to suspend our thoughts; to put a hold on our assumptions and beliefs. This can only be achieved through the practices of meditation and mind training. Left on its own, the mind will mess with you and your life.

> *If we perceive things as they really are, whether people, situations, or events, or our own selves, we will be in a better position than someone who substitutes thoughts in place of reality. People who do not perceive reality find themselves struggling to control an imaginary reality and suffering the consequences of the inconsistencies between what they think is there and what is actually there.*
>
> VICTOR SANCHEZ, *THE TEACHINGS OF DON CARLOS*

An Attitude of Dialogue

Since Bohm's introduction to dialogue we have been offered many tools of positive communication—nonviolent communication (developed by Marshall Rosenberg in the 1960s) and appreciative inquiry (developed in the 1990s) are two primary ones that seem to me to come from Bohm's model. Both nonviolent communication and appreciative inquiry are available through books and workshops. Appreciative inquiry tends to be for organizations, while nonviolent communication is more geared toward individuals. There are also truth circles where you learn to dialogue without giving advice or promoting any personal agenda. For more on these check out Parker J. Palmer's books *A Hidden Wholeness* and *Healing the Heart of Democracy*. Ideally, everyone would be exposed to these methods at home and in the work environment.

As meaning makers we engage in dialogue, a kind of intentional conversation, with each other with the sole purpose of creating a *shared meaning*. Bohm points to how these shared meanings are what hold people and communities together. This takes a willingness to let go of trying to force our ideas on each other, or our always attempting to convince or to even have the other understand you—the sole intent is to reach a common ground of meaning. We each have to give up our need to be right, our desire to win others over to our side or to convince anyone of anything. We need to be less focused on our own opinions and how to get these across. Instead we open up to a genuine conversation with others. Because this may sound foreign to most and maybe impossible to you, use this as a template of intention; work with this idea of dialogue as best you can. I liken this to one body—several minds. When we appreciate that we are sharing a body we have to find a way to claim a shared purpose, as shared meaning to our conversations.

All the exercises in this chapter are about getting to this place where we are engaging in more fearless conversations with each other by letting go of our pain stories and assumptions. Ideally, you are consistent in challenging your own beliefs, assumptions, and projections so that such dialogue can take place.

In short, entering conversation with *an attitude of dialogue* is to do the following:

- Open your mind and heart to a listening posture
- Hold an intention of creating some shared meaning from the conversation
- Give up your need to win, to be right, to make a point
- Be willing to challenge (and give up) your fundamental assumptions
- Take on the fearlessness of an open heart, let go of defending your opinions
- Think of you and the other as "one body" with respect to the individual "parts"
- Be ready to participate
- If in a group, sit in a circle*

---

*Any kind of processes I facilitate, even my workshops, are held in circles. When asked what I need for a presentation I always request that the room be set up in a circle, if possible. This evens out the playing field. There's an invitation to be mutually influenced when we gather in circles.

- Be receptive to being influenced by the other
- Be willing to continue the conversation, or come back to it, until some shared meaning is created

For our conversations to lead to some kind of shared purpose, there needs to be an underlying appreciation of yourself *and* the other. Some of this can be achieved through shared storytelling; further appreciation can be cultivated in our daily conversations with those around us.

The Profound Wisdom of Appreciation

It is very difficult to be creative or open or hold a real conversation with another when we are attached.

Attached to our views
Attached to our assumptions
Attached to our expectations
Attached to certain objects
Attached to how we are perceived
Attached to being understood
Attached to each other
Attached to our *shoulds* and *should nots*

As we each discover in our own ways, we can't take two paths at the same time—that of being attached to our views and the path of intimacy with another.

We crowd out the other person, or true compassion, when we have to be in control (by having our views understood or agreed with, for example). So our ability to really show up in our conversations and to experience some real intimacy comes with an attitude and approach of *nonattachment*. Too often instead of showing up and being present (curious, vulnerable) we hold some kind of agenda through our attachments. Or as Bohm mentions, we have a tendency to want to recruit or convert people to our way of seeing the world. Any place we try to get others to understand us (instead of trying to understand them) there is attachment.

In place of being attached we can take on the attitude (take the path) *of appreciation*. This appreciation creates more of an open hand rather than a closed fist that holds on to its subject of attachment. With appreciation there are no *shoulds* or strong expectations of the other person. Also approach *yourself* with an open heart of understanding and appreciation. Commonly, a lack of appreciation for others reflects a lack of appreciation for oneself.

A lot of difficulty in relationships comes when we don't feel (and maybe are not) understood. There may be a lack of mutual influence and we can't seem to get beyond trying to change the other's mind. This can be true in any relationship. We put a lot of our energy and attention into trying to get the other to understand and ultimately to agree with us. This has broken down a lot of marriages because, instead of putting energy into understanding the other, couples start to focus on and point out their perceived differences. John Gottman, professor emeritus of psychology at the University of Washington, has found that couples with a ratio of fewer than five positive interactions for every negative one are likely to get divorced. In all of Gottman's studies on marriages it is the *perception* of the other that was used to predict marital stability or likelihood of divorce. The more favorable the perceptions, the more secure the relationship. Furthermore, his research showed how couples could get caught in the negative loop of criticism, defensiveness, stonewalling the other, and even feeling contempt for the other. To transform our personal relationships we first want to have the motivation to do so. And motivation comes from the zero point. As Leo Tolstoy said, "Everyone thinks of changing the world, but no one thinks of changing himself." When you decide that changing yourself *can* change the world, one relationship at a time, you will see all your relationships transforming before you. When we can let go of having to be right, of having to prove a point, a wonderful thing happens—we open the way for a connection with the other and with our own happiness.

Here is a practice I use when attachment to be understood or to be right tries to take hold of me (particularly in relationships to significant others).

Letting Go of the Need to Be Right

+ When you find yourself in an argumentative dynamic ask yourself: *Do I want to be right or do I want to be happy? Do I want to be right or do I want freedom?* Let these questions guide your experience.

+ Focus your attention on the question while then *choosing* happiness and choosing freedom over the need to be right. When you consciously say to yourself, I choose freedom, your mind and entire psychophysical system begin to let go of the need to be right (or understood). This creates spaciousness inside you and within the conversation. You find yourself letting go of wanting to convert the other to some view or to have them understand you.

+ Let the choice of happiness or freedom make way by letting go of the need to be heard, to be right, to make some point.

+ Then let something remarkable happen . . . a place for real dialogue.

Some Advice about Advice

There can, at times, seem to be so much between us and intimacy with another. And we have been so thoroughly trained by our families and culture to give advice and feedback to others, mistaking that as being intimate and helpful. If we always feel the need to give others feedback, which ultimately drains us of our energy, we won't have much left for our creative pursuits. Furthermore, the need to give advice keeps one focused outside oneself, takes us away from the zero point.

Explore an Alternative to Advice

+ Begin with an awareness of how often you are giving advice. You can begin with the advice you give yourself. Notice when you are in the mind of giving advice and how this feels in your emotional and physical body. When giving advice to others, also notice the energy of the other person when you give advice. Most of us just want to be heard.

+ Then after a week of bringing awareness to this, practice taking some measures to not give advice. Can you go ten days without giving any feedback or advice to others or to yourself? This practice of withholding advice and feedback prepares the way for a new way of being in the world, a more attentive, curious, listening stance rather than one that is always dissipating energy out.
+ Instead of giving advice, listen to the individual's entire story without jumping in with feedback. Instead of giving advice or feedback, practice:

> Listening until the person is done speaking. Allow for a bit of silence.
>
> Asking a question. (Make certain it is not with a twist, where you are really giving advice or feedback. And no "why" questions—why did you do that?) Ask *what*—what was that like? Or what do you make of that? Or simply, what do you feel about that?
>
> Asking yourself if what you want to say is really improving on the situation.
>
> Focusing on what you might do differently (not what the other should do differently).
>
> Writing a response in your journal (especially if there is a lot of emotion around your response).
>
> Listening some more.

+ Only consider giving advice or feedback if you are specifically asked for it.

Not giving advice or feedback will feel unnatural at times, especially since the habit to do so is strong. This tendency to share our opinion, to give feedback, is in the current of our culture. We have been socially conditioned to constantly give and receive feedback to the point where we find it difficult to consider relating in other ways. I often get the question, "How can I not give my children advice? Are they included in this practice of not giving advice?" Yes, they are. You may come to realize how many arguments are avoided when you find another way to communicate with your children, and how much more they have to say to you.

Transformation
through the Spoken Word

If love is the answer, could you please rephrase the question?
WRITTEN BY JANE WAGNER
FOR LILY TOMLIN, COMEDIAN

In Japan, it is said that words of the soul reside in a spirit called kotodama, or the spirit of words, and the act of speaking words has the power to change the world.
MASARU EMOTO, JAPANESE SCIENTIST
AND AUTHOR OF THE HIDDEN MESSAGES IN WATER

What we say out loud matters. The spoken word gives words' meaning more power and influences everyone, including yourself; all who are in earshot. We have habitual ways of speech that really interfere with authentic presence. What we say flavors everything. Our habitual speech reflects our self-perception, but we are often oblivious to what we are actually saying out loud.

In the I Ching a superior person is "substantial in his or her word." This refers not only to what we say to others but also the inner dialogue we carry on with ourselves. The words we use with others of course reflect our inner dialogue. To help transform a habitual way of speech, which is based on a belief or assumption we hold, start with not verbalizing the inclination. For example, let's say you habitually ask *why*. Asking others *why* usually brings things to a painful point. The *why* question basically asks for someone or something to blame. (See below for more on this.)

Simply break the habit of *expressing* a negative verbal pattern to others. Every time we express such verbal patterns they get strengthened. This will loosen up the inner dialogue of this negative pattern as well. In this case you can replace the "Why did you do that?" with a *what* question: "What do you want?" or "What's going on?" So, "Why don't you try this?" becomes "What do you think about this idea?"

Another example of habitual speech is when we lead our comments with *I think*. Often what people mean when they say "I think" is "I know." *I think* communicates a wavering, an invitation for someone else to step in and make a choice for you. "I *think* I want to try that" sounds quite a bit different from "I *know* I want to try that." Or simply, "I *want* to try that." When you only think you know, then others can easily step in and hold a conviction in your place. Resistance also arises where we hesitate.

Exorcising the Why of It All

> *Nor again must we in all matters demand an explanation of the reason why things are what they are; in some cases, it is enough if the fact they are so is satisfactory.*
> ARISTOTLE, *NICOMACHEAN ETHICS*

As you open up more and more to the creative life, you let go of any need to know the *why* of it all. Internal work, transforming our assumptions and related patterns, is not an investigation into why things are the way they are—why you were hurt, why you are stuck, why you repeat this and that, why your mother didn't want you. To focus on the *why* results in the blame and shame game, because the *why* question really asks who is to blame. Try in your present conversations to release the whys—why are they doing this, why don't they do what I want, why are they the way they are, why, why, why? When we ask others *why,* it more often than not feels like a threat, and as a result their defenses go up. The *why* of it all will only take you further away from the energy and resources of the moment and away from living a more authentic life.

Instead, we need to focus on the *what* of it all. What happened? What is happening now? What is the relationship between what happened in the past and what is being repeated now? What wants to happen now? What led me up to this place in my life?

Through work with others on their psychological and spiritual issues, I realize that one does not have to know why someone did this or that (or even have specific memories of a precipitating event) in order to heal from the pain of the past, or to uplift the present situation.

+ + +

Why Wonder Why?

Three wanderers were walking on a path leading out from the deep woods and into the green, growing meadow and beyond. The path was long and narrow, with a diversity of terrain on each side. As they walked, they came upon a broken jar. One could see that the jar, when intact, had been ornate and beautiful. It had golden thread throughout and all the colors of the rainbow subtly burned into it. Next to the broken jar was a large rock.

The first wanderer approached the jar and the rock and immediately got angry. She demanded to know how such a thing could have happened. She asked herself, did the rock hit the jar or the jar hit the rock? She felt she had to know, but neither rock nor jar spoke. She stood there, angry and scared, and she didn't move.

The second wanderer looked at the jar and immediately became depressed. Why would God let such a thing happen? Why did this beautiful jar have to be ruined in this way? Why is this here on the path? Why did I come across it? Why, why, why? This wanderer went into a deep state of confusion and depression and also did not move.

The third wanderer saw the rock sitting next to the once-beautiful jar and simply noticed what had happened. The jar was broken. The rock was next to the jar. She realized that she didn't know the how of it because it had already happened. She didn't really care about the why of it because it wouldn't answer any of the more important questions. She just noticed that the jar was broken and what she could do. She bent down and picked up the broken shards, placing them in her pocket. She then moved the rock a bit to the side of the path and walked on. As she continued on down the path, the shards jingled in her pocket, making the sound of wind chimes.

The other two remained behind.

+ + +

As you acknowledge a given dynamic between you and another, the whys and hows of it may naturally arise. Notice these but do not spend much time with them. They will not generate movement and will likely result in you or the other feeling victimized and stuck. The why can take up a lot of time, energy, and speculation without much awareness.

Furthermore, the why is often part of someone else's story. Why someone hurt behaves the way they do is their story, so it remains out of your reach for you to do anything about it.

When you know the *what* of it all—for instance, that love is lacking in your life—you can take this information, use it to heal, and move on. You have the power to transform this energy like the third wanderer did with the broken jar.

Stolen Words

Remember the metaphor in "To Catch a Thief" in chapter 2 about the thefts in the bank? There is another great theft going on, one that steals our integrity, our energy, and our ability to be present. Words are being stolen right out from under us. When this happens, we find ourselves going right (metaphorically) when we thought we were going left. We find ourselves believing without reservation that north is up and south is down. We find ourselves being scared of someone because they are a Christian or a Muslim. We get angry when someone isn't "patriotic." We hold on to someone else's meaning of words. For example, we are taught that *selfish* is always bad and *love* is always good. (Many, many nasty acts have been done in the name of love.) All these stolen words are built on assumptions:

> War is patriotic, but peace is unpatriotic.
> All Republicans are pro-family, and Democrats are liberal.
> Climate change is a myth.
> It's not okay to have expectations.
> This hurts me more than it hurts you (as an expression of love).

We need to reclaim these stolen words and do so bravely and relentlessly. In our writing and in our speech we must use and speak out forbidden and stolen words, reframing them when necessary. For instance, "I am a monger of peace." This is a way to "be impeccable with our words" as Don Miguel Ruiz suggests in his book *The Four Agreements*. We need to use experience and witnessing to back up what we say instead of speaking like spin doctors. We can rely on facts—the ice caps *are* melting. These statements are validated by direct experience and evidence rather than assumptions and familial ingrained opinions. Einstein warned, "The only source of knowledge is experience." Basing our speech and conversations on experience and evidence means we need no spin to make it valid.

Another way to reclaim the meaning of lost words and concepts is finding the root meaning of words. Research the original intentions of a word. (The Internet is great for word searches!) Also, pay attention to the assumptions and the meanings intended when someone says something like:

I did it out of love.
This is what a patriot does.
This is what democracy looks like.
This is green.
That's a sin.
You're selfish.
I forgive you.
The penthouse is always on the top floor because the higher up you are the better. The better view is always from the top.
Dark is dangerous and bad.
You bring me down.
The northern countries are "on top," and it is always better to be on top.
Let's be friends.
He's a pagan.

Stolen words hold many assumptions and agreements and, usually, hidden deceptions. When we numbly agree to stolen words our creative expression is halted; stolen, too. If top is always better than bottom where does that leave the inhabitant of the first floor apartment, or the earthworm? We shut off our minds to so many possibilities when we lock ourselves in through holding such unconscious agreements about the meaning of words. Consider every word we carry as sacred and the words themselves a container of a potent elixir or poison. You carry this word around with you, affecting your psychophysical body as well as, when spoken, impacting the world around you. You release the elixir or poison from the bottle. When a word is stolen and we haven't claimed it back, then the vibration and meaning of the stolen word is the one carried in our psyches as well as the one heard and felt by others.

Maybe the volume of stolen words is just too great to tackle, just too premeditated to wrestle, just too much to even consider. You have heard the saying, "one day at a time." A good way to begin is to take a week or so to become aware of stolen words. Collect stolen words in your field notebook and write about them in your journal. After you have collected these stolen words, choose one or two at a time to reclaim or reframe. Just take one word or one concept at a time until it is transformed (at least in your life and conversations).

Another way to transform poisoned words to elixir is to listen for assumptions in someone's speech and help reframe words on the spot. When you do this you will witness the world transform around you. This transformation is much like the restoring of a prairie to a more natural and original state. We don't let one plant hoard the soil and light; we don't let a word's stolen meaning interfere with authentic dialogue. We are not robots to others' meaning of words. Break the pattern of agreeing to a stolen (and therefore assumptive) meaning of a word or phrase and allow for a diversity of meaning to beautify a prairie and a conversation. Listen deeply, and *speak up*. This can include (after listening to someone) a clear and strong statement of what you believe. Not with the intention of changing others' minds or giving them feedback, but to offer up your meaning based on personal experience. For example, after someone has captured a crowd with some religious or political speech with the intention of recruiting others, you may offer up a question or different view. A further example would be when someone uses a stolen word and phrase, like "born again" and they mean only one thing. You can use it in a new way, reframing it. For me, I am born again each morning to a new day.

Words and the stories they weave *are* the world.

✦✦✦
Trading Dialogue for Lodging

From *Zen Flesh, Zen Bones*, compiled by Paul Reps
and Nyogen Senzaki

Provided he makes and wins an argument about Buddhism with those who live there, any wandering monk can remain in a Zen temple. If he is defeated, he has to move on.

In a temple in the northern part of Japan two brother monks were dwelling together. The elder one was learned, but the younger one was stupid and had but one eye.

A wandering monk came and asked for lodging, properly challenging them to a debate about the sublime teaching. The elder brother, tired that day from much studying, told the younger one to take his place. "Go and request the dialogue in silence," he cautioned.

So the young monk and the stranger went to the shrine and sat down.

Shortly afterwards the traveler rose and went in to the elder brother and said: "Your young brother is a wonderful fellow. He defeated me."

"Relate the dialogue to me," said the elder one.

"Well," explained the traveler, "first I held up one finger, representing Buddha, the enlightened one. So he held up two fingers, signifying Buddha and his teaching. I held up three fingers, representing Buddha, his teaching, and his followers, living the harmonious life. Then he shook his clenched fist in my face, indicating that all three come from one realization. Thus he won and so I have no right to remain here." With this, the traveler left.

"Where is that fellow?" asked the younger one, running in to his elder brother.

"I understand you won the debate."

"Won nothing. I'm going to beat him up."

"Tell me the subject of the debate," asked the elder one.

"Why, the minute he saw me he held up one finger, insulting me by insinuating that I have only one eye. Since he was a stranger I thought I would be polite to him, so I held up two fingers, congratulating him that he has two eyes. Then the impolite wretch held up three fingers, suggesting that between us we only have three eyes. So I got mad and started to punch him, but he ran out and that ended it!"

✦✦✦

On the Edge:
Holding Difficult Conversations

Within our lifetimes we are called to hold difficult conversations. These difficult conversations come up at work, between friends and family members, counselor and client, student and teacher, and strangers, and, of course, within groups and between nations. It's important that we hold our seat with others and have these edgy conversations. But what we tend to do is have these reactive and isolated encounters with each other. We give our energy over to some hot issue without holding it in a larger context of the ongoing relationship. Reacting habitually to isolated issues results in little success. Only by responding to the changes within the big picture of the relationship can the overall relationship be improved. Isolated and reactive moments with others won't change the overall pattern because you are putting a Band-Aid on a bullet wound. Actually, once we are in a relationship with someone, ideally, we are in ongoing conversations. So first we want to enter these emotionally charged and challenging conversations with some sense and commitment to the bigger picture (the bigger story we are creating together, as it were).

Nothing happens in isolation—everything always takes place within a bigger picture. This also takes the stress off the importance of this one conversation, since an appreciation of the big picture will leave a way for a continued dialogue about the hot topic. So bring to these more edgy conversations a sense of what the big picture is for you or the both of you. For example, if you are fighting over finances, what is the bigger context that this issue shows up in? Is it a shared desire to live well into your retirement years? Also, when you are fighting about something bring the bigger picture in by naming some shared intention—"We both want to live long and well into our later years."

We also want to be able to hold these sacred, edgy conversations with ourselves, as in the "Profound Awakening through Inquiry Meditation" exercise on page 39. We may find that we hold these conversations in our dreams and in various altered states, such as through breathwork and shamanic journeying. Many a client has shared how they were able to speak their truths to others in their dreams! Another means is through spiritual journaling (challenging ourselves with the difficult questions). Living with the questions and doing some daily inquiry into our thoughts, habits, choices, practices, and intentions will help dismantle the habitual self in our conversations and relationships and bring forth opportunity for truly meaningful and open (albeit edgy) dialogue. Another place for such edgy conversations to take place is with the I Ching (the whole of chapter 6 is dedicated to this relationship).

Making Your Relationships Meaningful

To have your relationships be dynamic and meaningful there needs to be:

Honesty
Self-reflection
Love in the open
Mutual influence (through dialogue)
Showing up halfway
Responsibility
Ethics (ethical principles to guide you, especially in difficult dynamics)

Honesty is acquired through ongoing self-investigation. This and previous chapters have given many practices of self-reflection and inquiry. This self-awareness results in awareness of the other and a more true experience of intimacy. You have become more conscious of your inner world of beliefs, assumptions, and projections and are able to be in a more honest relationship with others.

✦✦✦

Love in the Open

From *Zen Flesh, Zen Bones,* compiled by Paul Reps
and Nyogen Senzaki

Twenty monks and one nun, who was named Eshun, were practicing meditation with a certain Zen master.

Eshun was very pretty even though her head was shaved and her dress plain. Several monks secretly fell in love with her. One of them wrote her a love letter, insisting upon a private meeting.

Eshun did not reply. The following day the master gave a lecture to the group, and when it was over, Eshun arose. Addressing the one who had written her, she said: "If you really love me so much, come and embrace me now."

✦✦✦

To *love in the open* means that most aspects of your relationship are out in the open. Not everything will be open for the entire world to view, but most everything within the relationship will be out in the open to each other. This would seem to be self-evident but it is not. When relationships end there usually are aspects of their relationship or self the participants kept hidden from each other. They didn't talk about their unhappiness, or they gave up on a dream only to regret it, or abuse in the relationship was done in secret. In the natural world disguise is only used as protection or to hide from predators. If you are in disguise in your relationship it is likely pointing to a serious problem.

A primary quality that goes into transformative conversations and is the cornerstone for any relationship is mutual influence.

It All Gets Down to This: Mutual Influence

Mutual influence is *the* fundamental foundation, the hallmark, to a healthy, dynamic relationship and each conversation within our relationships. Marriages, friendships, work relationships are all dependent upon this quality. Mutual influence depends on both people of the conversation being ethical, truthful, and open. A willingness to be influenced is dependent upon a vulnerability and curiosity toward the other; a genuine motivation to understand the other and then be influenced by what the other has to say. Both Gottman's research on successful and happy heterosexual marriages as well as the five-thousand-year-old philosophy of the I Ching highlight that our ability to be influenced by the other is critical for flourishing relationships. Mutual influence is dependent upon some level of respect and vulnerability with each other. In Gottman's studies of good marriages he refers to it as "allowing for influence." Because he studied only heterosexual couples, he emphasized how the male needs to let himself be influenced by the woman (because he believes this quality is more natural for women).

I find in my work within organizations that difficulty often arises when the leaders or employers (deans, bosses, supervisors, directors) are not open to mutual influence. They hold the expectation of influencing others but lack the skill of mutuality. The root of all relationships, even with your spiritual source, needs to be of mutual influence—give and take; a back and forth. *Mutual* means an authentic receptivity to the other. *Influence* means that we allow for ourselves to be impacted by the other. And this influence is felt and shown out in the open too.

Wherever there is difficulty in relationships there is likely a lack of mutual influence. To generate a mutual influence you must focus on opening your heart to the other through listening and understanding and then *allowing yourself to be altered by the other.* This encourages a genuine curiosity about the other (their stories, experiences, and ideas). In the creative process we bring in the "third thing" (the poem, the myth) to purposefully influence our perceptions and experience. (See "This Always Works: Bringing in the Third Thing or the Third Place" on page 182.) Without an influence this third thing could not benefit you in any way. It is through this mutual influence that we truly benefit ourselves, and others.

A mutual influence happens when you let your heart be moved by the other. Of course the word *mutual* implies that both are invested in this exchange of influence. However, you can practice allowing yourself to be influenced by the other, and this may transform any rigidity in the relationship. (Many tell me how it does wonders for their relationships with their teenagers. This mutual influence is felt by the young adult and builds their confidence.) This is like changing the dance rather than the partner. When you change the dance by offering up an attitude of receptivity to the other, then the other's dance changes, too. If there is a foundation of love and respect (what Gottman refers to as having an emotional bank account to draw on), your partner will have the internal resources to change their dance with you. If a strong emotional foundation is lacking, when you change the dance, the other may leave the dance floor. Living more intentionally and consciously in this way always results in transformation. Sometimes that transformation destroys the old to make room for the new; sometimes it transforms the old *into* the new.

> *The superior person opens his heart and mind*
> *To accept without prejudice.*
>
> TOAIST MASTER ALFRED HUANG,
> *THE COMPLETE I CHING*

Being influenced by the other is not about getting to a place where your relationships are always conflict-free. Conflict in our relationships can actually be a positive aspect, depending on what we do with it. Conflict can be very dynamic and creative, so don't work at eradicating it but try making it useful while engaging in it openly. Sometimes we are in relationship with people who are in conflict with themselves, or are suffering for a reason that is beyond our influence.

Letting Others Suffer

A teacher of mine once said that we have to allow our children to experience the effects of their lives. We can't follow them around protecting them from the disappointments and pain of life. We have to let them figure out for themselves how to respond to difficulty and how to handle disappointment. I nodded my head in agreement. Now, a couple decades later, a mom of a teenager, I don't find this quite so easy.

When I dropped my daughter off at school one day I witnessed an unkindness. (I know, I know, the school halls are full of them.) Instinctively, I wanted to leap out of the car and right the wrong. Even after the incident passed, I still wanted to find a way to fix it somehow. But I didn't. Instead I trusted her to navigate this unkindness in her own way. And I listened when she shared some of her thoughts about what happened. I did my best to not interfere by adding my opinions and attitude. (I withheld feedback.) Even in situations where I have needed to be more involved, it was important that I did so in a way that didn't violate her personal integrity.

I have had a lot of practice witnessing personal suffering in my practice as a counselor and spiritual teacher. I also witness parents who rescue their adult children from financial and personal ruin again and again. The adult children never quite experience the full consequences of their choices and mistakes, and so never learn the ability to transform difficulty into opportunity. Often these adult children find someone else to rely upon, usually someone who is drawn to codependent relationships.

Unfortunately, there are times it seems our world is strewn with suffering and difficulty, and there are no solutions readily available. My heart breaks a little every day witnessing all the pain in the world. I do my best not to add to the suffering. I do my best to be part of the solution instead of adding to the problem. I act in ways that demonstrate to my daughter how an adult responds to difficulty, and let her navigate the hallways of her life.

One of my favorite Buddhist teachings is given by Shantideva (695–743 CE), an Indian Buddhist scholar at Nalanda University and author of the *Bodhicaryāvatāra,* a long poem (sutra) describing the process of awakening the heart and mind. In this sutra he points out a practical way to mitigate suffering and to generate more happiness, and how living life from one's own side is a way to respond to the suffering around us:

> *To cover the earth with sheets of hide*
> *Where could such amounts of skin be found?*
> *But simply wrap some leather around your feet*
> *And it's as if the whole earth had been covered.*

The Gift of the Troublemaker

Ethical behavior is doing the right thing when no one else is watching—even when doing the wrong thing is legal.

ALDO LEOPOLD, *A SAND COUNTY ALMANAC*

When a troublemaker shows up in your life, you have the opportunity to let it pull you away from your creative intentions or use it in your creative and spiritual pursuits. A *troublemaker* can be a person, situation, or event that presents us with some difficulty. The troublemakers in our lives meet up with our internal enemies (false gods) of anger, fear, doubt, assumptions, arrogance, and other afflictive emotional and mental states. What happens too often is that we mistake the outside troublemaker as the problem. When we do this we miss the opportunity to transform the difficulty that presents itself within this situation.

Everything in life holds the potential to assist our creative and spiritual intentions, and to bring forth our fullest potentials. Shantideva points to how the understanding of unity, that everything is dependent, means that getting angry at things is really getting angry at an apparition, because everything we see involves projection. This translates into not being caught up in the appearance of things. Nothing is as it appears, since our beliefs, assumptions, and perceptions are all projected out onto the other.

Wherever I went, a new life begun,
hidden in the grass, or waiting beyond the trees.
There is a spirit abiding in everything.

WILLIAM STAFFORD, FROM "YOU DON'T
KNOW THE END," IN *THE WAY IT IS*

We habitually meet our troublemakers with assumptions about them, and we tend to take their behavior very personally. We somehow make it about us. There are many conditions that caused the troublemakers to behave in the way they did; it is unlikely to come down to just one reason. "Everything arises from conditions," as Shantideva reminds us in the *Bodhicaryāvatāra*. Nothing happens in a vacuum. So, let go of the assumptions, which only keep you trapped by the troublemaker.

The troublemaker typically addresses the place where we are the most stuck. This does not mean we are in agreement with abusive and hostile behavior or not bothered by the injustices of the world. Even the most advanced practitioners experience difficulty and witness injustices. The Dalai Lama deals with the issue of an abducted country, destruction of sacred property, abuses by the Chinese government, and the displacement of millions of his people. Yet he holds his seat, remaining engaged in life, meeting each challenge with compassion, wisdom, and presence.

He couldn't do this if he were caught up emotionally, habitually reacting to all these wrongdoings. Instead, he focuses on what he can do; he does the necessary internal work so he can benefit others. He realizes that we can only be responsible for our side of the equation. We can only create change from where we stand. When we are not caught up in personalizing everything, or making assumptions, we have the energy to really make a difference in the world, to bring love and compassion where it is most needed.

The most skillful means we have for dealing with the troublemakers that insult us, disappoint us, bully us, or get hostile or aggressive with us is to understand that they point to where we are caught up in a pain story. The troublemaker can be seen as one of your greatest teachers, also perhaps your greatest challenge, and your quickest means to heal the divide within and without. As Shantideva points out in the *Bodhicaryāvatāra*, "One should always look straight at sentient beings as if drinking them in with the eyes, thinking, 'Relying on them alone, I shall attain Buddhahood.'" We get to experience everything as a blessing or as a means for our transformation. We can make meaning with everything that is presented to us. In Native American mythology, the coyote is often portrayed as both the troublemaker *and* the ally. Troublemakers are our coyotes.

The I Ching reminds us that difficulty arises to help keep our focus on our spiritual principles instead of being caught up in outside circumstances. Difficulties can provide us with a means to return our attention to our spiritual practice and creative commitments when we have strayed from them. Therefore, we learn to receive our troublemakers as the blessing of divinity; as protecting our spiritual efforts and integrity. Through such transformational practices, our creative intentions and efforts become an ethical practice benefiting even those who trouble us.

Experience the troublemaker as someone just like yourself—someone who wants happiness, "same as me." They would not act this way if they were not suffering; they too want to heal the separation they feel inside. Can you feel compassion for that?

A man told me once that all the bad people
Were needed. Maybe not all, but your fingernails
You need; they are really claws, and we know
Claws. The sharks—what about them?
They make other fish swim faster. The hard-faced men
In black coats who chase you for hours
In dreams—that's the only way to get you
To the shore. Sometimes those hard women
Who abandon you get you to say, "You."
A lazy part of us is like a tumbleweed.
It doesn't move on its own. Sometimes it takes
A lot of Depression to get tumbleweeds moving.
Then they blow across three or four States.
This man told me that things work together.
Bad handwriting sometimes leads to new ideas;
And a careless God—who refuses to let people
Eat from the Tree of Knowledge—can lead
To books, and eventually to us. We write
Poems with lies in them, but they help a little.

ROBERT BLY, "BAD PEOPLE"

Bullies as Troublemakers

Bullies show up everywhere—through the Internet on Facebook and e-mails; they show up in national politics, and in our family gatherings. Bullies characteristically threaten others directly or indirectly. Perhaps they are threatening to expose weaknesses of yours to others, or imply that your job is on the line, or continue harassing you until you do as they want.

How are we to respond in an ethical and meaningful way to the bullies in our lives? How might our spiritual practice help us here? Ultimately, through our personal agreement we consent to be bullied. Yes, whether or not we are bullied depends on our response. Eleanor Roosevelt's wisdom comes to mind: "No one can make you feel inferior without your consent."

I've discovered that no one can bully us when we are strong in our principles and our focus is on what we are creating rather than some external drama (no matter how real). When we put our mind on ethical principles the bully cannot hook us because our attention and energy is on practicing a principle such as those presented earlier in "Navigating Your Life" on page 69 rather than the bully's behaviors.

Bullies try to manipulate events and people to get what they want. They often try to get us on the defensive. But they can only succeed with our consent. Don't consent. Sometimes we don't consent to bullying by taking action; other times we remain still and disengaged. We must each discern for ourselves how to respond to a bully or bullying environment. Bullies present an even greater challenge to our spiritual integrity when they manage an environment (work, politics, or family, for example). If we were raised in an environment where no one spoke up, we learn to be quiet to survive. Sometimes we learn to live under the radar of the abusers and bullies. But the bullying continues. So, living under the radar or not speaking up or feeling manipulated often means the bully is driving our bus and we are sitting in a back seat scared as they swerve about on the road.

Sometimes we have to do what it takes to get off the bus; other times we have to get our hands on the steering wheel. Here is a simple but effective way to disarm the bully.

Disarming a Bully's Grip

+ Stop and take a deep breath or two (don't react or make their behavior personal).

+ Realize how past painful experiences may be getting triggered and then take a broader view of the situation. What is really happening here? Don't get hooked entirely by this one isolated incident or person. Your life is bigger than this bully.
+ From this larger view, make a choice of how you are going to respond to this situation. What principle can you apply as an antidote?
+ Don't let the bully rush you (rushing others is a tactical way to control others).
+ Return your attention to something or someone of value to you. Spend time with someone you trust and love, or put time into a creative project.

I wanted the plums, but I waited.
The sun went down. The fire
went out. With no lights on
I waited. From the night again—
those words: how stupid I was.
And I closed my eyes to listen.
The words all sank down, deep
and rich. I felt their truth
and began to live them. They were mine
to enjoy. Who but a friend
could give so sternly what the sky
feels for everyone but few learn to
cherish? In the dark with the truth
I began the sentence of my life
and found it so simple there was no way
back into qualifying my thoughts
with irony or anything like that.
I went to the fridge and opened it—
sure enough the light was on.
I reached in and got the plums.

WILLIAM STAFFORD,
"THINKING ABOUT BEING CALLED
SIMPLE BY A CRITIC"

It can be helpful to have some understanding of what makes a bully a bully. The following is a portrait of an adult bully. As usual, add your experience and knowledge to the mix.

Portrait of an Adult Bully

Over the past several decades one of my areas of study has been narcissists. I would of course need several more decades to fully grasp the personal, cultural, and global impact of this psychological dynamic. My interest focuses on the impact this condition has on those around the narcissist and the ways loved ones, clients, students, and coworkers can get out from under the grip of this particular flavor of bullying. Fortunately, there is also treatment for those who suffer from narcissistic personality disorder. But the defense mechanisms of the narcissist typically prevent them from seeking help for themselves.

Everyone knows at least one person who is narcissistic (they often seek and hold positions of power). Evidence indicates that this personality disorder is on the rise. It can be very disruptive and painful when someone close to you—a boss, a family member, a colleague, or partner (spouse)—is narcissistic. It is likely that many adult bullies would be diagnosed with narcissistic personality disorder. So, I find it worth our time to explore this dynamic of narcissism and bullying.

If you would benefit from further insight into this and other personality disorders, I highly recommend *The Search for the Real Self: Unmasking the Personality Disorders of Our Age* by psychiatrist and educator James F. Masterson, M.D. Dr. Masterson describes that "narcissists often seem to be the people who have everything—talent, wealth, beauty, health, and power." He goes on to demonstrate how this personality disorder is based on a defensive false self that the individual must keep inflated (at all costs). This cost always includes other people. Underneath this defensive false self is someone who is miserable and deeply insecure.

Adult bullies appear to be the masters of their own lives. But this actually takes quite a bit of effort on their part. They have to continually defend, to bully, to maintain a false sense of self. "The defensive self is characterized by self-importance, grandiosity, and omnipotence."

Most adult bullies (narcissists), Masterson explains, "need control and perfection as a prerequisite to feel good about themselves." They believe themselves to be special and unique and bully those who don't support them in this grandiosity of self.

People are easily misled into believing this person is a remarkable scientist, doctor, architect, or politician because they tend to spend a great amount of time on their work. They appear to be involved in helping others, or creating something remarkable when in fact their "motive is to use these activities to fuel the narcissist's need for perfection and uniqueness." They protect their appearance of specialness with position, money, bullying, and a supporting cast of other people. They will (if their narcissism goes untreated) bully their way through life and relationships, while appearing to be living the ideal life. Adult bullies rely on a "massive denial of reality" to maintain their lives.

If being bullied seems to be a pattern in your life (and bullying is on the rise), and you feel you cannot break from the bully's grip, likely some *gaslighting** has been going on.

Gaslighting: How Bullies Get Away with It

> "Many folks with handsome faces are greater monsters than you," said Beauty. "Their ugliness is all inside them."
> NANCY WILLARD, *BEAUTY AND THE BEAST*

Bullies are often experts at gaslighting and can pull off a lifetime of bullying with the help of their victim's family and friends. Chances are most of us have been gaslighted at some point.

The term *gaslighting* comes from the 1944 Ingrid Bergman film, *Gaslight*. The bullying husband in the movie "gaslights" his wife by having the gaslights dim for no apparent reason and suggesting to his wife that she is imagining things, and doing other tricks to make her believe she is crazy, all while claiming to her, "It's all in your head." No one suspects

---

*The term *gaslighting* refers to a form of mental abuse in which false information is presented with the intent of making a victim doubt their own memory, perception, or even experience.

him of brutality because he is skillful at gaslighting others. Others assume his wife is going insane and treat her accordingly. This gaslighting of one's partner's family and friends further entraps the abused partner because everyone else sees how "nice" and "generous" the bully is.

Those bullies who are successful in their vocations are often quite generous with their resources. But this generosity is born from self-interest—to be held in esteem by others means they don't have to take responsibility for the problems within their personal relationships (or within themselves). They can pull this gaslighting off so well that the entire family (and further community) applauds the bully for their accomplishments while a loved one is being abused (and neglected). The gaslighting gives the surrounding friends, colleagues, and family members the message that the violations are minor (or mistaken) in comparison to the bully's successes and achievements. The gaslighting reaches a peak when the family then blames the one being bullied (as in the movie above, where others assumed the woman was crazy). This of course prevents the bully from ever accepting responsibility. Then, when the victim is finally free of the relationship the bully simply moves on to another congregation, job, or relationship.

Adult bullies will also gaslight their own past. They typically have a history of failed relationships that they blame on the inadequacies of the other. Bullies tend to jump from one relationship to another, not being able to handle the responsibility of solitude and aloneness. Basically, they need someone close to them to bully.

Recently someone shared the axiom: "Beware of the nice man with the angry wife," pointing to the gaslighting actions of a bully. I will add—beware of the generous woman with a depressed partner. Or, beware of the religious leader with a compliant following. Or, beware of the successful professional that can't work with a team, or the nationally recognized coach who abuses his position and students. Or, finally, beware of the mother with the Golden Boy (the one child who can do no wrong).

Accomplished bullies often have a kind of superiority complex—they see themselves saving the world, or being above others in some way or another. They feel entitled. They are never wrong. This demonstrates the victory of their gaslighting—they have even gaslighted themselves into believing they're special. However, underneath the bully's exterior hides a deeply insecure person who has to be in control lest they discover the basic condition of life, which is its uncertainty.

Breaking Free

To those surrounding the adult bully, I warn you that you have likely been carefully selected to be part of their world. When you no longer support the bully's view of themselves and their world you will be discarded in some way. The adult bully's world is black and white. The bully will always make the downfall of relationships about the other—and they do not respond to the dissolution of a relationship with self-reflection or sadness but with anger. They often try to get even with those who leave them. "Anger," Masterson explains, "protects them from their own insecurity." Anger keeps them from admitting any weaknesses. This makes for a dangerous situation for the "other," be it partner (spouse), employee, adult child, or friend. The narcissist "gets angry and aggressive. [Their] omnipotence and grandiosity are not joking matters [to them]." The bully has already eroded the confidence and trust of the spouse (or significant other); these last kicks from the bully will be harsh and possibly devastating. That is my reason for suggesting to those who are leaving an adult bully to get out quickly and cleanly. (Some have to leave a relationship like they are leaving a gang or cult—with a fast and deliberate exit.) There will be collateral damage in most cases. My intention is that the partner of the adult bully will have something internally and externally to build the rest of their life upon. There is a life awaiting you on the other side of this destructive relationship.

To the adult bully I ask—seek help for the real culprit of your failed relationships and anguish. I know that underneath your bravado you feel the edge of your own insecurity, depression, and fears. Start with Masterson's book. You will find compassion, understanding, and help there.

The first lines from a poem by one of Masterson's patients at the conclusion of her successful treatment are insightful: "I shied from what I considered real, building a world of my own, impregnable. I was unaware of the slowly decaying castle, a part of which would ebb away with every sudden storm."

Often in a bullying relationship we are robbed of personal time and space, and the best antidote is to take some time for ourselves.

Take Some Time

+ Take time to become aware of what is really going on inside and around you. This can only happen with some distance between you and the bully. Take a holiday from the dynamic (yes, even at the threat that they might hurt the dog or break your belongings).

+ Then once there is some distance, do some personal inquiry. Name what's going on. Is it bullying? Are you and others being gaslighted? What needs acceptance? The bottom line is take some time alone away from the bully and ask yourself: *Is this how I want to live my life?*

+ Name the threats that are being made against you and bring them out into the open to yourself. What is the worst of it? Can you see yourself on the other side of the threats? Let's say the bully threatens to kill the dog, or hurt someone you love, or wreck your career somehow.

+ Take some time to see yourself getting through it. Script successfully moving through it and script yourself on the other side. (See "Scripting Scenes for Your Creative Life" on page 203.)

+ Then, either on your return or from a distance, bring it out in the open to others. Reach out to others. Tell them what is going on and the threats that are being made or implied. Include reaching out to ones who are being gaslighted. This is the breaking point for many abusers and bullies—someone finally comes out in the open with the violations.

+ Ultimately, let go of the opinions of others. Typically the threats made by a bully include ruining others' opinions of you, whether explicitly or implicitly. So when you can let go of others' opinions as being meaningful to you, a better fate awaits you.

Public opinion is a weak tyrant compared with our own private opinion. What a man thinks of himself, that is what determines, or rather, indicates his fate.

HENRY DAVID THOREAU

Most of us carry an inner bully within us, a voice that rises up to rob us of the joy and intimacy available to us. This inner bully works very much like the outer one, gaslighting us into believing that we are less than we are. However, this bully follows us everywhere.

Early on in my mind-transformation practices, I found myself at times inundated with certain dark thoughts that just seemed to appear randomly and out of nowhere. They would show up at different times in my life and interfere with an otherwise pleasant time. They didn't seem to have any cause. Asking why they existed only generated more unhappiness on my part, so I decided to pay more attention to when they arose. Knowing that the problem is next to the wound, that the solution is within the question, I noticed how, if it weren't for these random dark thoughts, I would be feeling connected to my experience at the time. I would be more present. In fact, they tended to show up at times that would otherwise be particularly beautiful.

Every night the river sings a new song.

EVA-LIS WUORIO, *THE LAND OF RIGHT UP AND DOWN*

With the Inner Bully: You Become the Trickster

In this exercise you choose to become like the *heyoka,* a spirit in Lakota mythology that acts as a trickster. I have shared this practice with countless clients and students, and they report back how remarkable the results are; how this frees them from the inner bully.

✦ By now you are likely aware of the voice of your inner bully. If not, take some time to recognize the comments of the inner bully. Notice how you have a way of bullying and gaslighting yourself.

✦ When these negative, contrary, or dark thoughts arise in the mind, turn inward toward the thought as if to greet it. Know that this particular thought or belief would not be arising if the opposite weren't actually true. Your inner bully is giving some negative spin on a beautiful situation. (I found that the more insistent the inner bully was, the more remarkable the reality.)

✦ Then do a small internal bow and say "Thank you." You can add "You would not be showing up to bully me unless the opposite were actually true." Sometimes you may want to repeat "Thank you, thank you, thank you." This is all done internally in your mind as a way to transform the agreement there—you are tricking the internal bully! Let's say you are enjoying a wonderful conversation with a friend, and you begin to have thoughts about what an idiot you are, or how bad you feel about your body, or something along those lines. Identify these thoughts as flags and turn and face them. Bowing to them in gratitude, you say, "Oh, thank you, you would not be showing up if something beautiful weren't happening."

✦ Then notice and open up to what is really going on—touch the beauty of the moment. Turn your attention to your present experience. See what the internal bully was trying to keep you from experiencing.

You then become the trickster to the negative thoughts. You free yourself of a negative perception by not letting it block your view of reality, of the present experience. Instead it pulls you more into reality, because it becomes a flag that something beautiful, something real, is actually happening right now. With the Trickster you have taken back the moment. Soon that particular flavor of negativity will stop showing up—you have tricked it into silence, because it no longer works to distract you from the moment or to undermine your experience.

Oftentimes an attitude of acceptance when dealing with difficulty is the best antidote—acceptance with a twist, that is.

Acceptance with a Twist

Wisdom and foolishness are practically the same.
Both are indifferent to the opinions of the world.
JOSEPH CAMPBELL, *A JOSEPH CAMPBELL COMPANION*

Many claim that acceptance brings peace and happiness and plays a major role in healthy relationships. And I would agree that acceptance *with a twist* works wonders in creating lasting happiness. Acceptance of inward and outward conditions can keep your life from being hijacked by fear, resistance, negative emotions, and ignorance, as well as by the difficulty itself. Acceptance is an expression of generosity to self and others and can give us the ability to respond to life's difficulties with compassion and creativity. But what is really meant by *acceptance*—just going with the flow? Letting go and letting God? Does it always imply nonaction?

Acceptance with a twist gives anyone the ability to make meaning from any situation. Acceptance must be *active* to really take root in our lives. The first step in acceptance with a twist is to bring attention to what is going on, not to cover it up with some Band-Aid of false acceptance. When we are truly accepting of a situation we take the time to name what's really going on (global warming, personal suffering, hunger, anger, loss, resistance) and then we choose to do something about it. We don't linger about in a state of nonaction (and maybe hidden resentment) saying that we are accepting the situation when we are really resisting its existence.

There is too much passive acceptance—just going with the flow, or just *being* at times when what we need to do is speak up, act out, and join with others in a cause. (How I like to frame it is to be active in creating favorable causes and conditions.) Acceptance with a twist is dependent upon compassionate awareness of the actual dynamics of a situation or stressor, what you can or can't do about it, and the taking of some risk to transform any negativity. The *twist* comes with taking action that may or may not appear to others as acceptance.

As Rafiki, the spiritual advisor, teaches in *The Lion King* movie—sometimes the best way to learn acceptance is from a whack with a staff.

> ***Adult Simba.*** I know what I have to do. But going back means I'll have to face my past. I've been running from it for so long.
>
> *[Rafiki hits Simba on the head with his stick]*

Adult Simba. Ow! Jeez, what was that for?
Rafiki. It doesn't matter. It's in the past.

[laughs]

Adult Simba. Yeah, but it still hurts.
Rafiki. Oh yes, the past can hurt. But the way I see it, you can either run from it, or . . . learn from it.

[swings his stick again at Simba, who ducks out of the way]

Rafiki. Ha. You see? So what are you going to do?
Adult Simba. First, I'm gonna take your stick.

[Simba snatches Rafiki's stick and throws it and Rafiki runs to grab it]

Rafiki. No, no, no, no, not the stick! Hey, where you going?
Adult Simba. I'm going back!
Rafiki. Good! Go on! Get out of here!

[Rafiki begins laughing and screeching loudly]

Acceptance with a twist means you are willing to:

Rock the boat
Risk hurting someone's feelings (though this is not the intention of your actions)
Not worry about offending someone when it means keeping your integrity
Say it even if your voice shakes
Chance making a total fool of yourself
Not be invested in the response you'll get
Learn that the best protection is a vulnerability; go forward undefended
Say it loud enough for a crowd to hear (out in the open)
Be willing to lose your reputation over a cause

*Our desire for other people's love and admiration will
taint what would otherwise have been a powerful and
beneficial act.*

TRALEG KYABGON, *THE PRACTICE OF LOJONG*

Here is a teaching story that further illustrates acceptance with a twist.

✦✦✦

Is That So?

From *Zen Flesh, Zen Bones,* compiled by Paul Reps
and Nyogen Senzaki

The Zen master Hakuin was praised by his neighbors as one living a pure life.

A beautiful Japanese girl whose parents owned a food store lived near him. Suddenly, without any warning, her parents discovered she was with child.

This made her parents angry. She would not confess who the man was, but after much harassment at last named Hakuin.

In great anger the parents went to the master.

"Is that so?" was all he would say.

After the child was born it was brought to Hakuin. By this time he had lost his reputation, which did not trouble him, but he took very good care of the child. He obtained milk from his neighbors and everything else the little one needed. A year later the girl-mother could stand it no longer. She told her parents the truth—that the real father of the child was a young man who worked in the fish market. The mother and father of the girl at once went to Hakuin to ask his forgiveness, to apologize at length, and to get the child back again. Hakuin was willing. In yielding the child, all he said was: "Is that so?"

✦✦✦

Fortunately all these techniques in dealing with the inner and outer dynamics of bullying do positively transform our lives. When we become more aware of what is really going on and challenge our perspective we see the opportunities within and beyond our pain. We stop agreeing to being bullied or to bullying ourselves. But, none of us can transcend the difficulty in isolation; *we need each other.*

Tell Wally: Bringing It All Out into the Open

We can't live by isolating ourselves from others. We are on our own, but we can't do it alone. We live life from our side *in* relationships with others. We need to routinely hold intimate conversations with others. We cannot heal or transform or experience authentic awakening in isolation. We tend to hide when we are feeling resistant or experiencing shame, anger, sadness, or confusion. When we isolate, the negativity then breeds in secrecy and we tend to suffer more. (Remember that inner bully? She can really boss you around when you isolate).

It is best to gather at times with others who support your spiritual practice and creative aspirations. Our community and qualified teachers are integral parts of a reliable spiritual and creative life. It is better to spill it out to others than to carry and repress the questions and pain. This is the reason we each share our life story with others (as encouraged earlier)—to experience the mirroring and support of others. This is the reason we go to people and share our concerns, so that negativity and misunderstanding doesn't take root in our hearts and minds. This is the purpose of receiving oral teachings from a qualified teacher or help from a skillful counselor, so that we can be given guidance by someone who has themselves walked the walk.

Jangtse Choje Rinpoche at a teaching at Deer Park Buddhist Center in Oregon, Wisconsin, said, "The actual refuge is the dharma." He went on to say that the Buddha is the founder of the dharma (teachings; the actual translation for *dharma* is "known phenomenon"). The Sangha (circle of peers or practitioners), he pointed out, *sustains* the dharma. It is a skillful means to have our journey focused on the dharma, the teachings and practices. But even the teachings are best understood through the support of a qualified teacher and a supportive community.

Pat White Deer, a Native American elder, recently told me of a scene in the movie *Crocodile Dundee*. The reporter who brought Dundee, an

Australian bush man, to New York introduced him to a psychiatrist. Since he had lived in the bush his entire life the concept of a psychiatrist was novel to him.

"Don't you have any therapists there?" the reporter asked.

"Oh no," he replied. "When we have a problem we tell Wally [the local bartender]. Wally then tells others until everyone knows and problem solved."

Sharing our questions, difficulties, and stories breaks a cycle of isolation that is deeply rooted in our Western culture. We take too much to the grave. Asking questions of the teacher, opening up to others, challenging assumptions in public, and working ideas out through conversation is rich soil for a fulfilling and purposeful life. We feel our belonging within these conversations with each other. Not only do we not heal in isolation, we do not truly experience our humanity if we believe that we are in this alone. Rather than trying to figure it all out in isolation, put it out to "Wally." Hold the conversation. Ask the questions. Show up in gatherings. Receive more teachings. Make contact.

4

Even the Smallest Puddle Reflects the Moon

CLAIMING YOUR CREATIVE INHERITANCE

Wanderer, your footsteps are,
the road, and nothing more.
Wanderer, there is no road,
the road is made by walking.
By walking one makes the road,
and upon glancing behind,
one sees the path
that will never be trod again.
Wanderer, there is no road—
Only wakes upon the sea.

ANTONIO MACHADO,
POEM 29 OF "PROVERBS AND SONGS"

Finding true fulfillment does not depend on following any
particular religion or holding any particular belief.

HIS HOLINESS THE FOURTEENTH DALAI LAMA,
ESSENCE OF THE HEART SUTRA

Seek and Ye Shall *Not* Find

Some covet the idea of fulfillment like the gambling addict covets the big win. Do you know how the gambler becomes an addict? They have to experience at least one major win. This is the hook that gets them in a constant addictive search for the next big win. They had a taste of it and they want more. This is called *chasing the win*. Of course, the search for this next big win often destroys their lives and those around them. It is not so much the one win itself that harms them, but the continued attachments to having to have another big win (and usually an expectation of an even bigger win). They live in a constant search for their happiness and a relief from the addiction. (Research in the field of addictive gambling shows us that those who don't experience a big win early on are less likely to become addicts or even gamble again.) I have witnessed people create a similar dynamic in relationships; romanticizing a past relationship and then going in search of their "phantom lover." In our creative and spiritual lives we may do the same thing—build up what a creative life should look like based on some illusionary past experience of how things should be.

Our attachments to our past, and our illusions of how things are, can be dismantled through the simple process of living consciously and intentionally.

Fulfillment, living a purposeful and creative life, comes through a process of welcoming it, making room for it, not through seeking it like a gambler seeks a card game (or like we may pursue the imaginary phantom lover). Yes, at times we seek the truth like a woman with her hair on fire seeks the pond. But this is best only at the beginning of a spiritual or creative pilgrimage. You can liken this to the falling in love stage of a relationship or the beginning of creative pursuit. But we can't constantly be in seeking mode. A bird, as it is said, can't always be in flight. Once the initial urgency is gone, we need to know how to keep the creative energy alive. Studies reveal that we can't be seeking and creating at the same time. How can we be looking outside of our present experience and expect to create from within this present moment? Besides, we deserve much more than an illusionary promise of the next big win. Instead, we can live inspired and creatively open more and more to what each circumstance, each moment offers us.

We live a radically creative life by exploring the potentiality of the moment, and make claim to our spiritual and creative inheritances.

> *The master doesn't seek fulfillment.*
> *Not seeking, not expecting,*
> *She is present, and can welcome all things.*
>
> LAO-TZU, TAO TE CHING

This *Will Make Me Happy*

Research shows that we tend to get focused on the "one thing" that will bring us happiness—usually it is a possession, a relationship, or some experience like a trip to Hawaii or a raise. This is not to say these are not good things, but the happiness quotient simply doesn't last, so we move our attention, our focus, onto another object of our happiness. This is the illusion—nothing outside our self will bring lasting happiness—even writing a book or landing the perfect job or publisher. So that is the reason to develop inner states of well-being. These inner states become constant in an ever-changing outer world.

> *Most people believe that they would be happier if they were*
> *richer, but survey evidence on the subjective of well-being is*
> *largely inconsistent with that belief.*
>
> DANIEL KAHNEMAN, *THINKING, FAST AND SLOW*

The Focusing Illusion

The illusion is that "when I get this I will be happy." The focusing illusion includes putting our happiness on outward objects and circumstances and typically looks into the future. There is a lack of creativity involved because we are putting our energy in an illusionary state of *when*. This illusion also foregoes the zero point agreement to live life from your side because the focus of your happiness is on something outside of yourself.

We get what we thought we wanted and find it doesn't bring us the happiness or inspiration we expected, and we get discouraged and depressed. Or we go purchase another *something* that has gotten our attention or put our search engines onto another source in hopes that this will make us happy. Instead, we could come to an understanding of what brings us lasting happiness.

Buddhist philosophy and other mind-training practices, such as in the cognitive-behavioral sciences, identified this long ago—happiness is an inside job. This being the case, nothing on the outside will lastingly bring happiness—not another child, not a bestseller, not a new home, not a finished painting. Not even the right job. Happiness is something that takes place in the moment, a direct experience as a result of something you actively cultivated. It is ongoing and, therefore, creative. And whatever we manifest, no matter what form it takes, keeps changing. A published book, for instance, is like an adult child—the child may have left the home but stuff keeps happening! It's the creating, living the inspired life, and sharing your creations that bring you lasting happiness. Authentic manifestation is active in that you *are manifesting*—it's not what you *have manifested*. Authentic manifestation is relational. It is changing and impermanent like everything else. It's not the house or the written book that will bring you lasting happiness or further inspiration. It is the caring or decorating or living in the house that will give you happiness. It is in the sharing of what you have written, practicing what you teach, or getting onto the next novel that will keep you happy and inspired. Keeping your mind on how many "likes" you have on Facebook or how many books you sold on Amazon will keep you stuck in a loop of dissatisfaction. Even if you hit the bestseller list, your happiness and inspiration will still come down to what you do with what you have—the sharing of yourself with others. More on how to creatively manifest is addressed in the next chapter.

Instead of living mechanistically, the creative life is the result of uncovering the myriad possibilities inherent in each situation. We unleash our creativity and energize the dull places in life through the process of *seeing* and then using these possibilities. In order for us to see the possibilities, we must free ourselves from habitual and numbed states of seeing our world (techniques that were offered throughout chapter 2). We must offer up to ourselves the internal spaciousness that our creativity will need in order to flourish. We can't come up with new ideas or even a way out of feeling stuck if we are habituated to seeing in the same way. We have to give ourselves the freedom to think for ourselves, from our side, unimpeded by the agendas or assumptions of others.

There is actually a serious downside to focusing on the positive. This shadow side consists of the assumptions built into what we believe makes us truly happy. This is a form of "cult mind," where we accept some pitch of happiness as valid only to discover in reality that the focus of our attention did not bring us the happiness we expected. Each of us can do a personal inventory of past purchases that we thought would bring us increased happiness. How much happiness did this purchase actually bring you? Truth be told, all areas of our lives including love life, jobs, and pastimes are influenced by the focusing illusion of the search for happiness.

> *The monkey is reaching*
> *For the moon in the water.*
> *Until death overtakes him*
> *He'll never give up.*
> *If he'd let go the branch and*
> *Disappear in the deep pool,*
> *The whole world would shine*
> *With dazzling pureness.*
>
> HAKUIN EKAKU,
> "THE MONKEY IS REACHING"

A way to simplify this would be to say: Don't waste more time *searching* for peace, for happiness, for purpose—just let go. Give up the spiritual questing and dive into the moment. The poem above is like the story of the boy who, in his search, kept diving into the watery reflection of the pears he hungered for instead of noticing that they were up in the tree, in his reach all along. The mind being in search mode keeps us caught up in an illusion of what we think we want.

The searching mind, especially when desperately or constantly looking for happiness or even purpose, is sabotaged by the search itself. It gets caught up in some illusion of what is being offered when in fact there is a tree of plenty nearby. This is the reason it can be so difficult to give up our search for happiness and meaning in order to make our own happiness. So often it appears as if what we want is just nearly in our reach. (And those with a bounty seem so happy.)

The monkey can't let go of the supposed security of the branch it holds on to—and we each have our own branch. Titles, beliefs, expectations, and physical possessions are all branches that we hold on to while searching and reaching for an illusion of satisfaction. But it is only in the letting go of these branches of security that we have a direct experience of what we have been searching for. We can't make meaning when one hand is holding on to the branch of security (identity, assumptions) and the other is grasping for an illusion. We must let go and fall into our present moments.

The act of creating does bring us continued happiness; just so, the act of making meaning brings us fulfillment. Therefore, we put our inward and outward attention and energy on creating what we want. As we create and make meaning we bring our efforts out into the open, share them, and connect them with others; I refer to this as creative manifestation. *Creative manifestation* means that there is still action, still movement and participation in something—we are not clinging to an end result or object. We are always present and in the act of cultivating an ideal. Movement and participation are key to our ongoing enjoyment. This means we creatively manifest and then let go, we move on. Enjoy and participate in all the results of your efforts (money, friends, experiences), but don't remain attached to them, don't get caught up in an illusion of happiness.

> *Do the work, then relax, don't think—allow.*
>
> RAY BRADBURY

All the practices in this and the next chapter on creative manifestation nullify the focusing illusion and bring you to the manifestation of emotional, physical, and even material prosperity. But be warned, *anything* you want can take on the properties of a focusing illusion—even, "reading this chapter will make me happy." To creatively manifest happiness, abundance, your art, or a relationship, you must let go of the old stories (as shown in previous chapters) and live the active life. You must cultivate the conditions of what you want to manifest. You are now at the point where you can cultivate the creative life because you have made room for it through such internal practices as challenging assumptions. Next, fully release the searching mode mentality and see your creative life unfold, almost without effort.

Awhile back I talked with my husband, who is a wildlife biologist, about how people put so much energy, time, and money into *searching* for happiness. They get their minds set on something and their desire for it increases. He promptly said, "Tinbergen's research on prey selection."

Nikolas Tinbergen found in his research that tits (Paridae) tended to favor one kind of larval Lepidoptera at any given time—a fancy term for their favored food. He saw that the birds were actively searching for these particular species while ignoring other potential food sources (prey). He labeled this phenomenon "specific search image." This reveals a connection between Tinbergen's study and how we too tend to go in search of a given source of happiness, missing other potential sources. Even the search mentality itself is a hindrance. Humans tend to be very *search specific*; habitual in what we are looking for and the places that we look for it. We tend to become habitual in what we want, search for, and, as a result, find. This reflects a popular warning, be careful what you wish for. A more accurate caution is to be careful of what you are searching for.

As a therapist I witness people's unhappiness increase as they narrow their search down to finding a romantic partner, to weight loss, or to some other specific image that they believe will end their particular hunger. With young adults it is often the next electronic gadget (well, this is true for many adults as well). But if these brought us as much happiness as anticipated we would not begin our search for the next object of our happiness so quickly after obtaining the last one. This search intensifies when we have experienced some relief or happiness in the past from a given subject or experience (image). (Just like

Tinbergen's birds.) For example, in gambling addiction as I mentioned earlier: the person who once had a big win early on is more likely to chase the next win, ignoring all the other potential sources of happiness (and often after considerable losses).

This phenomenon explains the distance that develops between ourselves and what the given moment and environment truly has to offer us—we can't see beyond what we are searching for. People often speak of how unhappy they are with what they don't have, losing sight of what they do possess. What they possess is a moment filled with potentiality and options for making meaning and lasting happiness. (Consider how much money the gambling addict lost that could be used to create or experience something new.)

We all have a bit of the addict in us. Notice how advertisers trigger our search engines to want and search for their product. They trigger the focusing illusion—"here, buy this and be happy."

Ask yourself: Are you like the bird in the study, always going for the same source of nourishment (happiness, fulfillment) when something else might better feed you? What are other possibilities of where you can put your focus that you may be overlooking? Where are you the most habitual (this is where you are most likely in search mode)? Where are you putting your energy in seeking fulfillment from another rather than actively living a fulfilling life? (Consider the difference between the volunteer who went to Ecuador to help build bridges and the person that went to a shaman in Ecuador for insight into their purpose here on Earth.) How do you see yourself being spiritually or creatively fulfilled? (Hint: If fulfillment comes from some outward end result—beware, the focusing illusion is at play. If, on the other hand, fulfillment comes from the act of creating, then happiness is assured.)

Fortunately, unlike Tinbergen's birds, we have the innate ability to train our minds and to put our attention where we choose. We can be more receptive to the beauty and mystery of each moment and get the full spectrum of possibilities offered up to us in a given moment.

Fulfillment of the
Three Original Promises

We took our first gasp of breath and inherited three vows. A full life holds these as sacred. These "three original promises" call on our attention throughout life—each in its own right deserves our love, energy, and attention to live a truly fulfilling life. These three promises are to the self (mental, physical, and spiritual), to the other (family, spouse, friend), and to our creativity (our vocations and creative manifestations).

Our promise is to them; to be with them; to live with them, to hold ongoing conversations in all these areas. Each one needs feeding and watering, as it were. When one area gets too much attention, another promise may become wounded and deflated. How we keep our promises to one affects the other two. None of them are more valuable than the others. The promise to attend to yourself, to be with others, and to live an actively creative life are all equally valuable.

The question is how are we doing on each of our promises at any given time. I don't advocate for equality as much as I do for balance. Sometimes, when we fall in love with a project or person they get more of our time and energy. But if we were to forfeit our relationships consistently for our creative pursuits, for example, our relationships suffer. Or if we find ourselves in a codependent relationship or a job that doesn't allow for innovation, the personal and creative life suffers.

To live a meaningful life is to fulfill each promise consistently and throughout daily life. Everything can be fulfillment of a promise, even when there are dirty dishes to clean after a long day's work. But if we work hard all day and then give nothing to our spiritual or creative life, or to our relationships for that matter, everyone suffers. Each promise that is ignored sits in our psyche like a pebble in our running shoe. And this is a good thing—*that pain in your foot is telling you something.*

The promise to our self, to our creative and spiritual life, can make us uncomfortable and sometimes unhappy when we do not give that part of our life the attention it deserves. Fortunately, up until our death, we can go about fulfilling this promise. Right here, right now, outside your door, or among the dirty dishes in the kitchen sink, the promise to self can be fulfilled. This is living life from the zero point—you don't have to go outside of your daily life to have powerful creative and spiritual experiences. You don't have to jeopardize one promise for another. Your promise to the creative self is always ready to hold a conversation with you.

> *Some nights, stay up till dawn.*
> *As the moon sometimes does for the sun.*
> *Be a full bucket pulled up the dark way*
> *of a well, then lifted out into the light.*
>
> *Something opens our wings. Something*
> *makes boredom and hurt disappear.*
> *Someone fills the cup in front of us.*
> *We taste only sacredness.*
>
> RUMI

The promises work together in balancing our life as we fulfill them—ideally our vocation is an expression of the creative spirit and our ethical principles. It also matters that we bring our authentic selves into our work and take care of ourselves mentally, physically, and spiritually within all environments. Or in the case of our personal relationships, that we bring the same integrity to these as we might to our work relationships. We use these promises to remind us of what it means to keep life actively in balance.

Remember the practice of identifying and reframing stolen words? *Promise* can be such a word. Making a promise to ourselves or others can give the message of something we will have in the future, rather than something we are fulfilling in the present moment.

Promise or Con?

The three promises give us something to which we bring our attention to—how am I fulfilling the promise to live a meaningful life in my vocation or personal life? Promises give us something to move toward but inherently hold the danger of putting everything off into the future. One can ask, is this an authentic promise or a con?

We harvested sap one weekend to boil into maple syrup. The tree, the season, and the sap itself were rich with promise. The promise of finding a bucket full of sap, the promise of spring and warmer weather, the promise of sap being cooked into edible maple syrup. We lived in the moment of harvesting; enjoying the last of the clinging snow and emptying the buckets of watery liquid into the pot.

An authentic promise is one that is being fulfilled (at least in part) *in the moment*—like the promise in the harvesting of sap and the resulting maple syrup. A con, on the other hand, is mostly (or entirely) talk of what's to come without any real connection to a harvest. In a con there is no direct experience. Let's consider enlightenment, which could be either a con or an authentic promise. When you are actually practicing compassion, meditation, or other aspects that bring about enlightenment, then you are fulfilling the promise of enlightenment. If you are just talking the talk and there is little or no actual practice, then you are being conned (or conning yourself). You will notice that when there is no real practice there is no (or very little) movement around the promise.

It has been said by many teachers that the Buddha or God's love will be found in the practice. If what you want is love, practice love. If what you want is abundance, practice generosity. If you want to experience calm, then practice the meditation of calm abiding. There is a promise of peace and inner tranquility as a result of a regular meditation practice. There is a promise of happiness in the act of some creative endeavor.

When making a promise or when one is being made to you, ask yourself, what needs to actually happen to realize this promise? Be particularly wary of someone who promises something in the future that is contrary to what they are actually presenting in the moment. The addict may promise recovery, the abuser may promise love, the tyrant may promise everything. An apology is often a false promise—and is known as part of the abuse cycle (I apologize and promise never to do that again, I feel off the hook, and soon I do it again).

Don't give over your money, a commitment, your signature, or yourself to a promise that is not already being *activated in the moment*. Accept promises very cautiously, even when it appears as if the other may have the capacity to fulfill it. In making or agreeing to a promise be clear about your part in its fulfillment. Make sure the promise has legs, and get those legs moving every day. The tree doesn't promise its maple syrup. A living tree can make and fulfill the promise of sap, but the promise of that tasty syrup depends entirely upon the efforts of the harvester.

The illumination, the inspiration, and the fulfillment arrive when we are active. This can mean we are actively meditating, writing, walking, painting, teaching, or contemplating, to name a few. This is the reason it is vital to our creative and spiritual lives that we have places and times where we can be actively spiritual and actively creative on a daily basis. Too often we give over our creative energy and even our spiritual vibrancy to places and people that tire us out. Consequently, when it comes to our creative or spiritual promises we don't have the energy for it.

A Sufi saying that we should hold close is, "Within your own house dwells the treasure of joy; so why do you go begging from door to door?"

All that we behold is full of blessings.
WILLIAM WORDSWORTH

The Imposter Syndrome

We tend to put ourselves through more unnecessary distress and suffering than anybody else could possibly inflict upon us. Too many claim they are not ready or do not have enough education or experience to risk taking the next step in their life. Instead of taking that risk by taking that trip or writing that novel, they put it on hold. They go back to school (although they already have two degrees). They take a detour from their intentions. Most creative people encounter what I did in my late twenties as I ventured out on my own to build my private practice and write my first book. I felt like a big fake. Who was I to counsel people? Who was I to author a book? This is known as the *imposter syndrome* and is understood clinically as the psychological phenomenon in which people are unable to internalize their accomplishments. We just don't know our own talents! We are constantly limiting ourselves or letting outside circumstances limit us. My spiritual teacher at the time said that he would be worried about me if I hadn't had these internal struggles of inadequacy. He assured me that this phenomenon is common among the talented and educated and that we should be reluctant to trust someone who doesn't have such internal conversations.

When the imposter syndrome is activated we often put our life on hold; we tend to put things off because we don't believe in ourselves. Since creativity relies on one's efforts, you could say *everything* responds to this effort. But we resist such efforts and come up with many reasons for putting life on hold—an aversion to risk, fear of the unknown and of exposure, and the intimacy of the creative life. When feeling inadequate somehow we seek to keep ourselves safe in the norm of inactivity. In his book *The War of Art,* Steven Pressfield explores the battle between the unlived life and the life we live. "Between the two," he shows, "stands resistance." We put our lives on hold because we have to heal first, or get into the right relationship, or have enough time or money to create our masterpiece, or find the perfect land or home that will sustain our creative life (often in response to feeling inadequate as imposters do).

You get this, don't you? Clutter is often a manifestation of this agreement to put our creative life on hold. As the piles of paper, waste, and *stuff* accumulate; it gives us more and more things we have to get to before we can get to our creative lives. Then, the door closes and it is too late.

Many people share that they feel selfish when pursuing a dream or a passion. This feeling may actually point to how they are finally taking care of themselves. *If not now, when? If not you, who?*

From then on I took this psychological phenomenon of feeling like a fake as a pointer to just keep going. No one knows fully where personal inspiration originates. Most scholars and experts at critical junctures of creativity feel as if they don't know what they are doing. *But they keep going anyway*. And each of us can too. Anyone doing something truly inventive or creative will encounter this imposter syndrome or some flavor of resistance. Most will have ways to postpone their intentions. Rarely does anyone claim they know where their best stuff comes from, therefore we wonder at our own qualifications. Each of us can accept both our limits and these internal struggles as part of the creative process. The method behind creativity and success relies on our willingness to keep moving. This reminds me of one of my favorite quotes from Cervantes's Don Quixote: "Until death it is all life."

This means to take the time to reflect on what is worth pursuing in our lives and what we should terminate. Since only you know what your experiences are, only you will truly know what to keep and what to leave behind.

Maybe—It May Be *That*

How much of your life is held hostage by a *maybe*? Maybe I will get to that, maybe I like that, maybe I can do that. "I will think about that" is a maybe too. Maybe later. I consider most of our maybes as another way of saying *I don't know,* and another way of putting life on hold. Of course, at times saying maybe and sitting on the fence is the exact *non*action we need to take. But studies show for example that sitting on the fence too long in a relationship (beyond six months) can cause more distress and confusion. Better to just decide and live with the decision of no or yes. How many times have you heard others say, "I just *feel* so much better having made the decision"?

Lingering too long in the maybe realm is detrimental to our creativity. Think of it as a foundational aspect to your creative life: how can you build from a maybe? When we remain in a maybe for a prolonged stint of time, we become uninspired. Our clutter often represents maybes. Our maybes at their best are our future possibilities. But they remain only that—a thought of a possibility—and result in a sort of sleepwalking. An enduring lack of inspiration can lead to giving up, addiction, depression, hopelessness, and helplessness. It can also create a dependency on outside circumstances to make change possible, which becomes the focusing illusion mentioned earlier.

Thus, you want to become more and more conscious of what you are saying yes to, no to, and maybe to; and bring these out in the open. Often we keep our commitments or possible commitments to ourselves, reluctant to put it out there where others may hold us accountable. A meaning maker lives out in the open. We want to be ready, willing, and able to change our maybe to no or yes. This generates movement, inspiration, creativity, and confidence. A natural consequence of reading and using the exercises in this book will be to transform your maybes, opening you up to saying yes and to more real possibilities.

Evidence shows that such openness and creativity are dependent upon certain inner qualities such as trust, curiosity, personal illumination, tolerance for the unknown, enthusiastic effort, and confidence. Trust has shown up throughout this book as central to our ability to live creatively. For creative movement to take place, you must trust enough in yourself, trust in what you regard as your spiritual source, be it God or nature, and trust in the humanity of others to come through for you. Trust ultimately engages your creative intention—because with this trust, you continue to return to your intention. Trust is an expression of faith. As Frank Fools Crow states in *Fools Crow: Wisdom and Power,* "without faith there is no power and there is no movement." Usually when we are stuck in a lot of maybes or resistance, we lack either trust in ourselves, trust in others, or trust in a greater possibility.

Trust that we are the meaning makers we have been waiting for. Become clear on what you are saying maybe to, yes to, and no to, and witness the movement you desire.

Maybe, No, Yes

Is there anything lingering in your life (like a long winter) that begs for a jolt of energy? Does it seem that an *internal* winter is also lasting too long? If so, here is a simple way to do some internal spring cleaning that will generate positive movement in your life. Don't wait on the external thaw or the yes from someone else to make those desired strides in your life. If you want to receive the big yes from the outside world (*Yes, we want to publish your book; Yes, I want to exhibit your art; Yes, I want to spend some time with you; Yes, you are accepted into the school or organization*), first you have to clean out the clutter of the maybes that are holding you back. You have to be willing to turn your maybes into nos or yeses. Maybes should be a temporary oasis, not a place to set up camp. For example, if you are in a maybe relationship, you will not want to be on the fence for too long because the stress and dishonesty that results is far more painful and destructive than the open yes or no. Take out your journal and make three lists; a list of what you are saying no to, a list of your maybes, and a list of what you are saying yes to.

+ Start with the maybes. Take some time to make a list of everything you are saying maybe to. This includes all the things you are undecided about; the things about which you think we'll see, kinda, sort of, I'm thinking about it, it's a consideration, perhaps, could be, or I'll get back to you. Even the unused clothes in your closet or the unfinished art projects in your studio—all of these things go on your maybe list. (As a writer I hold myself hostage by a list of "maybe ideas"—maybe that is something I will write about.). Consider all the different areas of your life—personal, vocational, physical, spiritual, financial, artistic, relational, and so forth.

+ Next, turn your maybes into either a no or a yes. Start with the nos. Decide what you are not going to give your time and energy to. Go beyond just writing your nos down; do what you need to do to dissolve your commitment (and resulting energy drain) to this possibility. I sometimes say no to an idea by making a statement of gratitude for having the idea in the first place and then releasing it back out to the cosmos for someone else to follow up on.

+ Finally, get clear and open about what you are saying yes to. This asks you to be conscious of what you are truly committing yourself to—be it a relationship, creative endeavor, or spiritual pursuit. Come out in the open with what you say yes and no to. And for those lingering maybes, give them a deadline. Choose a date, or event, not too far into the future, where you will decide yes or no. By cleaning out the maybes and being clear about what you say no to, you have made room for the yeses in your life, and you will find an immediate increase in energy and inspiration around your commitments. Be intentional and conscious about your yeses.

✦ Keep your yeses conscious and active by reviewing them regularly and taking action on them.

Choose Yes and Move On: The Big Picture and the Steps Nearest In

> *After the final no there comes a yes*
> *And on that yes the future world depends.*
>
> WALLACE STEVENS,
> FROM "THE WELL DRESSED MAN WITH A BEARD"

Most times, there are many options provided to us; some are inherent in the situation, others lie beyond the given setting. We just have to be able and willing to look out beyond our limited perspective. And we do tend to limit ourselves in most, if not all, circumstances. Two common ways we do this are through our uncertainty of the outcome (we make negative assumptions of the outcome) or by lacking trust in our ability to proceed. We sense only risk but not the possibilities inherent in the risk.

To ignite awareness of the possibilities inherent in the situation, but that lay beyond the particular situation, we need to say yes to something big that moves our attention forward, and then, take the next step nearest in. The next step *nearest in* is the one closest to you, often the one that takes the most courage. If this "something big" were inherent in the situation it would be like the strawberry in your reach, like writing a poem and submitting it for a contest. If the big idea is out of sight or reach (in most cases it will be), you will first have to take a mental reach outside of the particular situation you are in; such as deciding to be a writer and making a living with writing as your central theme. At this point, you will have to believe in something that is not fully formed in its specifics and details. Fulfillment of any big idea relies on taking your focus off the teeth of the tiger (the limits) in order to see what other possibilities exist inherent in a bigger picture. Then after committing yourself to the bigger picture, identify the next step nearest in that takes you in that direction.

Say Yes to the Big Idea

Say yes to your larger idea, without being ready or having it all figured out. (Hint: What has been nudging at you for some time now?) Sign on the dotted line before you have all your ducks in a row. Commit to reaching for the strawberry or letting go of the branch and leaping into the great unknown. Absolutely every big plan involves leaping into the unknown, or reaching for what looks like a tasty strawberry. Living creatively means you will have to live with times of ambiguity. The risk in the reach is that you also lose your grip of the known and will soon be falling into something new. A death is certain to happen, but in this case it is the death of the security of the known. You may well have a map in your pocket but the speed of your fall will make it irretrievable.

Say yes to the big plan, the big idea, then, take the next step, and keep saying yes and then taking the next step *close in* unless it becomes clear that you need to go in another direction. When you face another direction you will be saying yes to something else. Don't get caught up in what you say no to; your energy and attention go to where you turn your gaze, to your yeses, and to taking the next step close in. Progress and inspiration are guaranteed as you focus on the next step of the great plan. Each one of my books was created line by line. Every success I have experienced has been taken in a leap of commitment first, followed by a series of close-in steps. When I show up to the page, I hold a general sense of the big picture but in the moment of creativity my attention is on this idea in front of me—this line, this concept. I would be in a constantly overwhelmed state if I greeted my writing with only the big picture. A lot of writers and others with big ideas give up because they don't know how to say yes to the creative life, to the next step nearest in. Instead they carry the big plan, the big idea around with them like a weight. Or, they try to skip the step close in, which is always the one with the most emotional risk and bigger payoff. For example, let's say you are working for an organization that has become a negative working environment but you have worked there most of your adult life. The next step close in might be to leave that job so that you can find work that is more fulfilling. This step comes with great emotional risk but has the potential for a very large payoff.

Another benefit from learning to acknowledge and then take the next step close in is that we experience the many smaller successes that lead up to the manifestation of the greater idea. And in truth, life is made up of moments and steps close in. Even when we are about to take a grand leap into the unknown, once we land on new ground many smaller steps will be what makes the leap worthwhile. The leap is in making the commitment while holding the bigger picture in mind, then taking the next step nearest in toward our intention.

Get in the practice of saying yes daily. Say yes to your big idea and then notice the next step that needs to be taken to move toward the big picture, now. Don't go jumping ahead to the third or fourth step in the process. Become clear what the nearest step in is and take that step. It actually takes more courage to take a breath and then take the next small step than it does to make claim to some big step that doesn't actually generate real movement. Choose to keep saying yes to each step, trusting that if something feels off, you would stop the process.

The addict in recovery understands how saying yes one day at a time to sobriety will bring about personal freedom. They can't just be saying no to drugs or no to gambling. They have to have something on a daily basis they are saying yes to, which initially is to their sobriety. Then once sobriety sets in, they can begin to say yes to another big picture and take one step at a time, one day at a time, to fulfill their new big dream.

When you change the way you look at things, the things you look at change.
MAX PLANCK, NOBEL PRIZE–WINNING PHYSICIST, CONSIDERED THE FATHER OF QUANTUM PHYSICS

This Always Works: Bringing in the Third Thing or the Third Place

Rightly used, a third thing functions a bit like the old Rorschach inkblot test, evoking from us whatever the soul wants us to attend to. Mediated by a good metaphor, the

*soul is more likely than usual to have something to say. But
the fact will count for nothing if we fail to recognize that
the soul is speaking or fail to pay attention to what it says.*
        Parker J. Palmer, *A Hidden Wholeness*

You have noticed by now that I use quotes, poems, and mythological
and antidotal stories. These are the *third thing* first introduced to me
in Parker J. Palmer's work. This third thing, *tertium quid* in elemen-
tal science, points to an unknown third element that arises from two
known elements. This unknown third element opens us up. Basically
the two known things are you and your perspective—then we throw in
the third element to awaken more possibilities. The third thing gives us
a wider view. These third things give us the ability to see the strawber-
ries that are within our reach. And, if we are stuck or in resistance, the
third thing can unstick us.

Evoking the Soul with the Third Thing

The third thing is that extra something that can shake up com-
placency, get you to think for yourself, and generate your natural
meaning-making abilities. It has the ability to arouse the hidden
gems inside the secret chambers of our souls. People use this to get
results—they bring in that third element to change the chemistry of
a situation. The third thing teaches "sideways" with a poem or a story
instead of hitting you head-on with an opinion. So rather than tell
you what the sky looks like over the Pacific Ocean after a storm, I will
read to you a poem and you can imagine it for yourself. Or, instead
of telling you how to open up to a particular creative idea, I throw in
a third thing—a story or a poem or a poetic quote that is sure to stir
up your own meaning. These, too, give you direct experience with an
idea because you are making the meaning yourself instead of trying
to digest someone else's take on something. And, it is a most remarkable tool for opening your view to more options. An antidotal story
or myth or poem that confronts and in some way answers a question
presents the solution sideways to the person rather than head-on again.
This sideways approach to problem solving allows for you to make up

your own meaning and solution. This takes the energy off the problem and opens you up personally and directly to other possibilities.

The *third thing* is brought in to shake up the old assumptions and posturing and open the inner doors to new possibilities. Third things can include poems, myths, fairy tales, poetry, narrative quotes, antidotal stories, lyrical music, parables, metaphorical or paradoxical stories, puzzles, and koans.* Oracles such as the I Ching are also third things. Acknowledging a third thing brings something new and different into the mix of your thought process and experience. It automatically opens the door to creative movement.

I recommend that you have many third things handy to inspire and encourage you. My writing space is filled with poetry books, fairy tales, myths, and books of koans and metaphors to stir and open my mind. I consult the I Ching when I am confused or stuck. When I go for my walks, I sometimes listen to songs that are sure to bring about some creative idea to help me see an old problem in a new way (thank you, Bob Dylan). When communicating an idea to someone else, include a third thing. Read them a poem that for you expresses what you are trying to get across. They may not go away with some cookie-cutter notion of your original concept, but they will have made something of their own from what you shared. It always works.

> *Thou hast only to follow the wall far enough and there will be a door in it.*
>
> MARGUERITE DE ANGELI, *THE DOOR IN THE WALL*

The *third place* is also recognized as a means to generate creative thinking and the visioning of new possibilities. This concept is mostly mentioned in community building and refers to the use of a third place outside of home and work environments. These third places then generate more creative interaction among people. Many companies now have used this concept of a third place successfully to offer up a location where their workers can meet across disciplines in

---

*A *koan* is a paradoxical anecdote or riddle that doesn't have an answer. It's typically used in Zen Buddhism to provoke enlightenment and creative thinking.

a common, more social setting. Much like the third thing, the third place can challenge your patterned way of seeing or thinking. For me, the third place can be a casual setting, like a coffee shop or an outside public garden. Locate some third places where you can meet with others (not always of like minds); where conversation and an exchange of ideas and story are welcomed. (I do not consider religious institutions or other places with strongly set rules and established processes to be suitable third places.) City parks, bookstores, community centers, college campuses, libraries, nature centers, museums, and local cafes with a place to visit all hold the potential for being a third place where creativity can be harvested. Ideally these places have in common a way for people to hold open conversations, are free or at minimal cost, invite a combination of regulars and new people to congregate, invite people to come as they are, and are in either a natural or welcoming setting where natural light, sounds, and sights are accessible.

There are also inner third places that can be places of discovery.

Journey to the Third Place through Transpersonal States

Transpersonal means to get beyond the personal, beyond the limits of our assumptions and of the physical body. Whenever one seeks to bring forth a creative vision through a transpersonal state, a qualified teacher, partner, or circle should be present to facilitate it and hold space for you. Chanting, breathwork (such as Stanislav Grof's holotropic breathwork, rebirthing breathwork, shamanic breathing, and pranayama breathwork), shamanic journeying, sun dances, ecstatic dance, various yogic practices, certain rituals, vision questing (extended time in nature), sweat lodges, and certain practices of guided meditation enable transpersonal and altered states that can bring forth a personal creative vision. On many occasions, I have witnessed the transpersonal effects of sharing one's life story with others as well.

To call upon a creative vision is to intentionally generate an altered state so as to receive personal and direct insight. This altered state allows you to temporarily get outside of your habitual mind and body. To bring forth a creative vision of your own, you must be the journeyer.

You must be the one to take a pilgrimage to the sacred internal third place. A qualified teacher and guide will hold the space for you as you travel to your internal Bodhi tree or other third place. In the case of sun dances and other sacred ceremonies, an invitation by those holding the ceremony, along with the proper preparation, is likely required. I recommend you do breathwork with a partner or in a circle so you can share your experiences afterward.

The creative visions and momentum you want are carried within you. Breathwork is one way of opening the inner doors. Your creative visions cannot manifest without you. In many spiritual traditions, when a vision comes to someone, it's believed that that person's energy has left their body and traveled to a place of wisdom. It is also important to know that our experiences when in a transpersonal state are directly influenced by our intentions going in. Take your creative intention with you, wherever you go, both inwardly and outwardly.

> *The pious will lack the means to open the way to the hidden lands. . . . Those who contemplate going will often fall prey to their fears and will lack the prerequisite courage. Those who do go will often be slandered by (others) who are envious of their good fortune. . . . For those who lack the auspicious circumstances to journey to these hidden lands . . . the beyul will remain no more than imagined paradises of enlightened beings; they will not manifest through contemplation and idle talk.*
>
> PADMASAMBHAVA, "THE OUTER PASSKEY
> TO THE HIDDEN-LANDS," QUOTED IN
> *THE HEART OF THE WORLD* BY IAN BAKER

While the *beyul* are the sacred hidden lands within remote parts of Tibet, Padmasambhava, an eighth-century Buddhist master, also refers to the inner *beyul* reached through various Tibetan tantric spiritual practices. In Ian Baker's memoir of his spiritual travels in Tibet's hidden lands, he emphasizes the corresponding internal pilgrimage that must also take place. To travel to these places, you must get beyond just talk and speculation. These inner hidden lands, with all they have to offer us, can be reached through exploring new inner and outer places.

As we continue to venture inward and outward, exploring all our possibilities, we are also likely to encounter disappointment.

Eat, Pray, Disappointment

She got the guy. He got the girl. She was cured. He won the lottery. She became a bestselling author. He was reborn. Happy endings abound.

These successes are splendid, but it's the disappointments too that can be the elixir of life—proof we are risking what we believe in. We really don't know what lies on the other side of our next step (this is the ability to live with the unknown), but some flavor of disappointment will be part of it. Life is never tied up in pretty endings. Something follows getting the guy, winning the lottery, or being reborn. Something comes after enlightenment.

Disappointment doesn't mean failure, or that you dreamed too big. It can just as easily mean you didn't dream big enough. More likely it means you are moving forward, taking that next step. It shows you have come up against an expectation, a limit, or a completion with one idea and are on the edge of another.

Instead of trying to change your thoughts from negative to positive, hold a conversation with the disappointment. This conversation allows for a natural acceptance (with a twist) of some limit we may be experiencing. Then within this conversation you can find a turning point where you can take your next step. Disappointment means you tried. But don't remain there; keep going. I doubt you have fully committed yourself to something or someone if you haven't felt some level of disappointment.

Disappointment points to a dream missed or still longed for—and it points to an invitation for more on our part. Disappointment is simply part of our human experience. In fact our lives are more likely to develop along the lines of how we respond and work with disappointments than with our successes. This is because every success, every happy ending, contains some disappointment.

The story didn't end in *Eat, Pray, Love*—a movie about a woman who goes on a journey of self-discovery—with her getting the guy; the movie and book did. She barely began her spiritual journey. We cannot just go on a thirty-day jaunt to find peace—to eat, pray, and then find happiness. The Hollywood version of life doesn't translate into our daily lives because too many see disappointment as a stopping point and give up when they encounter it. They turn away from a creative path when they don't get the outcome they expected in the time they expected it. They consider divorce or escapes way too early in the game.

Let's each take the next step in life, while keeping our eyes open for that which disturbs and disappoints, too.

What we strive for
in perfection
is not what turns us
into the lit angel
we desire.

What disturbs
and then nourishes
has everything
we need.

DAVID WHYTE,
FROM "THE WINTER OF LISTENING"

The Philosophy and Science of Creativity

If we knew what we were doing, it wouldn't be called research.

ALBERT EINSTEIN

The origin of the word *science* comes from the Latin word, *scientia,* further derived from *scire,* which means "to know." The science of inspiration, of creativity, of spirituality, then, means to have some personal understanding of how inspiration works, how creativity works, and how we can bring about direct spiritual experience. Scientists discover how something works through experimentation. Experience is our best evidence of what works and what does not work. And to experience something we have to be ready to explore new ideas and possibilities. There are many formulas and programs offered up to the hungry seeker that take away the responsibility of exploring and thinking for ourselves. Lots of money is spent this way. Buying into certain formulas simply because they claim themselves as "scientific" or "religious" is to relinquish ourselves as a meaning maker. In these cases we give the experimentation and knowledge over to someone else. Therefore to know the science of creativity (or the meaning of something) is to *become the scientist*—the one who explores and then becomes knowledgeable through discovery.

Not only is it scientific to question and explore but also science insists that we never cease our exploration. In "true science there is always room for discoveries," Bohm insists. And any one of us who gets hooked on a "final" truth is not expressing true science. Typically what happens is in our excitement over a discovery, personal or otherwise, we find ways to fit everything into this one realization. Either that, or we found a religion! (Because now everyone should share in our discovery.) Bohm encourages us to take on a *scientific philosophy* by understanding the "infinity of nature." This is a more scientific term for the Heart Sutra (discussed in chapter 5), meaning that nothing is set and permanent; everything is changing, evolving, and coexisting together. We can end a great deal of our suffering and add to our happiness and creativity when we tune into this infinity of nature—the tao of science and the science of spirituality—that every moment is offering itself up to you with more and more possibilities. The infinity of nature (natural law) speaks to how our hindrances are mostly man-made and how we overcome them (break through the finiteness of our self-imposed limits) by making meaning.

In this life of exploration, discovery, and then more exploration we are a vital part of the whole in its discovery and evolution. A discovery need not ever be a stopping point, whether it is a personal spiritual epiphany or a mathematical solution. We can thoroughly celebrate and integrate what we know into our lives, but let it open us up to what is possible next. If we hold on to our discoveries like children who found the hidden Easter egg, we will lose the opportunity of what is yet to be discovered.

Using the scientific model of discovery we give ourselves a plethora of choices or, in the most difficult of situations, an ability to reach for the single strawberry like the monk caught between the tiger and the cliff. Much in our culture attempts to limit us (intentionally or not) by casting a spell of distractions and "programs" that dull us down. To transform a pattern of limitations all we have to do is focus on our side of the equation, to change some patterned way of being from within and from our side.

Take a breath—because at this very moment as you regard even the *idea* of the third option (maybe even in a particular situation), new pathways of possibilities are being opened to you. Specific alternatives may already be coming to you because of your willingness to consider the concept of possibilities. Bringing to mind that there are likely other possibilities inherent either in or outside of even the worst of scenarios opens the mind to new ideas and perceptions. You are now more able to perceive more choices. You have made room for more opportunities, which want to emerge from this found receptivity to possibilities.

> *Attention to possibilities leads to intention for possibilities, which equals creativity.*
> DR. HENRY OLDS JR., EDUCATIONAL CONSULTANT

We are all full of so much potential and surrounded by so much possibility. We are all in our own way a part of, or a reflection of, the divine. Each of us matters; each of us is remarkable—even a puddle reflects the moon.

> *Enlightenment is like the moon reflected in the water. The moon doesn't get wet; the water isn't broken. Although*

its light is wide and vast, the moon is reflected even in a
puddle an inch long. The whole moon and the whole sky
are reflected in a dewdrop on the grass.

DOGEN KIGEN, THIRTEENTH-CENTURY JAPANESE
PHILOSOPHER

Another way to generate creativity and possibilities is by stealing ideas, like the puddle steals the moon in its own personal reflection.

Steal Like Picasso

A saying often attributed to Pablo Picasso is, "Good artists copy; great artists steal." You can't live the creative life without borrowing from the dead, or from the living. You must steal shamelessly from those who came before you and those around you now. Then you must make it your own. In making the material your own you get what you want—a personal and direct experience that is both creative and spiritual. We make meaning on the compost of others' creations, ideas, and lives. This book you hold in your hands includes material stolen from others. A large part of my life's work is to leave behind a truly rich compost pile for those who will live off my life, as I mentioned earlier. Whatever we leave behind makes up our compost. Our books, our art, our ideas, our children, our teachings, our attitude, our beliefs, our legacies all go into our life's compost. So there is a heritage of stealing that moves the world forward.

Just as importantly, in this culture of branding and trademarking, plagiarism, and the wild world of the Internet—how can we steal like Picasso to feed our creative spirit and bring our fire to the people? How can we justify stealing and do so without committing plagiarism? Ask yourself, how did we get fire in the first place? We stole it from some God or some animal stole it for us, or so the tales tell us. Through myths, legends, and teaching stories, *stealing always saves the day.*

Stealing is different from just copying or plagiarizing others. When you copy, you haven't put yourself into it. There are usually several other educators in my spiritual journaling classes, and I invite them to steal from me. I expect they will steal from me if they are truly inspired. When inspired they will take from what I offered and change it somehow. If they simply copied me, the results would come up flat (for them and their students). Like a copying machine, they would not add to what they took from me. If we only duplicate what inspires us, nothing truly creative will come of it. Steal what inspires you, then do something inspirational with this association. Make it your own somehow.

> *The secret to creativity is knowing how to hide your sources.*
> ALBERT EINSTEIN

So, once you have stolen a creative idea, or spiritual insight, *sit down with it until something new happens within you.* Everything worthwhile takes time. A good book has taken countless rewrites and revisions. A good friendship takes time together. An authentic moment of spiritual or creative inspiration is based on holding a conversation with "the other." If you want to understand something or have it show you something new, you have to sit down with it in long stretches. Then after some lengthy and often edgy conversations with yourself over an idea, meaning is made from your side.

> *Immature poets imitate; mature poets steal; bad poets deface what they take, and good poets make it into something better, or at least something different. The good poet welds his theft into a whole of feeling which is unique, utterly different than that from which it is torn.*
> T. S. ELIOT, *THE SACRED WOOD:*
> *ESSAYS ON POETRY AND CRITICISM*

Here, Steal These

✦ Read *Steal Like an Artist* by Austin Kleon. It is a great resource for those of you who want to increase your creativity. The first of his ten things nobody told you about being creative is "steal like an artist." He offers nine other pithy ways to create; to be your own meaning maker. Put it on your bed stand along with my other favorite book on creativity—Steven Pressfield's *The War of Art*. (These are probably better read with your morning coffee than your evening tea, though.)

✦ Find a spiritual or religious precept and make it your own by changing its meaning. Or, write a commentary of it with a unique twist all your own. Be warned! A dogmatic approach to religious or spiritual concepts dictates that we cannot alter them and that, instead, we should rely on someone else's interpretation of what yet another has said. You will rock the boat.

✦ Find a poem you like and, using its rhythm and subject, steal from it and write one of your own. I will often write an accompanying poem on the pages of my favorite poetry books. Sometimes I begin with the same first line to get me started. By the time I have my own poem (after several rewrites) the poem is entirely my own.

Aspiring from Within

The intention behind each action determines its effect. Our intentions and our actions affect not only ourselves but also others. If we believe that every intention and action evolves as we progress on our spiritual journey, then if we act consciously we evolve consciously, but if we act unconsciously we evolve unconsciously.

ALFRED HUANG, *THE COMPLETE I CHING*

As we choose to live intentionally, we evolve consciously instead of being involved unconsciously. But even more than that, we can constantly create from our intentions, and our lives will flourish from this intentional living. Intentions are an invitation to consciously explore and discover our life circumstances, putting us in the position of always creatively living life. Our intentions give us a big picture to move toward and the one step at a time to move forward each day.

Intentional choices create intentional, conscious results. Our intentions move us through a myriad of circumstances. Each action, as mentioned before, is motivated by our beliefs, assumptions, and intentions (hidden and conscious). *We aspire from within*; our intentions both create and call to us. Intentions recognize the principles of causality and dependent co-arising; happiness and suffering alike both arise from their own similar causes and conditions. Consciously held intentions are one of the most influential causal factors of our experiences. Instead of meeting a situation with a habitual response (being unconsciously involved), we choose how to respond with conscious intention. This conscious intention then becomes a major influence on the causes and conditions of our life experiences.

Most people use up a lot of energy simply getting from place to place (swimming in the ocean of life and not getting in the boat). Crafting and setting intentions gives you back energy lost in swimming about (and sometimes in place). Conscious intentions give us the boat to get around in, and we quickly find ourselves covering more ground (or water) with a life supported by intentions. They give us the energy to break through the armor that holds our true nature in; they give us the ability to express our inherent wisdom and creativity.

People often seek help from therapists or spiritual teachers because they feel depleted, fatigued, and discouraged by life and the choices they have made and continue to make. Use of conscious intentions retrieves lost energy; energy lost to past agreements and distorted, unconscious intentions. We can actually look at the results of our actions to know what intentions we are carrying around in our hearts. I make a distinction here and in *Wheel of Initiation* between intentions and principles. Principles are the oars of the boat or the reins on a horse. Intentions are the boat you ride in or the horse you ride on. Ethical and spiritual principles further direct your life.

> *It's not enough to be busy; so are the ants. The question is; what are we busy about?*
>
> HENRY DAVID THOREAU

We don't want to keep our intentions fixed because we find that as we live our intentions further, deeper meanings begin to emerge; we discover more meaning and purpose behind our intentions. The core meaning of the intention doesn't change (it is some aspect of living life from your side), but your intention changes what it brings out in you and your surroundings. When we set an intention, we set it as an entry point. We do not hold on to our intention like a zealous patriot holds on to a flag. Our intention is our reference point, guiding our experience but not insisting. Like a boat afloat on water it allows our energy to go into creating purposeful interaction with our surroundings instead of all of it going into the drama of just trying to stay afloat. Our life force goes into generating the energy of an intention; for example, "I bring joy into each situation," instead of being consumed by the drama or perceived problem at hand (such as reacting to someone being upset with you). Instead of reacting habitually, we hold an intention (a conscious purpose) and use it to help explore and guide our experience. This is the crucial point. Our intention comes out of some personal significance and we use it to explore and direct our experiences. Our intentions then become a major influence on how we explore a given dynamic and the resulting experience. We make meaning with our intentions, which then expand and deepen our experiences.

Personal Exploration into a Core Intention

I presently live guided by four core intentions. The intentions I live by presently are: I live life from my side; I attain the body, mind, and speech of awakening through the power of my efforts; I embody generosity; and I maintain the Lojong spirit. The exercises that follow here will help you create your own intentions.

What Do You Want?

+ Begin by journaling about what you want for yourself and in your life. (You have already practiced bringing more presence into your daily experience in "An Exploration into Presence" on page 20.) Here, write out the words, "What I want . . ." and fill up at least one page by completing this sentence. Instead of stopping to think, rewrite the words "What I want . . ." Don't let your pen stop moving, and don't stop to consider, just write. This bypasses the thinking mind and opens up to a free flow of ideas that may lie hidden in your subconscious.

✦ Next in this journaling exercise, take one entry from your list above and circle the wish that either repeats itself or sticks out as the most important one. Choose the one that, if you were to express this desire fully in your life, would result in a lot of your other wants falling into place as well. Write out a description of this one aspiration. Do your best to write it down in one succinct sentence. (Be careful not to mistake goals or affirmations for intentions.)

The sentence you just wrote will form the basis for your intention. The words we carry and use are potent tools of creation.

A goal or affirmation holds a different vibration and result than an intention. Too often we use goals to beat ourselves up, using some ideal we are trying to achieve as the bat. The ideal becomes a standard of measurement to compare ourselves against—too often we see that we are not this idea of ourselves.

An intention, on the other hand, can be more readily and easily aligned with a broader plan for your life. Instead of your goal being, "I am going to lose twenty pounds," your intention might be, "I live a physically, mentally, and spiritually active life"; or more simply, "I live an active life." This implies that, among other things, because you are active, you are less likely to be overweight. Intentions are designed to let you live each moment in alignment with your broader spiritual and creative aspirations.

Intentions are action oriented and, as such, energize and empower us. Living and acting from intentions is an optimal use of your energy. At any given moment you are either in alignment with your intention or out of alignment. When you are out of alignment, you are likely engaged in something that is robbing you of energy and making it difficult to initiate your intention. Your core intention will direct your experiences. An intention based in wisdom, action, and compassion draws to us all that we want to realize and gives us all we need to be meaning makers.

Create an Intention to Live By

✦ Begin with the wish you wrote in the prior exercise and design a full intention using verbs and action words. Use affirmative, active words that bring you into the moment. Make sure to leave out words that actually point to a difficulty such as anxiety or doubt. Instead use words that express freedom from the given issue or difficulty. Use words that point to how you want to make meaning in your life. For example, instead of "I live my life free of anxiety" write "I live freely, trusting my choices." Other examples might include:

I express beauty and harmony in my thoughts and actions.
I bravely create my truth.
I awaken to my creative potential.
I live life from my side.
I realize . . .
I act . . .
I attain . . .
I appreciate . . .
I express . . .

✦ Once you develop an intention, keep it strong in your mind. Do not divorce from it. Commit to an inner deliberation to hold your intention consciously throughout the day. Of course, you will create other intentions in your life, but if this is your first one, work with this one exclusively for some time, until you reach a familiarity with intentions. Your specific core intention sets and generates personal direct experience with the fulfillment of your three promises—personal (to self), relational (to others), creative (to vocations). Later you may develop and use an intention for each promise.

Have your intention be a pithy sentence that is easy to retrieve. Create an intention that will initiate you into a more engaged life; an intention that will allow you to explore situations more creatively and consciously. Once this core intention is set, it begins to uplift your entire life.

Some example intentions are as follows: "I experience appreciation with all life." Someone who felt unappreciated most of his life chose this intention. "I rejoice in the good fortune of others." This one was borrowed from the bodhisattva's precepts. This person often felt in competition with others. "I remain empowered in all situations." "I live an abundant life, doing what I love." "I express my creativity with all life." "I act authentically because I know my truth." This particular individual had lived in a marriage and life where he wouldn't speak up for himself. He found himself becoming less and less authentic.

Intention, Not Affirmation

Intentions are more than affirmations. Affirmations are typically "I am" statements, such as "I am beautiful, I am . . ." But evidence reveals that what tends to happen is we state a particular affirmation (*I am beautiful*), when we are actually thinking and generating its opposite (*I am ugly*). Then affirmations tend to trigger a negative emotional response and discourage us from acting positively.

With intentions we choose a verb and an action word to express our aspiration and motivation. This generates more accountability. It also encourages us to align ourselves, in the moment, with the given intention. Affirmations may not break through the layers of assumptions and habitual thought states we carry around with us, but intentions—comprised of conscious and purposeful word choices—directly influence our experiences in a dynamic way.

Ultimately, our intentions reach out to those we live with—our families and our communities. "I live an active life," for example, clearly benefits others as well as ourselves. An aspect of a conscious intention that makes it different from goals and affirmations is its altruistic quality. While it may be very personal (I live an abundant life doing what I love), its very nature will uplift the lives of everyone who comes in contact with the person expressing the intention. Your intention will enliven you and those around you.

Setting Your Intention

To set your intention means to create a bridge between your intention and your daily life—making your intention more real. When making homemade jams we want the jam to set so we can store it and eat it over a year's time. It is not jam unless it sets. The setting of your intention is to take the natural ingredients of your life, create an intention, and set it—making it usable.

Journaling to Set Your Intention

+ To further imprint your intention, journal about what your intention will look like, feel like, and be like when it is one hundred percent true. When this intention is fully realized, how will your life be different? How will this intention benefit others in your life? Does it have an altruistic quality to it? In what way will your life be more engaged, fulfilling, and active? What will be different when this intention is fulfilled? What does this intention allow you to explore and create in your life? Take at least a week with this intention, journaling around it, before you set it.

+ Close your eyes and say your intention a few times and pay attention to the physical and energetic sensations of the body to make sure that this intention really resonates with you. How does this intention feel in your body when you say it aloud? A timely intention will feel energetic, spacious, and good in the body; and most likely risky.

+ Then set this intention by claiming it as your core intention. Share it with your creative manifestation partners or write it out on a sheet of paper to display in a conspicuous place. This establishes (sets) this intention.

Your intention will naturally generate the desire to move and create. And it can be used as a guidepost—at any given moment you can check in to establish whether your agreements (attitude) or your actions are in alignment with this intention. Very soon you will be able to discover how much of your energy is going into your spiritual and creative life and how much is not.

> *You don't hear me yell to test the quiet or try to shake*
> *the wall, for I understand that the wrong sound weakens*
> *what no sound could ever save, and I am the one*
> *to live by the hum that shivers till the world can sing:—*
> *May my voice hover and wait for fate,*
> *when the right note shakes everything.*
>
> WILLIAM STAFFORD, FROM THE POEM
> "BELIEVER," IN *THE WAY IT IS*

The Wish-Fulfilling Mandala

The wish-fulfilling mandala is a simple tool that allows you to manifest your intention. You will experience immediate results through the use of this mandala. It's a simple practice to transform negative mind-sets and experiences to allow for direct spiritual and creative experience. It facilitates the transformation of pain stories, difficulties, and resistances into a way of living that is inspired by intention. It's a wish-fulfilling tool.

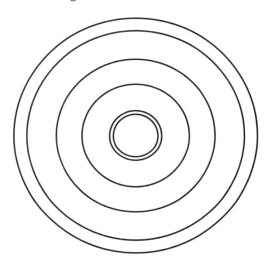

✦ Begin with the center circle. In this circle identify a strong assumption or pain story you hold that you know influences your inner and outer landscape. Identify something that you are struggling with. This could be about how you view yourself or the world around you. Consider it as a title to a pain story. Examples are: "I am never enough," "No one can be trusted," "I am not appreciated at work," "I can't finish what I start." Typically these will have a history (a historic pain story), which results in them seeming unchangeable. These pain stories prevent you from having direct experience with your true nature and creative intentions. They are at the center of the mandala because they hold a position of authority. They are also the *point of transformation*. When we name these, when we bring what holds us back out into the open, transformation begins. If you keep the pain story under the radar of your consciousness, you are not likely to transform it. In this case you are doing and thinking things on a daily basis that sustain it. You may want to journal around or review from previous chapters what holds you back or where you feel stuck. We start with a pain story that keeps us from our creative and spiritual realizations and move out from there.

+ The second thin circle is for coloring. Choose a color that you consider uplifting, transformative; a color that symbolically represents the transformation of pain. This color communicates to your brain and mind that movement is taking place around this hindrance. The psychology of color and its influence on us is vast. Color signals action, influences our emotions, and elicits a physiological response.

+ The third circle is made up of agreements that sustain the pain story; that support and endorse the particular assumption about yourself or the world. First write in your journal a list of cognitive and behavioral agreements that you have around this pain story. Cognitive agreements could include beliefs and assumptions. The difference is that there is an added energy around them—agreements are beliefs and assumptions that we invest in. They are like contracts that we have made with ourselves. So for example with the pain story of "I'm never appreciated," what are some agreements that sustain this core assumption? They might include: "I compare myself to others," "I don't believe in myself," "I think others are always judging me," "I expect the worst," "I don't believe others when they do compliment me." Notice how these sustain the pain story of "I'm never appreciated." Now write out some behavioral agreements that sustain your core pain story. For the same example these might include: "I don't risk signing up for new things," "I say no to most social invitations," "I isolate myself at home," "I get defensive at work a lot," "I complain to my spouse," "I take an antidepressant." After you have written down several agreements that sustain the pain story, write them out in the third circle. Notice how these keep your pain story, a core assumption you hold, active.

+ For the fourth circle, choose two agreements from the third circle, one cognitive one and one behavioral one, and write it out like this: "I no longer agree to . . ." (fill in with the cognitive agreement); "I no longer agree to . . ." (fill in with the behavioral agreement). To continue the above example: "I no longer agree to assume people are judging me" (cognitive); "I no longer agree to complain to my spouse" (behavioral). Choose only two because this keeps it simple and you will soon discover that these two are connected with the others. Success with breaking these agreements helps you break all the agreements that sustain the pain story. Just focus and commit to breaking your agreement with these two.

Now you have made room for what wants in and for the more creative self to emerge as well as for more possibilities. This dismantling of what holds your authentic and creative self hostage results in room for your intention. This is another reason to start with the pain story and its sustaining agreements—dismantling them makes room for you to fulfill your intentions.

+ In the fifth circle, write in your creative intention. This could easily be the one you already came up with in the "Create an Intention to Live By" exercise (remember, simple is good), or if you like, you could come up with another one. Then write your creative intention out in a favorite color. It may be something like: "I live an active and creative life." Or, to go with the example above, it may be: "I take an open heart into all situations."

+ Now, the final outer circle is made up of the two sustaining agreements of your intention. First identify in your journal up to five cognitive and five behavioral agreements that will reinforce your intention. Then choose two of the agreements from the journal entry, one cognitive one and one behavioral one, and write it out like this: "I *agree* to . . ." (fill in with the cognitive agreement); "I *agree* to . . ." (fill in with the behavioral agreement). To continue the above example: "I agree to assume more positively of others" (cognitive); "I agree to say yes to invitations to join others" (behavioral). Choose only two here to keep it simple. Again you will be creating the internal and external environment for your intention. As soon as you make this mandala and use it, you will have direct experiences with your intention— guaranteed.

Scripting Scenes for Your Creative Life

In cognitive-behavioral therapies, evidence reveals that what we hold in the mind directly influences our experiences. A well-known and useful treatment to alleviate anxiety is scripting a situation (scene) before you enter it. Here we bring together the science of mind with the influence of journal writing to help bring about what we want in our lives. You can make "scenes" from your intentions and write them out. You can script on a daily or weekly basis, or write a script for certain occasions. Scripting is a simple way to help us fulfill our three promises: to self, to others, and to our vocations. It is also a tool that helps us reframe what we assume. Through the mandala and scripting you can reframe your stories about yourself and the world. Where you once may have held on to the story about yourself as unimaginative, you reframe this lie (and other lies) with truth. Scripting takes the tool of visualization and gives it more fuel.

Sometimes we want to improve a situation, but we need more tools to reframe the stories we hold. Using the analogy of movie making, scripting is writing out the scene so the actors can step in and play out their parts. In your script, you will write out how a particular future scene will ideally unfold. Let's say you are attending a gathering and you want the event to go well. You want to behave according to your core intention. Script it first. Write it out in your journal how you would like the scene to go—include emotions, others' responses to you, all that you would like to have unfold in this situation. Include the outer and inner landscapes of this scene. Instead of heading into the scene with your doubts, fears, or negative expectations directing your experience, you gently carry this script in your consciousness. Often I take a moment in the morning to script what my day will be like. Throughout the day I hold on to my pithy intention as a way to direct the energy of particular scenes while letting go of expectations. In scenes that have a past pain story attached to them I take more time to script them out, working with them until I have them just right.

Whatever we consistently give our attention to is more likely to manifest in the world. You want your scripts to feel possible and to be possible, and you want them to be specific and uplifting as you read them. We have seen how we tend to script with our pain stories by mentally going over and over how things are going to happen and that what we get is more pain. Now when we script from our intentions we experience more happiness and success in our interactions with others. Scripting sets up certain cognitive conditions that open the way for uplifting experiences. This is living from the zero point.

Once a month I share my intentions and scripts with my creative manifestation group. (See "Joining with Others Freely: Creative Manifestation Circles," page 236.) Then the four of us carry the scripts in our consciousness for the following month. For the past twenty-five years, I've created a yearly script and scripting board of how I want my year to look. On New Year's Day, my family, friends, and I create scripting boards. These posters are images and words ("third things" like poems and quotes) that resonate with how we want the year to progress.* This gives us images that we can look at every day. These not only provide a reminder of our intentions but give us a means to gauge how our choices are in alignment with our scripting board. This is not a matter of passively making a board or writing a script and then sitting back and trusting that it all will magically come to be. This is a practice of creating through the power of intention and attention.

Take a Personal Inventory around Your Intention

Anytime throughout the day, check in and notice how your thoughts and actions are or are not in alignment with your intention. Check in by asking yourself, "Is what I am doing at this time in alignment with my intention?" (This is a yes or no answer.) This is particularly helpful if you are having some kind of difficulty. This attention to your experience and intention will give you the means to improve any situation.

If the answer to your checking in is no, how far off are you? What

---

*You may want to see my recent scripting board or connect with others who are scripting. To do so, go to my Facebook page on spiritual journaling: www.facebook.com/pages/Spiritual-Journaling/342474825771994?ref=hl.

steps can you take to align your life with your intention? If yes, how close are you? Are you fully living your intention? If you are continually out of alignment, a stronger commitment to your intention may be necessary. You have taken the time to create and set this intention, so chances are it is the best one for you at this time. As you live to fulfill this intention you are also creatively manifesting it. Know that the benefits of your living intentionally radiate out from you to others.

It Takes Courage

> *Start close in,*
> *don't take the second step*
> *or the third,*
> *start with the first*
> *thing*
> *close in,*
> *the step*
> *you don't want to take.*
>
> *Start with*
> *the ground*
> *you know,*
> *the pale ground*
> *beneath your feet,*
> *your own*
> *way of starting*
> *the conversation.*
>
> *Start with your own*
> *question,*
> *give up on other*
> *people's questions,*
> *don't let them*
> *smother something*
> *simple.*

To find
another's voice,
follow
your own voice,
wait until
that voice
becomes a
private ear
listening
to another.

Start right now
take a small step
you can call your own
don't follow
someone else's
heroics, be humble
and focused,
start close in,
don't mistake
that other
for your own.

Start close in,
don't take
the second step
or the third,
start with the first
thing
close in,
the step
you don't want to take.

DAVID WHYTE, "START CLOSE IN,"
RIVER FLOW: NEW & SELECTED POEMS

David Whyte expresses it so well in this poem—focus on taking the next step, close in, to fulfilling your intention. Use your scripting and your attention to your intention to decide what the next step close in is for you. Refer to your wish-fulfilling mandala to help you determine this next step. Your two behavioral agreements to break patterns or move toward your intentions are likely the next steps. What behavioral agreements are you breaking with your pain story? Take this next step. Or, what behavioral agreement sustains your intention? Take this as your next step. Choose one and keep it simple. It takes courage to take this closest, most immediate step because the big one out there is so far off. Saying to oneself, "My next step is to build my art studio," doesn't really generate any movement and soon can become overwhelming and discouraging. The closeness of the step we need to take makes it intimate and risky. If you can't afford a studio until you reduce your monthly rent or mortgage payment, the closest step may be, "I need to move out of this house." But notice how much easier it would be to keep all the attention on the big dream.

The ongoing agreement to live life from your side means to live bravely and actively. And you have a big picture of how this looks—maybe having your own studio someday, or your poems being published, or your ideas at work being used. But, in the case of your ideas being used at work this means that the *next step* is having an honest dialogue with your boss. Gulp! That's the close-in step. This takes more courage than any of the third or fourth steps out.

As David Whyte points out, don't mistake someone else's steps as your own. "Start with the step you don't want to take."

Life isn't about finding yourself. Life is about creating yourself.

GEORGE BERNARD SHAW

From Creation to Manifestation

Creativity is proof of life. We write. We paint. We garden. We restore prairies. We choreograph. We come up with ideas. And this, in and of itself, is personally fulfilling—to create and to be creative. But to leave your creations in the closet, or to limit yourself, limits your ability to transform the world around you. Growth has the stages of a germinating seed: from sprouting, to flowering, to releasing the next seed of creation. To fully flower means to bring our efforts out into the world—out into the open. Creation itself doesn't result in manifestation. *Creative manifestation* is first the flowering and then the releasing of our creations (seeds inherent in the creation). We create for the sole purpose of creating; manifestation is then another step in the evolution of a creative intention.

Creativity is the harvesting; manifestation is what you do with what you have harvested. Don't keep the harvest to yourself. (Don't do all of your dancing in front of the mirrors at home). People are happiest when they're either in the creative process or are sharing their creative harvest with others. In the I Ching, the character that has been translated by some as *the creative* is translated by Taoist master Alfred Huang as *initiating*. Lee Nichol, in his foreword to Bohm's book *On Creativity*, paraphrases Bohm's warning that if we fail to understand how essential creativity is to our lives, humanity may well perish from a lack of it. After all, it is through a continual open and creative stance, with a willingness to bring our creations out into the open, that our lives become truly meaningful.

> *We want to traverse the Unknown with a map—*
> *We want to know what to expect,*
> *or who we will meet up with.*
> *But how our mistakes will leave a trail*
> *that gives way to something new,*
> *or the greening along the path*
> *reminds us of something*
> *we might return to*
> *someday.*
>
> *Maybe there's a place that asks you to*
> *share a poem or song in order to receive a meal,*

or a good story might do;
You start in the middle and go from there.
Everything else will follow,
the same way life follows light.

As you walk on everything comes towards you.
You must offer up your poem, your song,
or your story
to be known. Forget your name.
Some will glance up from their lunch,
most won't.

But you repeat your favorite phrase,
over and over to the greening stranger,
like the chickadee or crow at dawn
and something beyond your glance
responds.

JULIE TALLARD JOHNSON, "AHEAD"

5

The Heart Sutra
and the Art of
Authentic Manifestation

Does the rose have to do something? No, the purpose of a rose is to be a rose. Your purpose is to be yourself. You don't have to run anywhere to become someone else.

THICH NHAT HANH, ON THE HEART SUTRA

Gate gate pāragate pārasaṃgate bodhi svāhā

HEART SUTRA MANTRA*

Manifesting a Path While Walking

Not in Utopia, subterranean fields,
Or some secreted island, Heaven knows where!
But in the very world, which is the world

---

*The current Dalai Lama translates the mantra as "go, go, go beyond, go thoroughly beyond, and establish yourself in enlightenment." For further reading I recommend the book by His Holiness the Dalai Lama, *How to See Yourself as You Really Are,* and Thich Nhat Hanh's book *The Heart of Understanding: Commentaries on the Prajnaparamita Heart Sutra.*

Of all of us, the place where, in the end,
We find our happiness, or not at all

WILLIAM WORDSWORTH, *THE PRELUDE*

To manifest, all we really have to do is be ourselves—*be who we already are*—let our inner world become manifest in the outer world. The origin of the word *manifestation* comes from the Latin word *manifestare,* meaning to "make public." To manifest we make public our intentions—our ideas, our creations, our aspirations, and our dreams—so they can interact with and transform the world.

Authentic manifestation is *creative* manifestation and comes *from* the zero point. Creative manifestation means having a direct personal experience based on our understanding of the interdependence of reality. Creative manifestation is an act of spiritual activism. It is ongoing; a process, not a destination. Perhaps you once believed that manifestation means having money in the bank or the house you always wanted. But this is a false and limited understanding of prosperity and abundance. Such manifestations are not inherently creative. When our manifestations are focused on outcomes, on an object (money), or a goal (relationship) we suffer because we seek this object and then become attached to getting or increasing this object. Typically when we have it we are quickly dissatisfied and begin to seek something new (even in the case of relationships). A wealth of possessions, a high social position, or even the perfect partner will never be an antidote to sadness, loneliness, or discontent. Wealth doesn't bring inspiration or happiness, because wealth (a high social position or a partner) is something wholly outside of us, and happiness is an inside job. In fact, evidence suggests wealth can be a greater hindrance than poverty (although poverty can generate physical obstacles). A lack of money and resources can be motivating whereas having them can actually make us less motivated.

Of course, creative manifestation is not limited to art; it includes anything and everything we want to bring into the world as well as everything we want to experience. Creative manifestation is evidence that we are in fact *living* an active life, since it happens when we open up fully to your spiritual and creative capacities in the moment. While spiritual practices are about transformation (of the mind), creativity is about expressing who and what we are. This distinction is valuable because in order to experience our spiritual and creative *manifestations* we want to understand, at least on a basic level, the message of the Heart Sutra. Our spiritual life and our creative life are intimately intertwined. The Heart Sutra gives us the ability to manifest our creative path *as we walk it*; to have peak spiritual and creative experiences in the context of our daily lives.

The Heart Sutra

Reliance on actions and their fruits
Within knowing this emptiness of phenomena
Is more wonderful than even the wonderful.
More fantastic than even the fantastic.

NAGARJUNA'S ESSAY ON
THE MIND OF ENLIGHTENMENT (C. 150–250 CE)

The Heart Sutra, or Prajñāpāramitā H□daya, is a core sutra in Buddhism. Translated from the Sanskrit *Prajñāpāramitā* means "the heart of the perfection of transcendent wisdom." The Heart Sutra points to how everything comes into being through a radical interdependence of all that is. We all have some understanding of this sutra from our own witnessing and reliance on nature—the cycle of the seasons and the ebb and flow of our lives. The Heart Sutra is the spiritual expression of the science of interconnectedness. Everything, including each one of us, is connected to everything else and everything is in flux. The reason we don't *feel* this connection is because we are limited by our view (based, of course, on our personal histories). As His Holiness the Dalai Lama said at one of his teachings on the Heart Sutra, "where there is grasping there is no view."* And most of us are caught up in grasping our assumptions or something we think will bring us happiness. Not only does this prevent us from feel-

---

*His Holiness the fourteenth Dalai Lama, "Womb of the Buddha: The Heart Sutra" (lecture, Indiana University, Bloomington, Ill., May 12–14, 2010).

ing our connection to all of life, it also prevents us from manifesting what does bring us lasting happiness. As the Tao Te Ching states, "The secret waits for eyes unclouded by longing." But when we free ourselves of the grasping and questing for something outside of our self, what we want is right here! Any time your view is unclouded (by assumptions, limiting beliefs, afflictive emotions, clinging, or searching) what truly serves you is revealed to you. Every time.

The Prajñāpāramitā Heart Sutra Mantra

The Heart Sutra is the essence of the Buddhist teachings but can be found at the center of science, ancient religions, and nature. The Heart Sutra is about holding an intimacy with all of life. As Zen master Eihei Dogen taught, "enlightenment is just intimacy with all things." The mantra, as a powerful statement of transformation, contains the vibration and meaning of the Heart Sutra within it—*Gate gate pāragate pārasaṃgate bodhi svāhā.*

Gate means "gone." Gone beyond suffering to freedom from suffering. Gone from forgetfulness to remembering our belonging to all of life. Gone from our feelings of separateness. *Gate gate* means "gone, gone."

Pāragate means "gone all the way to the other shore"—the shore of liberation. (Freedom from our habitual, lonely, and selfish states.)

In *pārasaṃgate, saṃ* means "everyone and every living thing," the *I am that.* We are each *that.* Nothing is exempt, every sentient being is invited over to the shore of liberation! We will all meet up on the other shore of belonging.

Bodhi points to our awakening and our ultimate realization of truth—that we are all connected. In this mantra we are awakening to our state of belonging through our interconnectedness.

Finally, we end the mantra with *svāhā,* which is a declaration similar to Hallelujah! Amen! So Be It! For me *svāhā* holds the exclamation of "Now! Here in this moment!"

Gone, gone, gone all the way over, everyone gone to the other shore, Awakening! Now!

The Paradox of Emptiness

Basically, what quantum theory says is that fundamental particles are empty of inherent existence and exist in an undefined state of potentialities. They have no inherent existence from their own side and do not become "real" until a mind interacts with them and gives them meaning.

SEAN ROBSVILLE, PHYSICIST, FROM
"BUDDHISM AND QUANTUM PHYSICS"

The previous chapters have helped us to understand that we have mistakenly relied upon our assumptions, memories of our pain stories, and outward appearances to navigate our lives. We can now begin to appreciate that there is far more to us and to our experiences than our perceptions would have us believe. Oddly, this "more," this good news, is often called the reality of "emptiness." This reality of emptiness is central to helping us transcend our limited views. And the understanding of emptiness is to grasp the meaning of the Heart Sutra and the zero point agreement.

Emptiness points to how we are empty of a separate, individual self, while at the same time full of everything. Form of any kind is empty of a separate existence but is full of everything in the universe. Let's revisit how we are all like a drop in the large ocean (the zero point), and how the ocean is in us. You can't separate the drop from the ocean or take out the ocean from the drop. The drop is empty of a separated existence. The drop, just as you and I, exists because of everything else that exists. The Sanskrit word for emptiness is *shinyata,* sometimes translated into "thusness." It points to how everything—including human existence—is dependent upon everything else existing too. That is to say, everything in this world is interconnected and in constant flux. So, the way to manifest our intentions is by tapping into this "thusness" and experiencing our intimacy with all things.

It's a big jump for people to understand the dependent nature of reality—no essence to anything, but at a fundamental level, just being able to recognize the mind that places qualities onto external objects and sees them within the object rather than as a mental projection can be a big "ah ha" moment. At the same time, we have to keep working with the relative nature of conventional reality to unravel the good from the bad, the positive from the negative. It's quite the process this delicate middle way.

CATHY KENNEDY, A FORTY-YEAR STUDENT OF THE
DHARMA WHO IS ALWAYS HUMBLED
BY THIS PROCESS OF DISCOVERY

Discovering the "Thusness" of Life

+ Practice this: Take some time to find anything that is permanent, unchanging, and could exist entirely on its own. (Of course you won't, but give it a try.)

+ Reflect on some possession that you like, your car for example. Notice first how it is impermanent (how it won't last). Consider also the impermanence of satisfaction you get from the car. (This isn't to say you don't get any satisfaction, but notice its flux and limits.)

+ Then consider how this object came into being through dependence upon specific causes and conditions: metal, factory workers, and so forth.

+ Now, see if this understanding of its *dependence* on other phenomena conflicts with its *appearance* as existing in its own right, independently. How can it exist wholly independently if it can only come into existence interdependently?

+ Contemplate this poem by Kabir:

> Inside this clay jug
>   there are canyons and
>   pine mountains,
>   and the maker of canyons
>   and pine mountains!
> All seven oceans are inside,
>   and hundreds of millions of stars.
> The acid that tests gold is here,
>   and the one who judges jewels.
> And the music
>   that comes from the strings

that no one touches,
and the source of all water.
If you want the truth, I will tell you
the truth:
Friend, listen:
the God whom I love is inside.

KABIR, "INSIDE THIS CLAY JUG," VERSION BY ROBERT BLY,
THE KABIR BOOK: FORTY-FOUR OF THE ECSTATIC POEMS OF KABIR

When we try to pick out anything by itself, we find it
hitched to everything else in the universe.

JOHN MUIR, *MY FIRST SUMMER IN THE SIERRA*

This wisdom of emptiness is profound in bringing about happiness because, even as the I Ching points out (see next chapter), everything is in a state of change and *potential*. Everything is capable of transformation. So this emptiness that the Heart Sutra refers to is the same as saying everything *becomes* based on everything else. Nothing happens in isolation. It gives you the ability to truly live life from your side as your part of a whole. The word *emptiness* tends to bring up all sorts of emotional reactions and misunderstandings for us in the West. I think this is in part because the idea of emptiness makes us feel less special, less entitled. But in truth it makes us uniquely capable of transformation and profound satisfaction. This is so because the cosmos is in an agreement to be mutually influenced. Remember how this dynamic of mutual influence is the foundation to a happy relationship? Well, we are in relationship with the entire cosmos (and it is with us). So you put out what you have (your intentions, your idea, your creativity) and the world responds and you respond to the world. It's a radical and beautiful dance of belonging and manifestation.

The fourth and final soul is the Nagila [essentially the divine
spirit in each human], the embodiment of the cosmic energy,
or Taku Skan Skan, that infuses the entire universe. Taku
Skan Skan means, "that which moves and causes all things

*to move." It is the original source of all things, the divine
essence of life. Taku Skan Skan is present in each being
through the Nagila, and it is the sacred thread that binds all
things and makes all beings relatives to one another . . . when
we understand Nagila, we can fully grasp the profundity of
the prayer Mitakuye oyasin: "We are all related."*

JOSEPH EPES BROWN, *TEACHING SPIRITS*

Since everything exists because of many interplaying phenomenon,
manifestation is never, ever dependent on one practice, one object, or
one formula. There are no tricks or secret methods to search for in
order to manifest your dreams. No one practice on its own will make
something possible. Your intention simply needs to interact with the
world to come to fruition. You simply go about making meaning with
your intentions. This is good news because it is through an appreciation
of the wisdom of the Heart Sutra, or of *Taku Skan Skan,* that we can
truly manifest our intentions. When we live aware of and active within
this interconnectedness we flourish.

Manifest in this Way

*Because persons and things are devoid of trueness of being
self-instituting, they are affected by conditions and are
capable of transformation.*

HIS HOLINESS THE DALAI LAMA,
HOW TO SEE YOURSELF AS YOU REALLY ARE

Manifestation is dependent upon your efforts. All your efforts then
become the causes and conditions that result in future creative manifestations. The more we can help set up the best causes and conditions
for our manifestation, the more success we will experience. Since everything exists dependently, one condition influences the others but isn't
solely the cause of one result. I look upon it like a tapestry—every thread
makes the piece possible. One thread does not make a tapestry, but one
thread is as intricate and valuable as its part in the whole. Remove a few

threads, or one significant one, and the tapestry is changed. Too many threads removed and it is no longer a tapestry.

> *Dependent arising refers to the fact that all impermanent phenomena—whether physical, mental, or otherwise—come into existence dependent upon certain causes and conditions. Whatever arises dependent upon certain causes and conditions is not operating exclusively under its own power.*
>
> HIS HOLINESS THE DALAI LAMA,
> *HOW TO SEE YOURSELF AS YOU REALLY ARE*

This is the meaning of the Heart Sutra and creative manifestation—that everything that is creatively manifested is based on a multitude of causes. You not only suffer from focusing on just one thing but actual failure ensures. Failure, disappointment, and corruption come from focusing on one thing—one result, one dynamic in the tapestry of life at the exclusion of all others. Our obsessiveness with finding the one person that will make us happy or the money to fulfill all our dreams or (you fill in the blank) leaves us wanting and suffering for more. As Geshe Sonam Rinchen writes in *Atisha's Lamp for the Path to Enlightenment,* "Contentment and a feeling of satisfaction are our greatest riches, our happiness, and splendor. Without them, no matter how much wealth we own, we will always feel hungry and impoverished."

This is the reason for *creative* manifestation—it's ongoing, dynamic, and meaningful. You are not setting your mind on one outcome or object that is static. It's about seeing how your creative manifestation, be it a recipe or a relationship, want to interact with the world. Creative manifestation relies on movement and interaction.

The Three Modes of Creative Manifestation

Creative manifestation leaves us wholly satisfied. This satisfaction allows us to create and experience more, but we won't be grasping to *get* or *have* more. Our creations are then manifested in this way:

- Our thoughts influence our experience and the impact of our manifestations.
- We begin with creating something, which is part of setting up the causes and conditions for our manifestations.
- Our creative manifestations are dependent upon many parts and made up of many parts (as in Kabir's "Inside This Clay Jug" on page 215).

These are the three modes of creative manifestation. The strongest of these are our thoughts; *how we perceive our manifestations* and therefore experience our manifestations. A condition of our creative manifestation is what we bring into it with our thoughts. Social scientists and physicists have revealed that the observer cannot be separated from the phenomenon being observed (known as the *observer effect*). Research even points to how the observer interacts with and affects that which is being observed. In Buddhist philosophy this has long been understood as the observer and observed dependently existing. In my limited understanding of quantum physics, nothing even exists *until* it is observed. This implies that manifestation is a direct result of one's consciousness. Either way, consciousness plays a major role in how we experience our manifestations. This is the reason for so much effort on thought transformation and developing awareness of how our assumptions and beliefs affect our experiences. Without attention to this you may create a masterpiece but manifest nothing—you may be led to the Bodhi tree but sit under it in a funk.

We create something; we help set up the causes and conditions of our manifestations. We paint the pictures and this sets up the conditions and causes for displaying them in a gallery. We study and practice compassionate listening and this sets us up for a beautiful relationship. We practice meditation and this sets up a calm and disciplined mind. All such creations begin from within, an intention or an idea, then on to the actual creation of the idea. The preceding chapter covered the "creative" aspect of manifestation—you have to actually create something. There is a lot out there about "attracting abundance." But you will experience more joy and prosperity in learning how to creatively manifest than in learning techniques of attraction. Meaning makers *create and manifest*; they fulfill their destiny by making meaning in the moment. Then our creative manifestations become the causes and conditions of others' manifestations, so everyone benefits.

Our manifestations are dependent upon and made up of many parts. By paying attention to the dependent-arising phenomenon your manifestations will become a more natural experience and one deeply connected to, and throughout, your life. This also gives us a template to work with—we can consider all that may go into helping set up the causes and conditions of a given desired manifestation. Every one of our manifestations comes into being based on a multitude of other people and conditions. With an awareness of this you can help create these causes and conditions. Nothing happens in isolation so the more you creatively manifest in the open, the more abundance you will experience. Furthermore, realizing and appreciating the phenomenon of dependent arising will allow you to have a grasp of the bigger picture that is unfolding in your life and the lives of others—how each of your creations is part of something bigger that wants to manifest in the world.

Simply put:

Show up
Create
Watch your thoughts
Transform your thoughts
See and appreciate the interdependence of life
Bring your creativity out into the open
Manifest as you walk
Let go
Enjoy
Repeat

To creatively manifest means to be aware that we each play a major part in the lives of those around us as well. As Martin Luther King Jr. said, "Whatever affects one directly, affects all indirectly. I can never be what I ought to be until you are what you ought to be. This is the interrelated structure of reality."

Reducing Yourself to Zero

Gandhi came to believe and demonstrate that any ability he had to improve upon the world around him occurred when he got out of his own way—when he met the world around him halfway and "emptied" himself out. He referred to this as "reducing yourself to zero." Reducing yourself to zero means you are in the motion of creative manifestation and have let go of your self-absorption. Reducing yourself to zero is another way to explain the zero point agreement and the Heart Sutra.

Creative manifestation only happens while we are engaged with others. Only when we can act in a way where we understand our self as a valuable drop in the ocean, feeling the oneness while giving our unique contribution to the greater good, will we truly live an active life. Gandhi believed deeply that to be of benefit we must experience this oneness with all beings. He believed it is our true nature to be connected and creative. Gandhi advocated too that the spiritual life is not about retreating to a cave or ashram. The spiritual life is to be explored within the context of our families and our communities.

Within the Buddhist philosophy we work on our enlightenment for the benefit of all beings. Bodhisattvas are known as "heroes of enlightenment" because they give up nirvana to return to Earth to help until all beings are enlightened. We could all *act as if* we are such heroes as Gandhi, Martin Luther King Jr., or another bodhisattva, here to help enlighten everyone to their true nature as meaning makers—starting with ourselves.

It Depends Upon

As a meditative exercise contemplate what one of your intentions or creations depends upon to become fully manifest.

✦ Take one of your creations that you want to manifest. Contemplate on that subject or intention (be it a relationship, painting, or written work) and use the "Basics of Inquiry Meditation" on page 47 to investigate all that goes into making this manifestation possible. Now that you either have the ideal (in the form of an intention) or have actually created something (like a business plan), investigate what it will take to make this fully manifest in the world.

✦ First consider what made the creation possible. What went into making it (the business plan, the poem, the relationship). Then realize what will make the creative manifestation possible by naming what such manifestation is dependent upon. What will make a poem creatively manifested in the world? (Hint: others will be reading it.) You will not be able to name everything, but open yourself up to as much as possible. Streamline your consciousness by writing as freely and as fast as possible.

✦ You can use the journaling exercise and repeat the sentence, "This manifestation depends upon . . ." See also, "I Am Ready," page 241.

It gets down to bringing ourselves and our creations out into the open whether it be playing an instrument on the street corner or helping set up some community project, while at the same time knowing there is more and more to create. Remember, we don't have to wait on certain conditions to emerge before we act; creative manifestation means to do so within the conditions of our lives as they are *presently*. Our creative manifestations come about in the same way anything and everything is creatively manifested in the natural world—through fully participating in *this* moment in *this* place.

> *The difference between what we do and what we are capable of doing would suffice to solve most of the world's problem.*
> MAHATMA GANDHI

So we are coming to understand that creative manifestation occurs through the *cultivation* of certain mind states and spiritual qualities. Instead of the attitude of *getting* something for our investments, we approach our desires to manifest certain experiences and resources in terms of *cultivation*—what are we cultivating? What are we nurturing in our life? What are we giving our energy, resources, and attention to?

Because whatever we are experiencing *now* is what we have been culti-vating up until now. So, for the remainder of this chapter, borrowing from principles within the Heart Sutra, I will offer you ways to bring all your creations out in the open; to creatively manifest *as a way of life*.

> *Do the thing to do it,*
> *And not for what it does.*
> *All of these, for instance,*
> *These words upon this page,*
> *Now exist as something—*
> *They'll go where they will go—*
> *Because I was the I,*
> *And dared to write them down.*
>
> DAVID ROZELLE, "DO THE THING"

Grit Moves the World

In Buddhist philosophy enthusiastic effort is considered one of *the* essential qualities to keep our practice alive and active. In spiritual practice, maintaining enthusiastic effort is imperative to the momen-tum and fulfillment of your spiritual intentions. Without effort there is no result. Even when something is given to us through grace it is likely a response to some effort on our part. We have to show up, and keep showing up.

> *Those who make enthusiastic effort*
> *Will not have difficulty accomplishing*
> *Every worldly and supramundane art.*
>
> THE BUDDHA, TAKEN FROM THE
> SUTRA ENCOURAGING THE SPECIAL WISH

Organizational consultants often refer to this as motivation. I like the simple term *grit*. We need grit for everything from making that thousandth breakfast for our family to finishing a novel. We need grit to raise a child well. We need grit to raise our self properly. We need grit to keep to our meditation practice. We need grit to create something new among all our losses and mistakes. We need grit to fight against the voices that try to steal our enthusiasm.

With grit we find that extra spice that gives the eggs a fresh taste. With grit we finish the novel (and write as many drafts as it takes for it to sing on its own). With grit we rejoice in our children. With grit we live an active life. With grit we return to the meditation practice because it is in the returning that we find equanimity. With grit we willingly begin again and again. And with grit keep our creative spirit alive.

Momentum Is Everything

The creative manifestation of a dream—the completed novel, the love of your life, or spiritual insight—will be missed if you sleepwalk through life. You have to wake yourself up *daily;* go past the comfort zone of your own habitats and habits. Grit is something that helps keep a momentum around your creative life so you will manifest.

A variety of spiritual and creative masters and scholars make the strong suggestion that it is better not to start at all than to start and not finish. Once you have chosen something to manifest and to bring out into the open—take it to its completion. Maintain enthusiasm right up to the end. Be careful not to be one of those who start out in lots of new directions without following them through to some result—don't write a book or a business plan only to keep it in the drawer.

> *Armor-like enthusiastic effort consists of being prepared to do as much, go as deeply, and continue for as long as is necessary to achieve a positive objective.*
> Geshe Sonam Rinchen, *The Six Perfections*

It helps to hold a persistent awareness of our motivation in pursuing a spiritual path or creative venture. What is the motivation behind the manifestation of your dream, intention, or commitment? What gets you to return to your creative life, to not give up on your meditation practice? (Earlier I pointed to the value of giving ourselves something to return to.) Our motivation will be the basis of whether or not we succeed. Our motivation, the reason we are choosing to pursue what we pursue, fuels our momentum. Rely on high-octane fuel. Know what motivates you and keep it up front in your consciousness, because once we bring our creations out into the open we are also confronted with more internal and external resistances (from self judgment to the jealousy of others). Remember your reasons for saying yes in the first place. We don't need fear to motivate us to return or stay with our spiritual and creative practices when we realize the benefits of our efforts. Enthusiastic effort to our creative and spiritual life can wholly be based on realization of the benefits. (And, of course, the lack of benefits when we are not practicing or being creative.) Both in the process of creation and manifestation you will need to rely on your enthusiastic effort, your grit, to keep you going because there will always be distractions and hindrances.

Write a Letter to Yourself

Sometimes we are afraid to keep going but can't quite name our fear. Here is an exercise that helps you recall earlier aspirations before you became afraid or stuck.

+ Journal or consider a time you were afraid, preferably an early memory (from childhood or adolescence). Remember as much detail as possible (writing the story out will elicit more recall).

+ Then write a letter to that child self, give advice (this one time is okay), offer reassurance that your child self is going to make it, give some hints of the successes ahead. Mirror this child's courage and abilities. Throw in a third thing—provide an antidote in the form of a story, poem, or quote. Make sure to address the letter to your child self and sign it from your adult self. Read it aloud to yourself while imagining the younger you hearing it.

+ If you haven't seen *The Kid*, a Disney movie about a man who meets an eight-year-old version of himself, I recommend it.

If you have gone far with something only to discover you are certain you are not going to finish it, consciously leave it behind. Leave it as the compost of what you will be putting your energy into. Maintain clarity around what is going to get your attention and energy once you make the choice of turning away from one thing and turning your energy toward something else. This is the threshold between what you once gave yourself to and what you are about to give yourself to. Impart your attention, enthusiasm, and participation to this new (or renewed) intention.

Keep rising up each morning with your spiritual principles and creative intentions strong in your heart. Everything you give yourself over to will give itself back to you.

> *Assistance is the universal immutable force of creative manifestation, whose role since the Big Bang has been to translate potential into being, to convert dreams into reality.*
>
> STEVEN PRESSFIELD, *DO THE WORK*

The Zero Point of Rejection

As we study the Heart Sutra we come to understand that the root of our suffering is in holding a wrong view. The Venerable Geshe Lhundub Sopa puts it this way: "When your view is obstructed by ignorance it results in attachment because you believe things exist by their own nature (that they exist absolutely and independently), and as a result, you grasp for them. You have a false conception, exaggerating something's worth. If you like it you want more and if you see something as unfavorable you exaggerate its faults." From a less exaggerated orientation we can even experience our rejections as assisting with our manifestations rather than as a hindrance.

Life is strewn with rejections and abandonments. Rejections show up as early as birth for some (no bonding with parents) and for most of us rejections are woven into the tapestry of life alongside missed opportunities, late starts, regrets, disappointments, and losses. It seems that rejection and abandonment happen to us, but in most cases we tend to abandon ourselves.

Too many times we lay the egg only to abandon the nest. Our clutter surrounds us as the reminders of abandoned promises. Dreams and commitments in the shape of files, outfits, unread books, notes, unfinished art projects, tools, magazines, recipe books, diet guides, exercise equipment, saved e-mails, supplies, unopened boxes, and the like are scattered about our outer landscape as abandoned roosts. Abandoned nests also come within the context of our relationships and social commitments.

I witness many abandoned nests in both the creative and spiritual life. For too many of us the enthusiasm comes only in the moment of making a commitment—the making of the nest and the laying of the egg. Then we get drawn away to another creative idea or spiritual practice, or become discouraged or impatient and leave that nest.

Lasting satisfaction comes from breaking the negative patterns that keep us in the loop of our exaggerated reactions to situations. If rejection or abandonment is a central theme in your life, you will tend to abandon yourself at critical times. In the writer's life this happens when we jump around from idea to idea but never quite complete that one idea. The next idea always seems better and we exaggerate its importance. But the original egg (idea or plan) remains dormant. In the spiritual life we get seduced by the latest spiritual fad rather than develop our own spiritual intentions. We then lack insights that endure over time. When we are trapped in ignorance we also tend to make it all about us. But the Heart Sutra reminds us that there are immeasurable causes and conditions at play here. This miserly focus on our self only increases our disappointment because we are missing the myriad of other possibilities inherent even in this time of loss.

The antidote to rejection or abandonment is to open up even further, take the idea or project as far as you can. Finish what you started.

Instead of starting something new, *begin again* with the original commitment. Bring enthusiasm to what you already said yes to. Then, even in situations where others reject you, you won't abandon yourself or the egg you laid.

So, the antidote to abandonment: *Don't abandon yourself.*

The zero point of rejection is in not giving up on your creations or yourself. In the previous chapter, through setting your intention, you chose the eggs you will bring to life. Now, continue to put energy into bringing your intentions out into the open. Make room for this commitment by emptying out any old abandoned nests. And be willing to say no to other obligations. (You prepared for this in the exercise "Maybe, No, Yes" on page 178.)

Making Room

+ This is a wonderful time to remove the clutter and abandoned nests from your environments. Clean out the clothes closet. Revamp your meditation or artistic space in your house. Don't continue to deceive yourself by saying, "I will get to it." You probably won't. Let go of everything you no longer use. Make room for the yes in your life by getting rid of what you have actually said no to.

+ Write about a time you were abandoned. Then rewrite it as an experience of acceptance and rejoicing. (Again, this is the profound technique of "re-mything" our stories, which actually helps open us up to the new, emerging myth. What you make possible in the mind becomes possible in the outer world.)

+ Write a rejection letter to some belief you've held but no longer accept.

+ Make a large circle on a page in your journal. Draw a line down the middle. On the left name all your commitments, projects, promises, possibilities, agreements—all your nests and eggs. Give this some time; look around your home (and closets) and into your relationships and calendar. Include everything. Then on the right side name the eggs you will bring to term. What on the left side is your clutter?

+ Share your creative or spiritual commitment with others whom you trust. Accountability helps keep us enthused (see "Joining with Others Freely: Creative Manifestation Circles" on page 236).

+ Journal writing prompt: Write about abandoned nests using the following words: *early migration, arrival, devotion, leafy twigs, kernel, liberate, sea foam.* This technique provides you with a few possibilities, a few different pathways for exploring abandonment. Just let the writing take you where it wants to—most likely it will result in greater personal awareness.

Rule of thumb: The more important a call or action is to our soul's evolution, the more resistance we will feel toward pursuing it.

STEVEN PRESSFIELD, *THE WAR OF ART*

Because the patterns that keep us asleep, that keep us abandoning our intentions, are deeply rooted, there will be deal breakers along the way.

Deal Breakers

Anytime we bring our creative manifestations into the light of day our deal breakers show up. There are always deal breakers in a spiritual effort or a creative commitment. What arises as a deal breaker for you? Be ready to break deals with old, deeply rooted patterns, assumptions, and the exaggerations that you carry. Be ready to break the deal with time spent following the paths of others rather than your own.

What's a deal breaker? The "deal" is an exaggeration about yourself and the world around you. The deal is a core agreement you have with a pain story, or some assumption about yourself or the world around you. The deal "breaker" is a specific agreement that can help you break free from whatever is holding you back. Typically, it's around the particular manifestation you are working with at the time. It can be understood as the apotheosis of your intention and creative manifestation. A transformation is taking place. A part of your egoistic self is crumbling as a result of an increase in your consciousness and actions. An old view of the world and its accompanying assumptions are breaking away. Your sense of reality may be changing, and the old view of yourself and the world need to be broken. The deal breaker usually shows up at a point where you either move forward on your intention and manifestation or give up.

This break (from the old) allows you to continue with your creative manifestation. When you are at this point something in your core is being shaken up. You are aware that if you keep living life the same old way, you will keep getting the same old result. Because the break is real (manifested internally and externally), this feels risky, scary, and uncertain. And it *is* risky, scary, and uncertain. You are stepping more into the great mystery and energy of the meaning of the Heart Sutra. But you must take that step and make an *outward* action that mirrors the inner awareness and shift. Make sure this doesn't remain only an internal awareness of what holds you back.

As "David," a client of mine, shared: "All my life I have had to figure things out. In fact, I expend quite a bit of time trying to figure things out—somehow believing that will make the difference. All it has actually done is keep me in my head, searching for reasons rather than just experiencing life. My deal breaker is not agreeing to the fact that I have to figure everything out first."

> *Resistance is not a peripheral opponent. Resistance arises*
> *from within. It is self-generated and self-perpetuated.*
> *Resistance is the enemy within.*
>
> STEVEN PRESSFIELD, *THE WAR OF ART*

Meeting Up with Resistance

Resistance can be what we move against, work with, or push through as we live and bring out our creative manifestations. In this way resistance is an opportunity—offering itself up to us every day as a means to remind us to stay awake, keep moving, enjoy, and participate. I imagine a fully realized human being may not need resistance but can act, live, and express without needing anything to move against. And indeed, as you manifest you have more energy so that when resistance arises (in all its various forms) you move through it with greater determination.

Understood in this way, resistance becomes a pointer to where we need movement in our lives. The moment you set a creative intention, resistance arises in one form or another. And now, when you are bringing your creations out in the open—resistance will surely show up. If you are truly engaged in your life and in your spiritual practice, resistance is a given. And it doesn't necessarily weaken, but mutates and evolves right along with your determination to creatively manifest.

> *Resistance cannot be seen, touched, heard, or smelled. But it can be felt. We experience it as an energy field radiating from a work-in-potential. It's a repelling force. It's negative. Its aim is to shove us away, distract us, prevent us from doing our work.*
>
> STEVEN PRESSFIELD, *THE WAR OF ART*

An easy way to name what you may be resisting is to look at your assumptions and agreements. You can review your wish-fulfilling mandala and the journaling around it. Your assumptions are what your resistance builds on and works with to keep you stuck. They prevent you from showing that painting, completing and publishing that book, joining that club, meeting that person, taking that walk, practicing that song, entering that poem in a contest, starting that business, moving to another state, or even trying a new dish at a restaurant. Resistance is like the omnipotent and omnipresent God—resistance is everywhere.

Every time you postpone, you are in resistance. Every time you knowingly act against your intentions, you are in resistance. Every time you overeat, watch too much television, overdo it at a job you dislike (or give too much of yourself to something you detest), spend lost time on the computer (or Internet), complain, get overwhelmed, give up on a creative project, don't put yourself out there, feel jealous, compete to beat someone else instead of simply doing your best, accumulate a lot of trinkets, don't throw out or recycle useless stuff, or blame your life on outside circumstances, you are in resistance.

In the process of creative manifestation, resistance comes up initially in response to your setting your intention. Ultimately, either your intention or your resistance will thrive and take root in your life. If you are not moving on your creative intention, then you are encountering some form of resistance. Each choice you encounter is either as an opportunity or a point of resistance. *Simply keep moving; take the next step in, bringing your manifestation out. Be an active part of the whole.* That's it; whenever resistance arises, just keep moving. Not only will you move through resistance, but you will enjoy the benefits of action. In my work with writers, it's their commitment to show up for the page every day that results in a finished book. And I have always found that when we keep writing our writing improves exponentially.

Anything that generates movement (physical, emotional, psychological, or spiritual) results in another successful battle won against resistance. You cannot be in resistance while you are in motion. One of my favorite books of all time, and one I borrow from a lot in this book, happens to be on this very subject: Steven Pressfield's *The War of Art*. It is not, however, a comfortable read if what you want is another excuse to postpone your manifestations.

A familiar last stand of resistance is the excuse to put off manifestation until you are ready—until you get that Ph.D., are in that perfect relationship, or get more training—until something else is taken care of (remember the false gods mentioned earlier). But there is no *there* to get to first. This is the place, *right now, here,* with whatever you have available to you now. This is the entry point, or the reentry point. Go!

Here is a story that for me illustrates how resistance can fool us by obstructing our view of what is truly possible. A meditation teacher offered this to us several decades ago when we were in the middle of a long and challenging retreat.

♦ ♦ ♦

The Door Out

There once was a woman who had been imprisoned for years. She had forgotten what she had done, but felt she surely must be bad to find herself in such a dark and lonely place. In her cell there was one window a few feet above her head. Each day around noon the sun would come through the window and give her about an hour of warmth and light. She would pull herself up and hold her face in the sunlight as long as possible and then drop down into the darkness when the sun was gone. Each day a guard would come in and feed her one meal. He would not greet her, and she assumed she was not to speak to him. She lived for each meal and for her one hour of sunlight. Had she looked around the cell when the light was coming through the window, she would have seen that there was no lock on the door and that she was free to go at any time.

✦✦✦

The Zero Point of Mistakes

What about when we make a mistake? What about when we fail? While all mistakes are workable, there are those mistakes and failures that are more workable than others. Some of our mistakes seem so unmanageable and disorienting. What makes this so?

When we live from the zero point all our mistakes are workable. When we follow the path of our own choices, even the poor ones, we can creatively handle the outcome. When we follow the path of someone else's choice for us (and are off the zero point), we are not necessarily motivated or even equipped to deal well with the consequences, especially negative results. We are more invested and knowledgeable in our own choices, so we have the motivation, internal dynamics, and resources to handle any difficulty that may arise. Our own choices, too, come from certain understandings about ourselves. In contrast, we don't necessarily have the internal navigational tools and motivations to handle the consequences of having taken someone else's path. When you make choices that are not really your own, you may find yourself lost. You will want to take the time to check in with yourself and ask, is this what I want? Is this my path or the path of another? Does this choice resonate with my intention?

Let nature set an example of the dangers in taking on someone else's path as your own. What if, for instance, a humming-bird followed the migration path of a Canada goose? Flying in the aerodynamic path of a goose's wings might make the migratory flight a lot easier for the little hummingbird, but what happens when the goose stops in Ballard County, Kentucky, to spend the winter feeding on waste grains in the frozen corn and soybean fields? The flowers and nectar the hummingbird needs to feed on through the winter are still several hundred miles south of where geese spend the winter. This is a big mistake for the little hummingbird to follow the path of a goose; maybe even deadly. We each must find and create our own migration pathway from here to there—from our intentions to our manifestations.

As a meaning maker our mistakes become part of the larger landscape of our life.

On the Edge of a New Frontier

One doesn't discover new lands without consenting to lose sight of the shore for a very long time.

ANDRÉ GIDE, FRENCH AUTHOR

This quote from Gide took on new meaning for me recently. Previously I interpreted it as losing sight of the old shore and crossing the ocean to the new land. It now means to lose sight of the shore of the new world and move more deeply into the frontier of this new place. You have to lose sight of the shore of the new world to truly discover this new terrain you have found yourself. You have to be careful not to be like the tourists who stay at the resort on the beach and don't really discover the new landscape around them.

Some are distressed that even after so much effort, and after having arrived in a new frontier of their lives, they are still struggling with familiar problems. Nothing has changed radically for them. They are still unhappy and discontent. Through investigation they find that they took into the new world habits, a mind-set, and behaviors from the pain story of the past. They found themselves on the edge of a new frontier and out of fear, habit, or distrust remained on the shore.

Most people die with their music still locked up inside of them.

BENJAMIN DISRAELI, NINETEENTH-CENTURY
BRITISH STATESMAN AND AUTHOR

Death also has the means to place us on a new frontier (if we let it). It places us on the edge of a new paradigm or world. But, so does all the life that surrounds the dying. My aunt Dora died a couple of years ago. Family, friends and, acquaintances gathered to celebrate her life, and I held brief conversations with them after a gap of ten, twenty, or thirty years had spanned between us. I shared in one conversation with a cousin whose smile I recognized still, after thirty years.

✦ ✦ ✦

The Blessings Book

"I'm writing down that one in my blessings book," she said after I commented on her beautiful smile.

"Blessings book?" I asked.

"Yes, at night I write down blessings, like the time when the guy sitting next to me on the airplane told me to sing."

"He wanted you to sing on the airplane?"

"No, he thought I should sing if I want to sing."

"Sure, of course you should sing if you want."

A small sliver of memory of her singing some thirty years back jumped into my mind. Wasn't she known for her striking voice?

"But my husband won't let me sing," she said, still smiling. "So I write it down in my blessings book."

I wondered (to myself) if it wouldn't be better to throw away the blessings book and instead get out the songbook and sing!

Start with a favorite song and go from there. Then she would find herself on the shoreline of a new frontier as well, where there are languages to learn, sights to discover, and where the internal landscape opens up to yet more possibilities. Once further into the new frontier the unknown insists that we pay attention. This invitation to go further in, away from the shore, is both frightening and exhilarating. You just don't know all that lies ahead, and it is this uncertainty that calls to the creative spirit. Living dynamically with death, with the unknown, invites us to put down the blessings book and go sing.

From here, as I write this story down, I can hear a woman's voice singing from far away, over the next peak. I think I will keep walking further in, away from the shore. What I hear and see makes my entire body shiver; she is singing a love song to her husband.

✦✦✦

Joining with Others Freely: Creative Manifestation Circles

For the past thirty-five years I have met within some framework of a manifestation group. These groups have always been four to six people who are close friends. My first one was back in the early 1980s through the Unity Church I attended in Minneapolis and was based on the Mastermind principles developed by the late Jack Boland.* We would use Boland's transformational system (what he called scientific or quantum prayer) and keep a Mastermind journal.† Boland also offered eight steps into Mastermind consciousness.‡ In part, these steps were based on the biblical quote from Matthew 18:20, "For where two or three are gathered in my name, there I am in the midst of them." I met in this way for about ten years; however, we created some of our own methods and dropped some of the original Mastermind principles.

My first group included a psychiatrist and a Unity minister. I enjoyed our shared prayers but also witnessed how our backgrounds and assumptions influenced what we embraced. I grew to reject some of the

---

*Napolean Hill, who wrote *Think and Grow Rich,* first wrote about the mastermind and insisted that it was an essential element of success originally taught to him by Andrew Carnegie. He called this mastermind the "third mind."

†All these techniques are still available but have evolved since then and can be found online. Some organizations borrow from this method as well. Be warned that many new groups make their own claims to the title "Mastermind" and want to charge money. However, you can simply use your own spiritual journal to script your intentions and those of your group, along with the methods I share here.

‡These steps are I surrender, I believe, I understand, I decide, I forgive, I ask, I am gratefully accepting, and dedication and covenant.

assumptions underlying Boland's methods but didn't throw the baby out with the bath water! I broke from my original group to develop my own version of a *creative* manifestation circle, based further on my experiences with groups, general system theories, Buddhist philosophy, depth psychology,* and the appreciation of nature. I began to teach my creative manifestation methods in 1993. Of course you too can steal from these simple methods and make them your own.

The bottom line is that gathering together with at least one other around your intentions will enhance your creative manifestations. Jack Boland referred to this as the making of miracles.

Bringing energy to the three promises—to self, other, and vocation—in a manifestation circle or partnership accelerates your creative manifestation. As when several people work together to cultivate a garden, more will get accomplished and likely there will be more to harvest. Because life itself is an amazing dynamic *system* where everything exists in relationship to everything else, the closer we are to each other the more we affect one another. Manifestation partners or circles, in their closeness, build up stronger causes and conditions for their intentions. Your intentions and visions are then also carried in the consciousness of your partners.

In such a circle, when we bring our creative intentions together we give them more momentum and a bigger playing field. Your partner's world is also fertile ground for your intentions. Our intentions reinforce each other's intentions and are built on the momentum of each other's aspirations and actions. We literally alter the causes and conditions in each other's lives deliberately through shared intention and visioning. And, since reality is understood as dependently co-arising and systemic in nature, each and every intention and resulting action is known to have an effect on the larger web of life. One's personal intention is integral to the awakening of everyone else in their circle and on outward to their families, towns, and ultimately the world.

---

*Depth psychology values how all minds, all lives, are ultimately embedded in some sort of myth-making in the form of themes or patterns. Mythology is the richness and wonder of humanity played out in a symbolical and thematic storytelling.

Setting Up the Circle

When you are gathering together to promote your aspirations you will find that the others can hold in their minds a purer view of what is possible for you because they don't carry your baggage, resistance, or disbelief. Of course they carry their own, but for you they can hold and envision something greater than you can for yourself. Ideally you can have up to six, but no more, in your circle. I find four to be the perfect number. You agree to meet only for the purposes set forth by your manifestation circle. This means that socializing is done in other settings, at other times. You can have it around a small meal if you like (in mine we make a seasonal soup). But don't have the meal take up too much of your time or focus. One reason four is a good number is that it is best if the group doesn't convene for longer than four hours. That's enough time to stay focused and attentive to each other's requests and to the process. You will want to agree to confidentiality and take time to discuss any other agreements that need to take place in your particular circle. I recommend that your circle agree to not giving advice or feedback, which is the antithesis of the mirroring we do in these circles. Also, agree to a set time that you will hold your circle and stick to it. Everyone in my circle remains aware that we meet for four hours. Ideally, you sit in a circle. I recommend you meet once a month.

You will bring to the circle one to four requests around intentions you have in your life presently. These can involve any of the three promises to self, other, and vocation. And it may be more beneficial if you had a request for each of these areas. You bring these intentions to be presented as requests to the others. These intentions should be what you hope for; what you want to have happen in the next month and beyond. What is it you want to creatively manifest in your life? I typically do have ones that represent my internal world (promise to self) and the outer world, promise to others and to my vocation. Also bring your spiritual journal or a special manifestation journal to write down your partner's requests as well as any wisdom you glean from the other's mirroring.

Mirroring

Mirroring is a key dynamic in Parker J. Palmer's Circle of Trust technique, which he offers in his book *A Hidden Wholeness,* and it is a central skill in all of my circles. This skill is essential in a manifestation circle. When we share our intentions with others, the others mirror back the potentialities inherent in our request, as well as what they intuitively know is possible. Sharing your intentions with a trusted circle is quite transformative in and of itself, because we are putting our biggest dreams out there to others. We learn to listen deeply to each other without projecting our internal struggles and assumptions on the other. (This was reviewed in the context of relationships in chapter 3.) When mirroring, you become the other's *terton,* which in Tibetan means a "treasure revealer." Those who can see and hear beyond illusions and assumptions can then reveal others' treasures to them. (Historically, secret texts, called *terma* in Tibetan, were hidden until such time that their treasures could be revealed to those ready for such knowledge.) As a terton, you can point the way to the other's inner hidden treasures and to what is possible for them. Those qualities were buried—but not lost—and have been waiting to be discovered. When you are mirroring, you are able to assist in this discovery, and as you do so you become a mirror outside your circle too; you begin to mirror throughout the course of your day. As a mirror, you realize yourself as a terton, transforming the world step by step.

> *We are all shaped by conventional culture. So we all come into a clearness committee [circle of trust] carrying a gravitational force that tries to pull our relationships back to fixing, saving, advising, and setting each other straight.*
>
> PARKER J. PALMER, *A HIDDEN WHOLENESS*

To mirror, we agree to put our full attention on the one who is sharing their requests, their visions for themselves. We listen deeply and intuitively, allowing for the vision and treasures to appear to us as they share. We can notice what comes up within ourselves, but we set that aside for the time being. When the person is done sharing, others one at a time will take turns mirroring their vision back to them. In so doing, they shouldn't make suggestions, give feedback, or counsel the person in any way.

When you are mirroring you can take some notes to help you gather the gems and requests into your journal. I have come to borrow from the process invented by the early Quakers called the "clearness committee" (more on this can also be found in *A Hidden Wholeness*). Its name comes from its ability to help provide needed clarity. In my training on the clearing process, I observed the power and medicine of being a witness for others. I noticed how those who have to share their opinions or give advice are often the ones protecting some strongly held assumption.

Your Creative Manifestation Circle

A manifestation circle exists to provide mutual support, encouragement, and visioning through mirroring possibilities to each other. Each mirrors for the others things that each would find difficult to perceive and envision for themselves. A circle is never intended to solve any problems or to heal each other, but to allow for personal and global transformation through shared visioning.

+ You will each take a turn checking in. This is not a time of conversation but one where you each get a chance to share how the past month has gone for you, particularly around your intentions and requests from last month. You will not be mirroring the check-in specifically but what you have heard can go into the mirroring exchange later on.
+ After everyone has checked in, each takes a turn to share their requests, intentions, and visions for themselves. Have up to four requests. After one person has shared their visions and requests, each person takes a turn to mirror the greatest potential and possibility with each request, seeing beyond the limits and resistances of the one sharing. In mirroring a personal vision and intention, we listen for the potentiality and very real possibilities inherent in this person's wishes. We reflect back to the other the qualities, strengths, and dreams being fulfilled. As an example, someone may share the dream of more peaceful relationships in their home. In their check-in they may have shared

some difficulties they have had around these situations. Then your mirroring could be, "I see your home filled with laughter and love. You all find time for one another and are uplifted by each other's presence. You are able to hold any difficult conversations with compassion for the other."

This process is repeated until each person has had an opportunity to share their requests, intentions, and visions.

✦ Each morning after you are done with your meditation you can review the requests, envisioning for your partners. This is a good time to script or review your scripts around your intentions. Sit for a few minutes visioning your greatest potential and that of your partners. And throughout the day, when your partners come to mind, their accompanying intentions and requests rise up in your consciousness as well, as do yours for them.

We can also align ourselves with an attitude of readiness. We can tell the world, "I am ready." I find this exercise particularly helpful when I am between ideas or when I am wanting to stir up enthusiasm with my creative ideas and intentions.

I Am Ready

✦ Write out the sentence, "I am ready."
✦ Repeat the sentence, "I am ready . . ." until something comes. Do not stop your pen to think, instead keep writing. Fill up at least one page; more if you are so inclined.
✦ Then at least one sunrise a week (several sunrises would be even better), greet the sun with "I am ready . . ." and recite your list.
✦ Add to it as ideas and commitments arise. Then take some time to journal your response or experience.

Your Destiny Story

Awhile back we went to see the movie *Rango,* a strange animated film about journeys. The protagonist, a pet chameleon stranded in the desert, meets an armadillo who is seeking the mystical Spirit of the West. There was one line that the armadillo said that struck me: "You can't leave your own story." You can't completely break from your destiny when you understand destiny to be like the tree in the acorn, the chicken in the egg, the butterfly in the cocoon. Just like every other living being on the planet, our destiny stories are not something we go in search of; rather we open up to them, removing the obstacles that interfere with this emergence or birth or natural transformation from within. This brings to mind a favorite quote attributed to Jesus through the gnostic Gospel of Thomas:

> *If you bring forth what is within you*
> *What is within you will save you*
> *If you do not bring forth what is within you*
> *What is within you will destroy you.*

We can't abandon our own stories. If we don't manifest our spiritual and creative inheritances they will likely destroy us from within. I know you know what I mean—that darn thing that keeps nagging us is trying to find a way out into the world! If we open the door and let it out, we will feel a lot better. When we do stray from our destiny story there are ways that attempt to bring us back to our true path, our deepest calling. Oftentimes there are two forces at play, one calling us to be true to something from within and another pulling to be a certain way in the world. After all, our stories are mingling and meshing with everyone else's stories. I think, when two or more destiny stories come to meet, like in a creative manifestation circle or in other intentional gatherings—miracles happen, books get written, inventions get discovered, and the world's true story of interdependence continues to transform and evolve.

In David R. Loy's book *The World Is Made of Stories* he writes, "We play at the meaning of life by telling different stories." As a meaning maker we also play at the meaning of our life through gathering with others, through an active relationship with nature, through the cultivation of our spiritual principles and intentions, and by consulting the cosmos through some reliable oracle. An oracle is a means into the bigger picture and a window into where you and I are within this larger cosmology, this larger story. The I Ching also offers up a different story so we can play at the meaning of our life. For me, the I Ching, the Book of Changes, is the meaning maker's oracle of divination and insight.

6

The Book of Changes

THE I CHING AND THE ART OF MAKING
MEANING OF EVERYTHING

The only way to make sense out of change is to plunge into it, move with it, and join the dance.

ALAN W. WATTS, *THE WISDOM OF INSECURITY*

Everything in nature returns, is born of, and lives within a cycle. In this way the world constantly completes itself. Acceptance of this allows one to come into the fullness of being at the appropriate time.

RICHARD WILHELM AND CARY BAYNES, *THE I CHING OR BOOK OF CHANGES,* ON HEXAGRAM TWENTY-FOUR, *FU*

The I Ching is thousands of years old and is believed to be the oldest book of divination. And, even though there are a vast multitude of commentaries written about the I Ching, no single person or philosophy can make claim that their interpretation is the definitive one.* There

---

*However, one of my most treasured translations is *The Complete I Ching: The Definitive Translation* by the Taoist master Alfred Huang.

are also more than a hundred different schools of philosophy on how to understand the I Ching and apply it to one's daily life. This allows you to choose a translation that fits your spiritual and creative ideals. The I Ching is a simple but powerful tool that helps the diviner create harmony between the inner self and the outer world. It offers a direct means to live from the zero point.

> *The universe is moved by a power which cycles endlessly from day to day. Such greatness endures for all time. As in heaven, so on earth.*
>
> RICHARD WILHELM AND CARY BAYNES,
> *THE I CHING OR BOOK OF CHANGES*

Simple Is Best

A consultation with the I Ching consists of creating a six-line hexagram. There are many ways to consult the oracle—casting yarrow sticks (once tortoise shells and animal bones were used), I Ching coins, pennies, homemade cards, or other stones or sticks. I use the plastic sticks offered in Frits Blok's little gift box and have made myself I Ching cards for quick reference. Simple is best. Better to make the consultation quick and easy to give yourself more time for studying and meditating around the consultation. Taoist master Alfred Huang's I Ching guide shares the Chinese saying, "The type of vehicle does not matter, so long as it gets you to your destination." Choose the method that works best for you. The results of your cast, or throw, can be converted to a number that will correspond to each line of the hexagram. This is repeated until all six lines have been cast and the hexagram formed. There are sixty-four possible combinations, or hexagrams, and the various translations of the I Ching name each of these and provide commentaries for the interpretation of each. Each I Ching translation begins with simple instructions on how to consult the I Ching and use the Book of Changes. A great little translation to start with is Brian Browne Walker's *The I Ching or Book of Changes: A Guide to Life's Turning Points.*

In its most basic presentation the I Ching is sixty-four hexagrams. All the other commentaries, names to the hexagrams, and descriptions are relative versions given by an author. More expansively, the I Ching is understood as a mirror of the universe; a microcosm. It is said to contain the universe because within the sixty-four hexagrams are held all possibilities. So when you consult and study the I Ching you consult with the substantial and changing possibilities that exist in the universe. As Taoist master Alfred Huang says in his introduction, "The main theme of the I Ching is that everything is in a process of continuous change, rising and falling in a progressive evolutionary advancement."

The I Ching creates an inner process of thought transformation, a way to engage in personal inquiry, helping each of us traverse the diverse territory of our humanity. It helps us *make meaning* by offering a larger and alternative view (story) of any given situation. Instead of limiting ourselves to one perspective (often based in our assumptions, history, and beliefs) we open up to a more expansive view. As mentioned earlier, the I Ching acts as that "third thing" providing us with more options. We can also discover other possible ways to navigate any difficult circumstance.

A Spiritual Friend

I have consulted the I Ching since I was sixteen years old, for a little over forty years. Shortly after my first initiation into the journey as a meaning maker (by being baptized with tap water), I discovered the I Ching. Although to this day it has met me halfway—it discovered me too. Literally, this little paperback, *Essential Changes: The Essence of the I Ching* by Omen Press, fell off the bookstore shelf at a critical time in my life. I wanted something that would help me deal with the rocky terrain of my teenage years.* And in its brief introduction the translator writes: "There is clearly a field for choice"—meaning, make your own interpretation. Since then the Book of Changes has been a constant companion, helping me navigate and make meaning throughout

---

*This resulted in my writing a translation for teens, *I Ching for Teens*.

my entire life. I offer up this chapter in part as an expression of my appreciation to this great and enduring spiritual friend and guide.

To a meaning maker the I Ching "allows one to come into the fullness of being at the appropriate time" as the chapter opening quote mentions. There is in fact a natural timing for everything in our lives, just as in nature. We are given insight into the best timing for us to hold fast or to let go. The best time to retreat and the best time to act. The Book of Changes gives us more to make meaning with within the diverse circumstances we find ourselves in. I refer to this as the oracle for the meaning maker, but it would best be expressed as the oracle that *allows* one to be a meaning maker.

The I Ching's core philosophy relies on the same interdependent reality found in nature and the Heart Sutra—everything is changing (thus it is called the Book of *Changes*) and all exists dependent upon everything else. Nothing ever happens in isolation. The I Ching shows that all solutions reside within the individual (the zero point), move out from there to intimate partnerships, then to the larger family, on to the local community, and outward to the global community. It also relies on the principles within nature—the four elements, the four seasons, and the natural laws of interdependence and impermanence. Finally the I Ching brings in the spiritual and mythical through the relationships between heaven and earth—the earthly and the divine archetypes. The earth principle represents the receptive, the receiver, and the heavenly principle represents the creative or the Creator/Giver.

In this chapter, I introduce the I Ching as an oracle to help you divine your life—to make meaning in times of plenty and times of lack, in times of confusion and clarity. I point to several translations, but will trust you to find one that matches and respects your philosophical bent. The I Ching does not come out of any religious affiliation and is more philosophical in presentation. Anyone, from a Catholic to a secular humanist, can greatly benefit from consulting the guidance of the I Ching. The I Ching allows us to embrace the many aspects of change in our lives.

A Healthy Dose of Doubt

If one has no doubts, why divine?

Cuo Qui-ming,
Zhou dynasty historian

Since its conception diviners have approached the I Ching to get past concerns and doubts. And we all encounter doubts at one time or another.

Our doubts can be productive or a hindrance in our desire to live meaningfully. When doubt is productive it challenges us to consider the situation or environment we are getting ourselves into (or have found ourselves in). For instance, you may doubt the prospects of something or someone. This doubt, used wisely, helps you to investigate further and discover for yourself the root of any concern. On the other hand, hindering doubt is like a drop of ink in water, making the water undrinkable. This doubt is *self-doubt* and permeates everything. Life itself becomes undrinkable for those who chronically doubt themselves. Fortunately the I Ching assists with both types of doubt. When we doubt ourselves, we can rely on the I Ching to find that leash of trust and inner wisdom on which to act. When we doubt the safety or integrity of a situation we can consult the I Ching for further insight.

A healthy dose of (productive) doubt can be an enriching and favorable state of mind. The uncertainty that you feel when this doubt arises can lead you to consult your own inner wisdom through the I Ching. The old myth around doubt and curiosity—that it killed the cat and that it will get you in a heap of trouble—is not only outdated, but it is a myth intended to control the congregation and keep naughty kids in line. Its purpose is to make you uncomfortable and unwilling to challenge what you are told.

In his seventh-century commentary on *Aryadeva's Four Hundred [Verses] on the Yogic Deeds of Bodhisattvas*, Chandrakirti tells the story of a ship's captain captured by an ogress.

✦✦✦

The Ship's Captain and the Ogress

The ogress warns the captain never even to look, let alone venture, to the south of her island. This admonition arouses his doubt and uncertainty about what he is being told. He becomes curious, so, one day he evades her watchful eyes and steals away to explore. There in the south, he finds the king of horses, Balahaka, who will carry you away across the ocean to safety on the other shore if you hold on to even one hair of his mane. And so the captain escaped from the island on which he had been held prisoner.

✦✦✦

Such positive doubt is a perfect navigational tool, a way to ignite a sacred curiosity that leads to other possibilities (or to consulting the I Ching). Positive doubt gets us to question, study, and investigate what we are told. We also question the appearance of phenomena and are not as easily fooled. When we listen to our doubts in this way we won't be so easily controlled or imprisoned by others' views. We will discover truth for ourselves and adventure out beyond the comfort zone of dogma put out by others. Besides, one person's religious experience or antidote could be another's imprisonment or poison. So, we can always consult the I Ching to explore what is truly possible.

> *To those devoid of imagination a blank place on the map is a useless waste; to others, the most valuable part.*
>
> ALDO LEOPOLD, *A SAND COUNTY ALMANAC*

Don't spend your life on someone else's island:

Question everything of significance.

Those who told you that curiosity killed the cat said so to control you.

Let all admonitions arouse in you a sacred curiosity of doubt.

Follow your doubt (your curiosity) to the other side of things.

Don't be held captive by others' beliefs or desires—*steal away and explore.*

In times of self-doubt there is that inner edge that arises within us, a hesitation to move forward or challenge what is going on around us but a desire to take some kind of action. This happens because we intuitively know what we want or need to do, but our doubts and fears overshadow our inner guide (like that drop of ink in the water). The I Ching, which represents the vast ocean of wisdom, the cosmic connection, is not hindered by our self-doubt and can help us to access the oceanic wisdom. A bead of ink dropped into the vast ocean is diluted and disappears.

Your consultations with the I Ching should always be uplifting and ring intuitively true for you. The feedback from the I Ching may be challenging, but it will never be negative or in any way hostile. If the commentary is in any way negative, find another translation. Your consultations should release you of your doubts, open you up to ways to explore your options, and move you through your resistances.

We can also solicit the I Ching to strengthen our spiritual practices, cultivate our creative intentions, assist in thought transformation, and quickly give us another perspective. I often consult it around my fiction and nonfiction writing. A wonderful book for fiction writers is *I Ching for Writers: Finding the Page Inside You* by Sarah Jane Sloane.

Every consultation will provide you with another, wider perspective to any situation and therefore make room for more meaningful interaction. The I Ching mirrors back to us how our inner world of beliefs, assumptions, philosophical perspective, and psychological nature are being displayed in the outer situation. It reminds us that such transformative work is always fundamentally an inside job from the zero point. Yes, you may end up leaving your job, but a change in attitude about yourself may need to take place first (or you would have already left). The I Ching points to the change in attitude that one needs to make in order to proceed with an outer change (in address, for example). Fortunately it also gives feedback on the environment in which we find ourselves.

Most people think of sprouts growing only in spring, but the ancient Chinese realized that there was a life force latent in the seed from the winter. . . . The little plant must overcome the pressure of the soil. There must be a wholehearted willingness to grow.

ALFRED HUANG, *THE COMPLETE I CHING*

I make no claim other than I would not have experienced so much success and happiness if it were not for this spiritual friend and resource. The I Ching allows me in any situation to live from the zero point, to make meaning with everything and anything and to creatively manifest on a continual basis right in the landscape of my present day life. It will help you make meaning but will not in any way dictate this meaning. After all, we have to interpret the meaning within the context of our life; no one else can do this for us. This is quite different from seeking advice from someone or a source that will make the interpretation for us and dictate what we should do about it. We can use the I Ching as an organizing principle since we are always in a process of becoming. The I Ching doesn't boss us around, insisting we go right or left. Each hexagram represents possibilities and potentialities to choose from in order to make personal and relevant meaning.

As in any healthy relationship, the I Ching insists on our participation and use of our own abilities and intuitions. It works when you hold a conversation with it that is reflective and contemplative. It relies on the principle of mutual influence and teaches how to bring this forth in all our relationships, even with your higher power and higher principles. It is the oracle to living the zero point agreement, as it will always point to what needs attention from your side of the equation. Your conversations with the I Ching will help you to develop your own personal philosophy, your intuition, and personal knowledge of how things work. The I Ching helps you to move on to the next step "close in" with more insight and resources. Such a spiritual friend!

Holding a Conversation with the I Ching

Since the I Ching represents the universe, these conversations are a way to interact with "all that is." Your conversation with the I Ching relies on your further trusting your significance within the whole. This relationship depends on your receptivity to being influenced by your consultation. The commentaries of the I Ching point to actual situations, concrete solutions, and specific antidotes by offering a potential model of *how to become* in each situation. They are not vague in their message but are presented in a way that allows you to make your own interpretation. When we live life in accordance with our interpretation, we strengthen our ability to hold the zero point conversation with all of life and to creatively manifest (or transform difficulty) in any situation.

Each hexagram points to a theme and principle that is unique on its own but is always interacting (coexisting) with the other hexagrams and other elements of your life. That is the beauty in transforming one aspect of our life; all other aspects are somehow transformed. You can keep things simple by focusing your conversations with the I Ching on one topic until that topic is transformed and improved. Work on what is in front of you now, trusting that you are transforming and improving many other aspects of your life as well.

There is a popular axiom that basically goes, it is the student who must choose the teacher, not the teacher (or sage in this case) who chooses us.

Meet the Sage of the I Ching

Early on in my study and conversations with the I Ching, I came upon the voice of the I Ching, which several interpretations refer to as the Unknown. Other translations of the I Ching refer to this source as a Sage, or the Sage. I began to refer to this source as the Great Unknown. I found that in using the I Ching, the Great Unknown didn't respond to shallow or frivolous concerns. And in the case where I was stubborn in my learning the Sage would stick with the same topic until I reached some understanding. (This often meant I would receive the same hexagram several times in a row.)

In my long-term relationship with the I Ching, I have come to feel the Sage's presence, to sense this wisdom and potentiality that surrounds me and is in me. Often following my consultation I am surrounded with a tangible sensation of this oceanic presence and wisdom, which when I was younger felt like an embrace from the Great Unknown. Something tangible responds to my consultations, and you will find this to be true for you too. After you have consulted the I Ching consistently for some time you will develop your own unique relationship and ongoing dialogue with the Sage of the I Ching, who will awaken your inner sage.

A Few Basics

We begin with heaven (Ch'ien) and earth (K'un). Heaven is represented in yang energy and earth is represented in yin energy. Yang and yin—the creative and the receptive—are present in all of life and are the foundation of all the other hexagrams. Where heaven (the creative) and earth (the receptive) interact there is unlimited potential as to what can happen. These two central hexagrams of heaven and earth, yin and yang, represent for the inquirer all the possible developmental and evolving situations of the universe and are, therefore, inherent in any given situation. The two hexagrams themselves are what produce the sixty-four images of the hexagram—everything is born from the interaction between heaven and earth.

> Dark, yielding, devoted, accepting of guidance. The image here is of Earth's ability to nourish all living things as they willingly surrender to the nature of the world.
>
> WILHELM AND BAYNES, THE I CHING OR BOOK OF CHANGES ON HEXAGRAM TWO, K'UN

The relationship between heaven and earth, active and receptive, yang and yin creates a basic system of an impermanent and changing reality of which we are a part. These inherent patterns within the hexagrams of the I Ching are found in all aspects of life, which are always changing, always expanding or contracting. Consulting the I Ching allows you to tap into this system as a way to visualize and understand where you may be in this ever-changing, dynamic universe. It is a snapshot of a moment or aspect of time in your life, which you get to take a look at and retrieve insight about through the patterns that are inherent and changing in that particular picture (or story).

I Ching is translated as "the book of changes." *I* means "change" and is understood to be the underlying principle of life. *Ching* is translated as "scripture" or "book." We then access the basic and fundamental principle of existence when we consult the I Ching. This allows us to make meaning with the master meaning maker (the Tao, the Great Unknown, Brahman, God). I am convinced that this is the reason some religious fundamentalists consider such an oracle as evil or "occult" (in the negative reference to the word). They fear and resist the personal empowerment that such an oracle can give us. With the guidance of the I Ching we could evolve into autonomous self-reflecting individuals who are free from dogma or a dependence on one teacher or doctrine! In contemplating and applying the commentaries of the I Ching we discover *for ourselves* the many mysteries and possibilities of the universe.

> *The Book of Changes is more than just a book. It is a living, breathing oracle, a patient and all-seeing teacher who can be relied upon for flawless advice at every turning point in our lives. Those who approach the I Ching sincerely, consult it regularly, and embody in their lives the lessons it teaches inevitably experience the greatest riches that life has to offer.*
>
> BRIAN BROWNE WALKER,
> *THE I CHING OR BOOK OF CHANGES*

Ask and You Shall Receive

Here I offer you the basics in consulting the I Ching. Give yourself at least twenty minutes for each I Ching consultation. The Sage of the I Ching typically teaches us by suggestion, never with a harsh slam to the head. Therefore, be clear about what you want and you will receive answers.

+ First write in your journal a paragraph or more describing the particular situation you are consulting around. Don't formulate the question yet; write about the story surrounding the concern.
+ Then write out what would be helpful for you to know. What do you want insight around?

✦ Come up with one simple and pithy question taken from your journal entry. Clear questions result in clear answers. This part of the query is worth the effort, since the response will be based on the how and what of your question. Consider what topic or dynamic you want to explore. Then design a question in a way that isn't going for a yes or no response. In other words, don't ask *Will I get the job?* but instead ask *What would be a next step in making this job more possible?* As mentioned earlier, *what* questions will result in more insight. Here are some examples:

> What wants to happen?
> What should I pay attention to?
> What is my biggest obstacle with this idea?
> What would be helpful for me to know in this relationship?
> What could I do to improve the situation?
> What do I need to pay attention to here?

✦ Now write your question down in your journal. Notice, just as you did in coming up with your intention, whether you need to revise it to make it even pithier. Remember that the more vague you are the less you get; the clearer you are the more clarity you will receive.

✦ Then frame your question with, *What would like to happen in a meaningful way, together, at this time in my life?* Initially I would write this part of my question out, too. Then I would simply hold this framing question in my mind as I toss the coins or sticks, along with my question. Let go of any expectations and let this framing question guide you through the consultation. So your question may be like this: *What can I do to improve my relationship with my husband during this time of transition? What would like to happen in a meaningful way, together, at this time in my life?*

✦ Open yourself up to receive answers from the Great Unknown.

✦ As you read your consultation, notice your thoughts and what else arises in the mind, including dreams and images, as they are likely relevant to the consultation. Then take the time to journal any particular insights. Some people choose to have a special I Ching consultation journal. My consultations are weaved throughout my spiritual journals.

✦ This is also a good time to do some inquiry meditation around the particular principle the I Ching may be presenting to you.

✦ A good finish to the consultation is naming an action you will take as a result of the consultation. Decide how you are going to use the lesson to make meaning in a given relationship or situation. Let the consultation you receive from the I Ching influence you. Embody it through action.

Through your ongoing conversations with the I Ching you open inner doors to a new and wider story of your life.

The Bigger Question

> *We must use time wisely and forever realize that the time is always ripe to do right.*
>
> NELSON MANDELA

The I Ching always responds to the bigger, underlying question if there is one. Since there are a multitude of causes and conditions to any situation and everything is in a flux, your specific query may not reflect what needs the most attention. You may find yourself confused by the reading and unable to make relative sense of its meaning. Recognize that there might be a bigger question here that needs attention first. In this case, it is answering your question by attending to the bigger issue. For example, you may ask about a given relationship, but it is clear that the reading is pointing to another situation (you either know this intuitively or something in the reading triggered this awareness). When this happens, the I Ching is pointing to something that needs addressing before you can really generate the desired movement in the situation you first consulted on. Also, remember to pay attention to what or who may come to mind when you are receiving the consultation. If you are consulting about work, but your spouse keeps coming to mind as you read the text—trust this. Trust that the wisdom of the I Ching (and your intuition) is pointing to where to apply this consult. You may want to do some additional inquiry as to what that bigger issue may be by tossing the coins or sticks for further insight.

Success in Life

When the water starts boiling it is foolish to turn off the heat.
NELSON MANDELA

Your consultations with the I Ching will enhance your imagination and creative efforts, resulting in more successes. You will experience more and more creative abundance. As Brian Browne Walker says, you will prosper from these consultations.

You will experience peak creative moments. And when you are at the top of your game, or mountain, stay ever present and awake. This is not the time to lie back and just soak in the good vibes of success. I think this is an aspect that can be overlooked or misunderstood in the I Ching—within the changes, the fluxes of life and its circumstances, when we are at a peak moment of success and receiving some kudos because of it—this is *not* the time to "turn off the heat," as Nelson Mandela would say. Keep the heat on. A common response to success or peak experiences is to just lean back and enjoy our abundance. Enjoy the peaks, but don't stop the momentum of your life because of it. The I Ching also recommends that this is the time to really strengthen your spiritual and creative resolve, to not get lazy but instead stay active while you enjoy your successes. There will be a natural ebb and flow to consider—a bird can't always be flying, and if you keep the heat on too long the water will boil down to nothing. Here again the I Ching relies on nature's timing; on the ebb and flow that happens in the natural world and helps the student of the I Ching to tap into the organic current of life.

This current of life is at times experienced in the synchronistic messages we receive through the I Ching and that we encounter in our daily lives.

Synchronicity:
The Conversation with the Tao

Synchronicity can provide us with confirmation that we are on the right path, as well as let us know when we are not.
JEAN SHINODA BOLEN, THE TAO OF PSYCHOLOGY

We must admit that there is something to be said for the immense importance of chance.

CARL JUNG, FOREWORD TO WILHELM AND BAYNE,
THE I CHING OR BOOK OF CHANGES

The I Ching contains the same underlying principle as the Heart Sutra—that there is an essential tenet that connects everything to everything else. Everything arises conditionally. Nothing occurs in isolation; everything is interdependent. Equally so, built into every action are reactions; for every cause there are effects. The synchronistic encounter or event is an *effect* and its cause includes your I Ching question, your intentions, thoughts, dreams, or prayers that preceded the synchronicity.

Basically, a synchronistic encounter is a *meaningful* coincidence. It is a causal encounter that cannot be logically explained but is responding to some internal issue or question (like your question brought to the I Ching). Synchronicity is present in every I Ching consultation. In fact, each toss of the coins or sticks results in a meaningful coincidence with a hexagram. The lesson you are given happens through a synchronistic encounter with your question, the coins, and the resulting commentary of the given hexagram.

As Jean Shinoda Bolen says in *The Tao of Psychology,* "Synchronistic events are the clues that point to the existence of an underlying connecting principle." Meaningful coincidences will get your attention, so you don't have to go searching for them. They come to you from the Tao (the Great Unknown) and are helpful pointers on your path. Following your I Ching consultation they occur sometimes in response to the consultation and the meaning you have made from it. Pay particular attention to meaningful coincidences after consulting the I Ching, both as a practice to strengthen this ability and to receive help. Don't search for these external encounters—simply notice what comes up, *what gets your attention.* If you consult about someone and then run into him or her, what does this person represent to you? It may be that you are meant to do something with this person; it may mean that this person simply holds symbolic meaning for you. When you consult the I Ching or have a synchronistic encounter you obtain a reflection of what you already intuitively know. So, you decide.

Synchronistic encounters arise like road signs telling you *this road is a major detour, reconsider your plans,* or *keep going.* Wherever they show up, they are here to help you on your way. Just as the natural world also relies on intrinsic timing—a cycle of creativity and rest, the waxing and waning of the moon, the rising and setting of the sun—your synchronistic encounters with the I Ching and beyond will help you with your natural timing. There is a time to move and a time to stay put. There is a time to say no and a time to say yes.

We can interpret these consultations and synchronistic encounters symbolically *and* logically. This means that we have both a symbolic and a psychological language to work with. Connect the I Ching's message to your life in a logical way, as in how it influences your actions. At the same time consider its symbolic meanings. The I Ching is rich and diverse in its symbolic offerings, and many books, including Master Alfred Huang's, give commentaries on each hexagram's symbols.

The qualities that are brought forth through our consultations with the I Ching are the qualities and principles that are pivotal to a meaning maker—awareness, acceptance (with a twist), compassion, ethical discipline, perseverance, tolerance of differences, detachment, inner truth, intuitive wisdom, reliance on the natural world, conscientiousness, and inner independence. Inner independence in particular acknowledges the zero point. It is the cultivation of the principles that underlie the zero point agreement that gives us this inner independence in this complex and shared universe.

Let him that would move the world, first move himself.
SOCRATES

7

The Eleven Core Principles
of the Zero Point Agreement

Zero
Is where the Real Fun starts.

There's too much counting
Everywhere else.

DANIEL LADINSKY, *I HEARD GOD LAUGHING:*
RENDERINGS OF HAFIZ

Right understanding is the only solution to both physical
and mental problems. You should always check very
carefully how you're expending your energy: will it make
you happy or not? That's a big responsibility, don't you
think? It's your choice: The path of wisdom or the path of
ignorance.

LAMA THUBTEN YESHE

There are eleven pithy slogans that can be used as practice points and reminders of the zero point agreement, which is to live life *from your side.* These are accessible to anyone from any religious or spiritual background, as well as those who live a more humanistic or secular lifestyle. These are not exhaustive or to be used as clubs. They are simply pointers, references to help in living life from the zero point. Each of these are brought out throughout the book but can be more quickly referenced here. Pithy intentions, slogans, and principles can redirect the mind, in the moment, in a beneficial way.

1. Take Full Responsibility for Your Experiences

The price of greatness is responsibility.

WINSTON CHURCHILL

This has been covered throughout the book and is the basis for living life from your side. If there is a magic pill to happiness, this is it, because when we take responsibility for our life and our experiences so much becomes possible.

Inherent within the principle of taking responsibility for your experiences is the agreement to *be willing to do whatever it takes.* You take full responsibility for your life experiences by doing what it takes in the moment to bring forth your best. Be willing to do whatever it takes to bring your creative or spiritual intention to fruition. Be willing to live from the zero point, be willing to do what it takes to realize the Heart Sutra. Enter situations with a clear purpose of accountability.

"Whatever it takes" will arise as you further pursue your intentions and creatively manifest. This accountability will touch every area of your life and bring forth the tight spots where habitual states are strong. (In part because we can't be certain ahead of time what the "whatever" is.) When we are willing to do whatever it takes, we leave the comfort of the known and open up to the vast possibilities in the unknown.

You can make this commitment to yourself ("I am willing to do whatever it takes to [now state your intention]") in your journal or outwardly to your creative manifestation partners. I recommend this be part of setting your intention as described earlier. When you are truly committed to an intention you are willing to do whatever it takes to fulfill it.

The modern dogma is comfort at any cost.
ALDO LEOPOLD, *A SAND COUNTY ALMANAC*

2. Find Freedom through Personal Investigation and Examination

Self-inquiry is an ancient practice for exploring the potency and beauty of our own interior nature and discovering who and what we really are. *To be who you already are* means to *explore and discover* who you are. So much of our experience comes down to the condition of our mind. Your true and lasting happiness is dependent on your attitude and what you focus your mind on. Mind training through investigation and examination goes beyond just having the fresh perspective that some counseling session or workshop may give us. We need to be willing and able to examine our lives in general terms and investigate our mind-sets, choices, behaviors, and circumstances in more detail. This is an ongoing process and particularly helpful at times we feel stuck or unhappy. This principle is about developing the skills of personal inquiry so we can further understand the causes and circumstances of our experiences.

This is not about being obsessive about our thoughts. On the contrary, it is about utilizing methods to train the mind. These methods are found throughout the book and will free the mind from the self-absorption of worry, anxiety, self-hatred, depression, anger, and fear.

3. Take Refuge in Wholesome and Strong Intentions

When you take refuge in wholesome intentions you turn your mind into an ally. To take refuge in wholesome and strong intentions means you rely on positive intentions to make your life meaningful. In taking refuge you let intentions be the guiding force in all your interactions. Taking refuge is a matter of commitment. In taking refuge we recognize that a purposefully driven life benefits others. In taking such refuge in your wholesome intentions you are committing yourself to a creative life. Grounded in your intentions and principles, you are not distracted from your creative and spiritual pursuits. One of my first teachers reminded me and my fellow students that *energy follows intention*. This means that our lives follow our intentions. Intentions act like the taproot of your life—deeply nurturing you and those around you in a forward motion. (See chapter 4 for more on intentions.)

> *The Buddhist understanding of karma emphasizes intentionality as the key to self-transformation.*
> DAVID R. LOY, *THE WORLD IS MADE OF STORIES*

4. Work with Your Strong, Disturbing Emotions

Work with your own strong, disturbing emotions first. Examine emotions that upset you the most, as they arise. Strong and disturbing emotions will only get stronger if we don't interrupt them. Practice working with a strong and repetitive emotion like anger, jealousy, or disappointment. Notice when it arises and how. Become aware of how this internal affliction harms you and others. Examine how it interferes with your creative and spiritual life. The idea is to work gradually and thoroughly with one disturbing emotion at a time until you are less and less disturbed by them. Use the different practices in this book to disrupt the pattern of reactive emotions.

Changing Your Emotional Response

The mind, fortunately, is trainable. We can learn to locate the culprit of our suffering through mindfulness of our cognitive processes and the emotions and behaviors that result. We can retrain the mind to focus on such inner qualities as compassion, tolerance, and patience. How then is it we feel so pushed around by our emotional states and outside experiences? Observe your mind and experiences in the following way and then decide what is driving your experience. Is it your circumstances, your emotions, or your thoughts?

+ Borrowing from the cognitive-behavioral model, we start with a *situation* (a friend's funeral), then we identify a *thought*, a mental response (she had a good life; I will miss her, but her suffering from cancer is over).

Next, we notice an *emotional response* based on the cognitive response (I feel sad and relieved; I feel grateful our paths crossed). And then we have the resulting *behavior and experience* (I celebrate her life).

✦ Use this awareness technique to understand one of your afflictive emotions and reactive states. Begin with a painful situation in your life story (my father belittled me), to which you have a thought response (I came to believe I was worthless). You create assumptions (I must change myself to please my father and others) from the emotional content (feeling inadequate, feeling shame), resulting in the behavior and actions (always trying to please others).

We can't change the past. But we will keep repeating it if we continue to live by the beliefs and assumptions set in response to past events. Notice also that the original belief and assumption really aren't your fault. There is no need to add to the pain by shaming yourself. Your original thought response is understandable when you consider it in the context of your story. Be kind as you dismantle these beliefs and assumptions. Most of our habitual beliefs and assumptions are linked to an original belief that helped us survive or interpret a difficult situation.

5. Maintain Your Inner Integrity

My feeling is, the better we feel about ourselves, the fewer times we have to knock somebody down in order to stand on top of their bodies and feel tall.

ODETTE POLLAR, *DYNAMICS OF DIVERSITY*

The greatest gift, from which all other gifts come, is your personal freedom and happiness, your inner integrity. Taking the time and effort to focus on your well-being isn't selfish but necessary if you are to be of any real benefit to others. When we feel good about ourselves we express this contentment outward in our lives. This slogan encourages you to give enough time to the promise made to yourself, to care for this one precious human being—you. Each day do something that is uplifting, self-nurturing, or fun.

Inner integrity is based on inner independence and effort on your part to be happy while not getting caught up in self-pity or self-absorption. (Someone living from the zero point doesn't complain.) This means that you are not using the zero point principle, or any practice, to strengthen your self-absorption. This internal integrity reflects an understanding of the principles within the Heart Sutra and the I Ching. Only you can break through any self-enclosed view of the world. Your entire life happens from the zero point, but it is in no way all about you.

6. Live as the Meaning Maker

Of course this entire book speaks to this principle. We can only make meaning from the zero point. So here is a bit of wisdom from Lewis Carroll in *Through the Looking Glass*.

"I can't believe that!" said Alice.

"Can't you?" the queen said in a pitying tone. "Try again, draw a long breath, and shut your eyes."

Alice laughed. "There's no use in trying," she said. "One can't believe impossible things."

"I daresay you haven't had much practice," said the queen. "When I was your age, I always did it for half an hour a day. Why, sometimes I've believed as many as six impossible things before breakfast."

7. Show Up Halfway for All Your Relationships

This slogan is essential to successfully living from the zero point and maintaining healthy relationships. Showing up halfway means respecting the personal boundaries and integrity in all relationships. To show up halfway we have to become aware of this halfway position in our relationships. We want to be able to find this halfway point and live our life there with others. I encourage my clients to locate this halfway mark in their relationships by imagining an invisible line between them and the other—and then to notice when or how they are crossing over the boundary.

Ask yourself, where is this place in my relationships and communications with others? What does it look like to go past halfway? What does it look like to hang back from this meeting place? Hanging back means you are isolating yourself or are not truly committed to that particular relationship. There can be no communication or intimacy with "the other" if we are not meeting them halfway. We can also make the mistake of going *past* the halfway mark in our relationships. When we go past halfway we are typically being codependent, crossing personal boundaries, and doing or taking on too much. In these relationships you find yourself resenting the other, getting overwhelmed with responsibilities until you become exhausted. We also tend to go past halfway when we do not trust the other to show up. One of my favorite lines in a song is from the Minneapolis singer, Claudia Schmidt. She sings about being in a relationship way past its expiration date and says: "I've gone so far past halfway that I met myself coming back." It is better to wait out at the halfway point than to cross the boundary to try to get what you want. Live your life from your side at this halfway place and notice who shows up.

You will find this principle in the I Ching as well, where we are guided to meet even the Creator halfway. In relationship with your spiritual source not showing up halfway means you are not in an active relationship with this source. How do you expect to experience sacred connection when you hold yourself back? When we go *past* halfway in our relationship to our spiritual source we don't allow room for the Great Unknown to help us.

8. Reflect on the Preciousness of Human Life

Most of us have the opportunity for liberation because, unlike all other sentient beings, we humans have an inclination of basic intelligence, which is primarily our ability to develop our wisdom and compassion. We have

this special ability to differentiate between good and bad.
We can obtain an understanding of cause and effect.
GESHE LHUNDUB SOPA, FROM AN ORAL TEACHING ON
THE PRECIOUSNESS OF HUMAN LIFE

Recognizing the preciousness of human life is about recognizing the amazing opportunity this life offers us.

We can use the four reminders borrowed from the Buddhist philosophy to help us appreciate the opportunity of this life. These reminders address our emotions and have the power to motivate and inspire us. They are familiar and fierce in their truth. Despite their value we can easily forget them, replacing them with quite a different set of assumptions. These reminders are wake-up calls, jolts to our smugness, they are the voice of reality as it speaks through our immediate experience. As we go through them, we are saying to ourselves, *remember this; consider this; stay tuned to these universal truths.* Such reflection is a form of visualizing reality—seeing the frame that holds the big picture in place. These reminders open us up to a bigger reality than the small one we may cling to. By rehearsing these reminders (perhaps coming up with your own versions), you can bring them into your awareness so that they can inform and guide your experience.

- Remember the opportunities inherent in having a human life. Enjoy and appreciate this rare opportunity that this one life has to offer. You have a chance to make something of your life. You have the ability to think and act. All the opportunities and conditions in your life can and will change, but while you have these reminders you recognize your life as a precious opportunity.

> *This free and favorable life, very difficult to obtain,*
> *Brings the accomplishment of the purpose of human*
> *existence.*
> *If the benefits are not achieved now,*
> *How will such an opportunity arise later?*
>
> THE BUDDHA

- One day you will die. Everyone you know will die too. Death cannot be avoided; it comes to us all without warning. Even if we live a long life, it is still brief like a bubble on water. Everyone expects to live longer than they do. Someday your somedays will all be gone. To face death with integrity live your life fully without regrets or complaints.

> *The life of beings passes like a flash of lightning in the sky. It goes quickly, like water tumbling down a steep mountain.*
>
> THE BUDDHA

- Whatever you do, good or bad, has a result. This reminder points to the science of interdependence and how our karma, our actions, will come to fruition in this and possibly future lives. We are continually experiencing the results of previous choices and actions—both our own and others'. What you do or don't do matters.
- The search for happiness outside of yourself will cause you to suffer. You can't escape disappointments and suffering entirely. Part of our humanity is feeling incomplete and dissatisfied. However, the root of our suffering is expecting something outside ourselves to define us. Do your best to accept your limits while living fully.

> *As you proceed through life,*
> *follow your own path,*
> *birds will shit on you.*
> *Don't bother to brush it off.*
>
> JOSEPH CAMPBELL,
> *A JOSEPH CAMPBELL COMPANION*

9. Cultivate a Spiritual Practice

You acknowledge and have a spiritual and ethical practice you rely upon. This principle has been fully covered in chapter 4. You live life fully and actively from your side using your chosen principles.

10. Depend on the Natural World

Nature is a constant source of inspiration to help you to live life from your side.

> *I, the fiery life of divine essence, am aflame beyond the beauty of the meadows, I gleam in the waters, and I burn in the sun, moon, and stars. . . . I awaken everything to life.*
>
> HILDEGARD VON BINGEN,
> *LIBER DIVINORUM OPERUM* (BOOK OF DIVINE WORKS)

This *viriditas,* or "greening wisdom" of Hildegard of Bingen, a twelfth-century nun who has since been canonized, expresses that we rely on nature not only for our physical well-being, but must also understand nature as our teacher, as our guide. This is fundamental to living life from the zero point. As Ernest "Nick" Hockings, Ojibwe tribal member and educator, said, "People who understand the spiritual nature of the environment begin to see things, the interaction that everything has with everything else."

This principle emphasizes the fundamental wisdom in having a strong connection with nature. In his book *Zen Mind, Zen Horse,* Allan J. Hamilton, M.D., warns us that "we became outcasts from the natural world."

This principle means that part of our spiritual practice and daily routine involves, at the very least, some contact with our natural surroundings. We depend on nature as teacher and spiritual friend. In turn we hold a determined recognition of nature's reliance on us to live ethically and in a principled manner within this greater context of nature. We cannot be creative, wholly human, or ethical when we view ourselves as separate from the natural world. To live life from our side means we claim this inheritance, this connection to all that is, by fulfilling our part in it—which means to live intimately with our natural surroundings.

Coyote Says, *"Go Tell It on the Mountain"*

> *Pilgrimage to the place of the wise is to escape the flame of separation from Nature.*
>
> AN OLD SUFI SAYING

A coyote visited us one morning. She was likely a voice in the previous evening's singing and howling that awoke me. There she was, walking up the driveway toward the horse pasture. I went outside to get a better look, expecting her to run off. Instead she stopped, turned to look at me, and stood there. So we stared at one another for a while.

"She's too bold," my husband commented.

I thought as I stared back how the coyote must think *us* too bold. Her ancestors probably warned her of our impudence; "They build and pave and live wherever they want. They are too bold. They never flinch."

Perhaps our house sits on the mounds of her ancestors or on top of a once favored hunting ground.

We looked at each other for a few more moments until she began to slowly walk off, sniffing the ground and checking out a collapsed soccer ball abandoned in the pasture. She strolled along the cornfield and gradually disappeared into the golden-brown cornstalks, like a phantom; like a reminder and as something to make meaning from.

These encounters with the natural world cannot be replicated anywhere. Nothing whatsoever can take the place of experiencing the natural world. Not the most beautiful temple or church. Not even the most remarkable art or music (which ultimately tries to copy nature).

The Zero Point of the Natural World

Nature is always living from the zero point and can teach us to do so too. In terms of creativity, time spent in nature or with animals awakens our right brain and as Dr. Hamilton explains, "provides us a unique opportunity to mute our left hemisphere." Any time we are relating to the natural world we give ourselves an opportunity to get some respite from our habitual selves. In nature we tend to let go of the worries and without much effort heal the sense of separation we carry around inside of us. Remember that the Buddha experienced enlightenment outside under the Bodhi tree; the beatitudes were offered outside, as were most of Jesus's teachings; Native American vision quests, too, take place under the natural night sky. I find that if I was previously stuck in my writing or some other creative pursuit a walk outside or time spent with our horses always frees my mind.

+ Uninspired? Get outside. Engage in a conversation with the natural world. Hold a conversation with a local tree and your head will be on fire with ideas. Don't know what you want? Take a walk out in the prairie or through the woods until something inspires you. Need to get outside yourself and experience a connection to all that is? Spend time with a horse. All our encounters with something more primitive, natural, and instinctual will awaken these same qualities in us.

+ When you return from this conversation with the divinity of the natural world drumming through you, find some time to write about your experiences, thoughts, or emerging inspiration in your journal. Who and what is showing up? Is coyote showing up for you these days? What has the wind brought to you recently? What is getting your attention? Did cricket come calling? What do you keep bumping into on your morning walks?

I don't think there is anything to distinguish us from the wild and natural world except for our misguided belief that we're above or separate from the natural world. We use tools to make our lives easier, but so do a whole bunch of other primate species.

WILLIAM E. ISHMAEL, WILDLIFE BIOLOGIST

✦ ✦ ✦

The Tiger and the Fox

Adapted from an old folk tale

Once there was a man who longed to know his place in the world and how to listen to God's wisdom on how things worked. So he went for a long walk through the woods and saw a fox that had lost its legs and he wondered how it survived. He waited and watched. At dusk he saw a great tiger with some wild game in its mouth. He had eaten much of it but left the rest near the bank where the fox hid and rested. When the tiger left, the fox emerged from his hiding place to happily eat.

The next day the man watched again and saw the tiger once again provide a meal for the fox by leaving some remains near the pond. The man was moved by how nature provided for the fox by means of the tiger. He thought, "That must be it! I am meant to go sit quietly in the woods and God will provide for me all that I need as well." So the next day he went out to a deep spot in the woods where he sat himself up against a tree and waited. He waited for God to bring him what he needed and believed God would take care of him in the same way the fox was taken care of. Many days and nights passed, and the man was on the verge of starvation, hopelessness, and death. As he lay his head down in defeat he heard a voice—"Wake up, foolish man, open your eyes to the truth! Follow the example of the tiger and stop imitating the fox!"

✦✦✦

11. Rely on Qualified Teachers

A qualified teacher is someone who exemplifies a way of life for you. This is mostly true in your spiritual life but holds true in your creative life as well. One of my best teachers was a writer and poet.

At some point it will be worthwhile, if not necessary, that you receive some teachings through an embodied master. When we plan to meet with a spiritual teacher, or gather in a group to do spiritual work, the truly transformative experience will be in what we discover within ourselves. The meaningful journey of life can be deepened and supported by a skillful teacher or dynamic circle of peers.

I have dedicated a great deal of my professional life helping students and clients find safe and dynamic places to experience healing and transformation. In each one of my previous books I offered up guidance ranging from finding a skillful psychic or counselor to keeping yourself safe in a group situation. I find that more growth, insight, and transformation happen within circles conducted by a qualified teacher or counselor. A great teacher or counselor is a treasure to have, which is my reason for including this as a principle within the zero point. I would not have gotten this far, or done this well, if it weren't for the qualified teachers offering me guidance and instruction along the way. This brings to mind the Lutheran minister who baptized me with tap water as well as the teacher I find in my consultation with the I Ching. However, I learned well from the false prophets and teachers too. A few years after my baptism by tap water I was condemned to hell by a Baptist minister, and I've experienced more than one false shaman use fear to try to recruit me.

I want for you to find the true teachers among the false ones. And in my book *Wheel of Initiation* I give an extensive checklist for consideration. In brief, a true teacher will mirror your greatest self and point to the myriad possibilities available to you. When necessary she will use a sharp stick of truth; other times a sweet song. I agree with Fools Crow, who says that the teacher/healer has the smallest part in the process of a successful healing experience. The healer comes with the bells and whistles, while the student transforms himself, and the rest is spirit at work.

Finally, I love this advice I have heard and given to people about choosing a teacher or counselor: Witness how they treat their own family.

> *Whichever step of the staircase you enter upon, the journey will, in its own way and own time, lead you to all the other steps. The only requirement is that you continue to put one foot in front of the other—one thought, moment of interest, and effort after another. That is all teachers really require of their students. They have trust that the teachings will unfold their results naturally, if the student will only grasp the opportunity.*
>
> GESHE LHUNDUB SOPA WITH DAVID PATT,
> *STEPS ON THE PATH TO ENLIGHTENMENT*

The Zero Point Principles

In summary:

Take full responsibility for your experiences

Find freedom through personal investigation and examination

Take refuge in wholesome and strong intentions

Work with your strong, disturbing emotions

Maintain your inner integrity

Live as the meaning maker

Show up halfway for all your relationships

Reflect on the preciousness of human life

Cultivate a spiritual practice

Depend on the natural world

Rely on qualified teachers

8

Planting Lotuses in the Fire
LIVING THE MEANINGFUL LIFE

Soil tilled dark, planted unseen,
feigns death at first light.

But punched below, new seeds riot
against the crown,

While earth, plowed topsy-turvy,
thrusts back, out of sight.

What would be green begins in blackness,
upside down.

DAVID ROZELLE, "WHAT WOULD BE GREEN"

We don't receive wisdom; we must discover it for ourselves
after a journey that no one can take for us or spare us.

MARCEL PROUST, FRENCH NOVELIST

Spiritual Activism

There is a river flowing fast,
It is so great and swift that there are those who will be afraid.
They will try to hold on to the shore.
They will feel that they are being torn apart and will suffer
*   greatly.*
Know the river has its destination.
The elders say we must let go of the shore, push off
Into the middle of the river,
Keep our eyes open and our heads above the water.

ATTRIBUTED TO AN UNNAMED HOPI ELDER

Our ability to make meaning relies mostly on our ability and willing-ness to hold conversations with the world around us. Some interactions will be obvious in their ever-widening impact, others will not. Each conversation we hold will have an influence. This goes beyond having meaningful dialogue with others, to being in conversation constantly with yourself and the world. Spiritual activism is the creative act of showing up in intimate and open conversations with everything around you.

Ten years ago . . .
I turned my face for a moment
and it became my life.

Sometimes I go about pitying myself,
and all along
my soul is being blown by great winds across the sky.

OJIBWE SAYING

Throughout my whole life, during every minute of it, the world
has been gradually lightening up and blazing before my eyes
until it has come to surround me, entirely lit up from within.

PIERRE TEILHARD DE CHARDIN,
FRENCH PHILOSOPHER AND JESUIT PRIEST

Eleven Conversations

A while ago I set out the aspiration to hold eleven conversations. I felt too isolated and protected living my life as a writer and counselor. These conversations, outside of the work environment, were to be purposeful in that they were to open me up to a deeper understanding of others, as well as to enable me to speak more openly with others. They were also meant to be purposeful conversations in that they were an expression of my intentions. Some conversations took quite a bit of courage on my part. But writing a list of eleven people with whom I would hold intimate and open conversations was just the motivation I needed. The first on my list was a neighboring farmer whose evening lights kept the night sky lit, thus hindering the natural darkness and beauty of the evening. (One reason I chose to live out in the country was to enjoy the natural light and dark.) I intended to ask (for a decade) if there was a way to not have the light on at all times. Another was with Parker J. Palmer, the author of *A Hidden Wholeness* and, more recently, *Healing the Heart of Democracy*. My intention was to meet with him face-to-face since I have enjoyed the teachings offered in his books and recordings. It just so happens he lives in Madison, only a fifty-mile drive from me.

It may seem that one conversation holds more value than the other, but fundamentally this isn't so. For me, each one of the eleven conversations held their own intrinsic wisdom and value. Each one made a difference in my life. Each conversation opened me (and I hope the other) up to more possibilities to explore. Each conversation made my world bigger and increased my understanding of the other while breaking through various assumptions I held. In my conversation with the farmer I learned that there is an ongoing threat of his farm equipment being stolen. Therefore, the light remains on. This challenged my assumption that he kept the light on for other reasons. Turns out he has had thousands of dollars worth of equipment stolen over the years. I also discovered that this is quite common. I still long for the natural darkness but hold a more compassionate understanding around the interfering light. The conversation led to my challenging other assumptions I held about him and other farmers.

Having these conversations with others also allows for mutual influence to take place. We benefit when we allow ourselves to be influenced by others—even if it is only in understanding their story (whether we agree with it or not). For instance, since the farmer didn't take down his nightlights after our conversation, the "outcome" wasn't me getting what I wanted. The conversation—through the exchange of story and being influenced—is the purpose. So when we go into these conversations with our intentions in mind we do so with an open heart that is willing to be influenced by the other. We are not really holding a conversation when we are not being influenced—or when the other is totally unwilling to be mutually influenced as well.

Any open and intentional conversation we have with others will challenge our assumptions and self-absorption.

Treat Every Conversation with Others as if It Is Your Last

A young woman of eighteen who came to see me for counseling wanted to tattoo a large tombstone on her body along with the initials of her deceased stepfather. She said they didn't get on well and that her last words with him weren't kind. She considered this her amends. I recommended she find another way to deal with her past than permanently branding herself. In my counseling sessions I hold the attitude that this may be my final (and in some cases only) conversation with this person. That way we don't get caught up in the less consequential issues and can focus on the purpose of their asking for my help. This makes for some intense and purpose-driven conversations.

Treating every conversation and interaction as if it were our last invites us to invest more in what we say, and in what we don't say, to each other. This integrity with our words would ideally include all forms of Internet communication. Not only may it be your last word with that person, but on the Internet all communications are held captive for future review. I like using the four reminders provided earlier to direct my conversations with others.

Getting Off the Tour Bus

My conversation with Parker J. Palmer is sprinkled throughout this book.* I would say, too, that his wisdom is salted throughout my life. His teachings and writings on living the active life, his courage in using the word and concept of spirituality when it comes to our education and creative life, and the example he sets constantly draw me to his work in the world. And more recently, his book *Healing the Heart of Democracy,* has given us an approach to heal the wounds of our communities from the zero point—from what he refers to as developing the "habits of heart."

In our conversation, Parker spoke of how we all want to be invited to take a spiritual, meaningful pilgrimage, but it can take time to first hear the call and then to actually take such a journey. We have been told so long that we can't figure it out for ourselves that we need others to lead the way for us. "So many of us (including clergy and teachers) are like spiritual tourists remaining on the tour bus. As the educators, spiritual teachers, counselors, and clergy, we are the 'tour guides,' pointing out the window. We say, 'See over there, that is where Jesus was born, or see that tree, that is the Bodhi tree where the Buddha obtained enlightenment.'" The guides and the tourists stay on the bus because they are afraid or don't know how to get off. For many it is all they know.

But Parker points out that "everybody wants to get off the bus." Everyone wants to be invited to take a real spiritual pilgrimage of their own making. We each want to experience spiritual truth for ourselves. We each have our own version of the *Mona Lisa* or a great poem inside us to bring out. Each of us wants to know how to plant lotuses in the fire instead of only reading how others do so. "Most spiritual teachers went into the profession to go on their own spiritual pilgrimage, to have their own spiritual experiences—so we can become quite isolated as tour guides. We need to help people off the bus but feel stuck ourselves. This will be a slow process so don't give up."

---

*All the quotes in this section are taken or adapted from this conversation with Palmer on December 15, 2011.

We first have to get ourselves off the bus. We need to give up our search for meaning and our reluctance to navigate the terrain without the protection of our assumptions or some set dogma. We need to stop settling for the comfort of the air-conditioned bus and feel the heat of personal exploration. To get off the bus we simply have to engage in real conversations with each other and the world around us.

Everyone wants to share their stories, hold conversations with the world around them; sit under their own Bodhi tree. "We can create bridges between us by simply sharing our stories," by holding the conversations; by engaging in dialogue, as David Bohm invited us to do. In *Wheel of Initiation,* the sharing of one's life story is central to the initiatory pilgrimage. We make meaning through the conversations we open up to on a daily basis. Parker reminds us, "There is no right or wrong here, nothing to defend, this is just a sharing of story." Each conversation is a story within a bigger story. Each conversation gets us and others off the bus, as we engage in real dialogue with one another. Out in the open we can discover the world anew, every day. Our conversations can be with all sentient beings, as well as trees, gardens, rivers, our own bodies, and so on. In so many ways it all really gets down to our willingness to show up and hold these conversation out in the open with whoever and whatever meets us halfway. Each conversation we hold can be an invitation to the other to get off the tour bus and into direct experience with the divinity in each of us.

This includes conversations with those who are on *and off* the bus. "The youth see the other horizon, and we need this perspective, this vision. The teachers and elders have the wisdom of how we got here, but we are over the arc and can't see the eastern horizon." So our conversations need to take us to that "third place" mentioned earlier, where we will meet up with others who hold different and widening views as well as opposing views. With an approach of sharing stories, listening compassionately, reaching for understanding (rather than to be understood) we will experience the intimacy we crave.

I have eleven times eleven times eleven more conversations to hold. I look forward to each one. (I consider this book as a start of a conversation with you.)

Once we are off the tour bus let's do our best to stay off the bus and create more bridges between us all through continued open and honest conversations. Keep the conversations going until everyone is off the bus.

> *That you are here—that life exists and identity,*
> *That the powerful play goes on, and you may contribute a*
> *verse.*
>
> WALT WHITMAN

My Conversation with God

At the age of fifteen I was condemned to hell by a Southern Baptist minister. I stood before him in my shorts and T-shirt, I admit scantily covered, as he announced my banishment. Once I was censured, he turned his back on me to greet the next parishioner as he received each of them coming out of the sanctuary. They moved by me like souls on the assembly line for Christ. It felt much like the receiving line at a wedding reception where you don't mention to the bride that the groom is a scoundrel. You congratulate. You give or receive a blessing and you move on.

Being my fifteen-year-old self, I told the minister I didn't agree with his take on Jesus. This minister, who had to be in his late fifties (the age I am now), did not know me. He did not know how I tried to let Jesus into my heart. He did not know I had already spent years reading and studying the Bible. He did not know I was on a long-term spiritual pilgrimage. He did not know I prayed every day and that I already practiced yoga and meditation. All he knew was that I didn't agree with what he was proselytizing to all the other steamed-up listeners—that, basically, unless you are reborn you are in deep trouble. You must view yourself as a lowly sinner and beg for God's mercy. I can't recall the entire sermon but it included words like *blood, Christ, sinners, redemption,* and *everlasting life for the few.* During the sermon he invited those up who were letting Jesus in; those who were willing to announce their rebirth. Oh, how grand it would have been for all if this young woman who sat in the farthest row of sinners could make her way up to the front and be saved.

I didn't move. It would have been dishonest. I didn't feel anything but rebellion. Not a Jesus in sight.

After being publicly condemned, I stood for a while in a bit of a daze. An elder of the church approached me. "Don't worry dear, he can get pretty zealous. God talks with him every day," she said convincingly.

At first I thought she said *jealous*. Later I looked up the word *zealous*, not knowing what it meant. Apparently he was committed, dedicated, hard-core, eager, ardent. My rebellion converted into fear. After all, God makes a daily visit to this man, I thought. What if I was missing the one opportunity for salvation? What if this was my one chance to guarantee a secure and happy afterlife? Would you just shrug it off and walk away? Wouldn't you want to confirm a place in heaven, feel as if you belonged to something bigger than yourself? Where do you want to spend eternity?

As this story goes I went back to the church the following day and found it open. This was back in 1971 when church doors were left unlocked. I went in and prayed. Okay, I begged. I begged to whatever God was listening to please show me the way, give me something to go on. I begged for that "Jesus in my heart" feeling. I begged for some sort of revelation. I spent a few hours there alone until later that morning the elder came into the church and we talked. She set up a time for me to visit with the minister for an hour before his lunch.

You can guess how that went.

He didn't see before him a child with a beggar's heart. He gave me scripture. He recited commandments. He told me not to dance with a man until I was married. I sat and listened and felt my lowliness. After our one-way visit ended I left. Then the elder got my address, and for a year she and I would write each other. I poured my teenage heart onto paper, and she would kindly send me books, scriptures, and a few supportive words. Turns out a few of the books were worth my time, but still Jesus never showed. I continued to feel the pain and eagerness of the search. Hell was looming out there for me and all my loved ones. That brought up another concern of mine back then: Even if I were to find a way to secure a heavenly place, what about those in my life who didn't care about the afterlife? What about those who were not even attempting to make room in their hearts for Jesus? What about their souls?

A year passed when I finally wrote the minister himself. After all, he talks to God. Every day. By then I needed a direct line. My brother was more and more troubled due to his schizophrenia, my boyfriend was drunk most of the time, and my parents absent. I sent out a three-page letter to the minister. I asked him to intervene for me since he had a direct line to God.

And then I waited.

Several weeks passed before I got a letter, longer than usual. While I waited, I sat up nights reading the Bible and going over the books the elder sent. *Ring of Truth* by J. B. Phillips is one title that I haven't been able to discard even now after forty years. Finally the letter arrived. It was bulky. As it turns out, it was thick with scripture and notes from the elder. It did not make any mention of the letter I sent to the minister. Not a word from him.

On that day something broke open inside of me (something escaping out rather than being invited in). I realized then that no one person holds a special relationship with God. There are no closed fists or one size fits all when it comes to God or a means to the afterlife. I also gave up on the idea of searching for ways to set up room for Jesus in my heart. (I can sense the panic arise in many a good Christian as I put this down in writing!) I really don't think Jesus minds. I began to reject the premise that someone's path can adequately determine another's; that someone can direct the meaning of another's life.

I took the letter out to our backyard, which back in the '70s was an aging apple orchard on the brink of extinction. I looked out and had my own conversation with God. It included a few wrathful words.

I planted my first lotus in the fire.

We plant our lotuses in the fiery ground of adversity, knowing the flower will bloom. Lotuses symbolize our ability to take root, grow, and blossom even in unfavorable or hostile conditions. They are another symbol of the zero point in that they bloom from within. We *become* even in adverse conditions. Actually, we *become* not so much in spite of adverse conditions but in conversation with them.

On the Brink of Illumination

On the brink of illumination,
the old ways are very seductive
and liable to pull you back.

JOSEPH CAMPBELL,
A JOSEPH CAMPBELL COMPANION

This brink of illumination could be as simple as understanding what your next step is in your life or it could be the result of years of spiritual inquiry. Or both. It could be the result of a deal breaker (mentioned earlier). The brink could be brought about through a conversation with a Southern Baptist minister or a conversation with a respected elder like Parker J. Palmer. Either way, this brink, which is possible at any moment, is a precarious and dynamic spot to find oneself. The word *brink* implies risk, even danger. But the danger isn't in taking the step into illumination but allowing ourselves to be pulled back into the old ways. (The danger is our tendency to get complacent and return to our seat on the tour bus.)

We could say that on the verge of fulfillment the old ways try to seduce us back into compliance. There needs to be an ongoing effort to stay awake, to have attentiveness be an underlying intention in all we do and experience. Be willing to always pay attention, hold those conversations, and plant that lotus in the ground of diversity.

As a meaning maker every day is the brink.

The Transcendent Action of Generosity

The six perfections of Buddhism, or *pāramitās,* are also known as the six transcendental actions, and they are generosity, ethical discipline, patience, enthusiasm, concentration, and wisdom. I consider these the six conditions for living a creative and ethical life, reflected in different ways in the eleven principles of the zero point agreement.

When we say that pāramitās are known as transcendent
action, we mean that our actions and attitudes are performed

in a nonegocentric manner. Transcendental does not refer to some external reality, rather to the way we conduct our lives and perceive the world—either in an egocentric or a nonegocentric way. The six pāramitās are concerned with the effort to step out of the egocentric mentality.

TRALEG KYABGON

Putting yourself down or holding yourself back is egocentric and stingy. Expressing yourself in a creatively open way is nonegocentric and generous.

Checking In with Your Intentions

To make sure that you are not falling back into an egocentric mentality (or getting back on the bus), you can periodically check in with your intentions. Pay attention throughout the day to whether your thoughts and actions are in alignment with your intention. If they are not, focus on how you can change that.

Start with Yourself: End with Others

So let's start with the action of generosity. The more generous we are with ourselves the more we will have to offer others. (You can't dry out the well and expect to nourish the village.) Generosity begets creativity because creativity at its core is a generous act. Furthermore, generosity in its specific manifestations makes room for your creative ideas to flourish.

Stinginess, on the other hand, makes you withhold your creativity. A stingy attitude limits your perspective of possibilities. Here are some common themes of stinginess:

- When we compare our creative efforts to others we bully ourselves into not taking action.
- When we hold the belief that "If I let this (idea, money, creation) go, then I will have less." In reality, letting go makes room for what wants in and is a way of giving to others.

- When we tell ourselves that "This has been done or said before" as an excuse not to explore old territory in a new way.
- When we confuse fear with humility: "Oh, this isn't good enough to continue working on or to share with others."
- When we misunderstand codependency for generosity.*

Take time to notice how your different ways of "not doing," of not taking the next step in your creative life, lack generosity. A simple act of generosity automatically generates movement in your creative life. How? Explore this idea through some act of generosity and witness the positive results for yourself.

The generosity that results in creativity is unattached to outcome, to our plans, our perceptions, and assumptions, or to how we think we are perceived by others. By overcoming such attachments our generosity increases along with our happiness, creative energy, and satisfaction.

> *The creative impulse of Van Gogh, a great genius, was simply loving what he saw and then wanting to share it with others, not for the purpose of showing off, but out of generosity.*
> BRENDA UELAND, *IF YOU WANT TO WRITE*

The perfection of generosity is the foundation for all the other perfections. First continue to be generous with yourself (keep the well replenished), and then apply acts of generosity within your creative life. Then reach out to others in conversation. This points to how phenomenon comes into existence through a multitude of causes—a generosity of causes.

> *One cannot achieve a rich and extensive result from a single cause.*
> GESHE LHUNDUB SOPA, *STEPS ON THE PATH TO ENLIGHTENMENT*, VOLUME 3

---

*Jack Kornfield's book, *A Path with Heart,* has a chapter entitled "Generosity, Codependency and Fearless Compassion" that discusses this in more depth.

Our satisfaction and happiness is dependent upon such a generous state of mind, as well as the stories we tell ourselves, and our willingness to explore possibilities.

A Person of Significance

The purpose is to strengthen our mind, so that we can step outside our solipsistic state and freely enter into the wider world.

TRALEG KYABGON, *THE PRACTICE OF LOJONG*

When we bring more generosity and love into our life circumstances and conversations we become a person of significance. As a result of our dedication to training our minds we bring integrity, joy, creativity, depth, and meaning to all our interactions with others. We understand ourselves to be the tour guide who has gotten off the bus. We are the teachers, the elders, what the I Ching refers to as the Superior Person. We are the spiritual stewards. We carry the expectations of a leader into our interactions and relationships. Our expectations not only affect how we see reality but also affect the reality itself, according to Edward E. Jones, a psychologist at Princeton University who reviewed the research on expectancy.*

Full engagement in the movement called democracy requires no less of us than full engagement in the living of our own lives.

PARKER J. PALMER, *HEALING THE HEART OF DEMOCRACY*

Spiritual Stewardship

Spiritual stewardship means maintaining an ongoing intention that arises from the altruistic desire to take personal responsibility for uplifting our lives and bringing benefit to others. Every action we take then

---

*Edward E. Jones, "Interpreting Interpersonal Behavior: The Effects of Expectancies," *Science* 234, no. 4772 (October 3, 1986): 41–46.

holds this underlying spiritual intention. In life as a meaning maker, we have each made a very real (karmic) agreement intention to ourselves, and to all sentient beings, to live from the zero point. Our choices and behaviors will continue to reflect what's in our consciousness and what we choose to cultivate. What will you choose to cultivate?

Sometimes we hold our spiritual aspirations and principles in our back pocket, not really constructing a life from them. Back-pocketing our principles and intentions can become a form of passive resistance to staying awake (to staying off the bus). This often happens when we identify with such titles as spiritual steward or bodhisattva or yogi instead of continually *cultivating* what these titles represent. Saying we are meaning makers says that we are moving more and more into a natural and active state of being in the world. We have evolved past the spiritual quest. We are the movement. We are where life happens. We are the zero point. Transformation then takes place on a regular basis in our daily lives.

A Daily Practice

The Bodhisattva Vow is a living vow that we reaffirm every day, not just once in a lifetime.

LAMA SURYA DAS,
AWAKENING THE BUDDHIST HEART

Have some kind of daily practice (meditation, journaling, walking) that reinforces your creative and spiritual life. Review the four reminders, recite your intentions, or observe some other practice offered up earlier in this book. Don't waste this precious life time by putting things off or ignoring the *daily* call to be active in your spiritual and creative life. Remember, none of us know the day or hour of our death. So let's not be frivolous with the remarkable opportunity of this day.

God is primarily a Creator. He seeks to create new life, and His kingdom generates a continual source of new energies and possibilities. This is why, on an experiential level, no human being ever reaches the end of his inner journey; for, as the kingdom begins to become a reality within him, there is generated from within a host of new possibilities which his consciousness can fulfill. So the life of the kingdom is dynamic and continually evolving. This is the inner meaning of the story of the great catch of fish in Luke 5:4–7.

JOHN A. SANFORD, *THE KINGDOM WITHIN*

The *Real* Holy Grail

If we remain stuck in the search for meaning (individually and collectively), we will continue to destroy the world around us because in our search for the holy grail we ignore our other responsibilities. This quest for meaning was (and still is by most) looked upon as the epiphany of a spiritual life. Everything becomes secondary to our search for our version of the holy grail. In this search many are searching for a meaningful experience, others for what makes them happy. The quest for purpose permeates our culture to the point that there is more money being made by people offering ways to help you *find* your purpose than in connection with people *activating* their purposes.

Of course the real holy grail has been with us all along. As expressed in a popular Chinese proverb: *If I keep a green bough in my heart, the singing bird will come.*

We must give up the personal and global myths that continue to endanger our personal and collective survival. The search for the holy grail is the old myth. The search for meaning is the old paradigm. Meaning is made by keeping the green bough green.

We hold the power to rewrite and re-myth our outdated legends and histories. And through this re-mything a new world is born.

The Old Myth

This story is from a book of myths and legends about quests. It represents the old myth. It represents the obsession to "find oneself" or to "find one's purpose." It shows what we have to give up in our search for the holy grail.

✦✦✦

The White Bird

African story from *Mythical Journeys,*
Legendary Quests by Moyra Caldecott

A hunter came to a pool to fill a gourd with water. As he bent down he saw the reflection of a white bird behind his own face on the still, silvered surface. He was astonished at its beauty and its size and looked up at once, thinking that he would indeed be honored if he could return to his people with such a bird. A chief would be proud to wear its feathers.

But the bird had already flown away over the tall, dark trees of the forest and was out of sight.

He set off in pursuit, leaving his family, his friends, and his tribe; nothing diverting him from his determination to find the bird.

He never caught another glimpse of it, but wherever he went he heard news of its passing.

He came at last to a great mountain with snow on its top. The people in the region thought they had seen the bird on the summit.

He began to climb, but found that his progress was becoming slower and slower. His limbs ached. His breath came with difficulty. He had not noticed it, but in the long years of searching he had been growing older. Now an old man, he could barely climb to the top of the mountain.

Finally he reached the summit and lay there in despair. His life had passed and it seemed to him he had achieved nothing.

"Oh, Mother!" he cried. And again, "Oh, Mother!"

A voice seemed to answer him. "Look up," it said. "Look up!"

And he looked up.

Spiralling through the air toward him was a single, shining white feather. With tears in his eyes he reached up and grasped it.

With the feather in his hand and a smile of contentment on his face, the hunter died.

✦✦✦

In the above quest, the hunter didn't even seem to enjoy his day-to-day experiences as it always came down to him missing the white bird. Because of his energy being spent in pursuit of the white bird, he didn't even notice his life pass by. He made little or no meaning from his day-to-day life. His spiritual quest was further motivated by his desire to be recognized (honored) by others. In his quest for the white bird he lived continually at the will and determination of outside circumstances.

Re-mything

+ You may want to sit awhile and contemplate what you make of the old myth. What do you think and feel about what the hunter did with this experience? What did he want (what was his motivation) in getting the bird? What if he had made a different meaning of the white bird, how would his life have been different?

+ How does this myth in any way represent you? Have you spent time away from loved ones in pursuit of your version of the holy grail? What to you is a holy grail? Who or what are you going to call out to with your last breath?

+ This can be a powerful "third thing" in groups where you are creating a new myth together. Read the myth out loud, then open up for a dialogue around its meaning. Then have everyone take the time to rewrite (re-myth) a new myth from this old myth.

+ Those who wish to can share their new myth. (Practice dialogue, or listening without giving feedback, as discussed in "Explore an Alternative to Advice" on page 132.) After everyone has shared their new myths you can open up to another conversation around the shared meaning and messages in the new myths.

Who cares about wealth and honor?
Even the poorest thing shines.
My miraculous power and spiritual activity:
Drawing water and carrying wood.

LAYMAN P'ANG, CHINESE ZEN MASTER

The New Myth

Now is the time to take the old myth and re-myth it, making it your own—the myth of our times, the myth of the meaning maker. The new myth, of course, is the one you are living, creating, and choosing for yourself. This new myth won't take you away from your life but open you up more to your life.

✦✦✦

The White Bird and the Gift

From Amy Schertz, artist and family therapist,
and Henry Johnson,
writer and family therapist

Once upon a time a young hunter was kneeling down at a local watering hole, gathering water for his family. He enjoyed helping his family in this way but felt there must be more to his life than gathering water. As he dipped a large gourd into the clear lake, he saw in its reflective waters a large white bird flying overhead. The great bird's reflection danced on the water and then disappeared from view. Just so, he felt the bird reflected something about his life. But what?

The hunter then remembered a story his grandfather told him as a small child of a great white bird that visited him at a time he too was discouraged. His grandfather was a medicine man who knew the language of the animals, "The white bird told me, we all have something to give." The bird told him that everyone, just like every living thing, is born with a purpose. On the spot, the young hunter felt a great sense of enthusiasm to return to his tribe and share his talents of drum making and dream weaving that he had in the past kept mostly to himself. Up until now he had felt embarrassed to share what he thought were not worthy gifts.

He filled the gourd with fresh water, and thanked the bird, though it had flown off. As he lifted the full gourd from the pond he saw that a white feather from the bird had landed near the pond's edge. He picked it up to keep as a reminder to share his gifts of drum making and dream weaving with his tribe. Filled with gratitude and enthusiasm, he carried the gourd of water back to his people, without spilling a drop.

✦✦✦

There is a community of the spirit.
Join it, and feel the delight
of walking in the noisy street,
and being the noise.

RUMI, *A COMMUNITY OF THE SPIRIT*

Join the noise. Plant your lotuses in the noise and fire of your daily life. Give up the questing *for* and become. As meaning makers we create and manifest meaning *as we walk, where we live.* We discover who or what we are within our families and communities, within the "noisy street" of our lives.

At the turn of dusk
the light leaves
a strip of day

writing its silver line
across
the distant hill.

Sometimes everything
has to come
down to that
one
thin line

so you can touch
that knowing
inside you.

Sometimes it takes
the turn of light
to dark
to know that

always, the

search for light
is already carried
in our secret heart.

No one else may know
how sometimes
when the last breath
has left
the body

someone in the room
has drawn something new
from the breathlessness
on
that silver line
between us.

There is no leaving
even as the last of the light
disappears from view

for, there is a dawning gala
in all that is arriving
on the crest
of the other side.

JULIE TALLARD JOHNSON,
"THE PILGRIMAGE"

Acknowledgments

My acknowledgment and gratitude start at home. I am deeply grateful to my husband, Bill, and my daughter, Lydia, for their ongoing support and their ability to keep me grounded. I thank the land and all its creatures for offering up to me daily lessons on belonging and meaning. And to the animals who share our space—our companion dogs and horses and our laying chickens. I witness life around me living from the zero point.

One purpose of my life is to let others know of those among us who are creatively engaged in uplifting the world around us. Parker J. Palmer, author of *A Hidden Wholeness* and *Healing the Heart of Democracy,* is one such person. His books, workshops, and online resources flavor each page of this book and fortunately each day of my life. Thank you, Parker. I am also fortunate to have other mentors and teachers "close in" who have influenced and supported my work: Geshe L. Sopa and Geshe Tenzin Dorje of Deer Park Buddhist Center; Bert Stitt, a true visionary of what is possible; Anne Forbes, Trees as Teacher guide; Tracy Wells, Thai massage therapist; Debra Morrill, shamanic healer and my Bindu breath partner; A'cha'rya Jina'neshvar (James Powell); David Rozelle, poet and philosopher extraordinaire; Mike Bougneit, shamanic dreamer; Kathy Steffen, the best of writing teachers and friend; Cathy Kennedy, a humble voice of truth; Steven Pressfield, author of *The War of Art* and *Do The Work*; Tracy Thaden, fellow explorer and meaning maker; Laurel L. Reinhardt, Ph.D., joy coach and soul sister; Kate Larkin, writer and editor extraordinaire; and, finally, Bill Ishmael, wildlife biologist and nature's advocate.

At its core this book is an invitation to hold ongoing conversations with the world around us. In that, I thank my sister Jeannie Retelle, who was willing to show up and hold intimate and open conversations with me. You are beautiful.

Finding the writings and works of David Bohm, first through His Holiness the Dalai Lama's teachings, later through his own books and lectures, was for me finding a spiritual friend in the scientific community. His spirit and message live on in me.

Of course there is a bounty of souls who have influenced the making of this book, and their poetry, quotes, and wisdom are peppered throughout. I am deeply grateful to the voices of David Whyte, Lama Zopa Rinpoche, Irvin Yalom, Allan J. Hamilton, M.D., Walt Whitman, Pema Chodron, Victor Sanchez, Paul Reps, James Masterson, M.D., Aldo Leopold, Traleg Kyabgon, Austin Kleon, Alfred Huang, Ralph Waldo Emerson, His Holiness the 14th Dalai Lama, Joseph Campbell, William Stafford, Black Elk, Gandhi, and Thich Nhat Hanh.

To all those who have sat in my circles or in one-to-one conversations over my thirty-five years as a therapist and teacher, I am grateful for the depth and intimacy of each conversation. The "mutual influence" comes through in these pages.

The conversations and soul of this book could not have happened without the creative efforts of those at Inner Traditions • Bear & Company. The best of people are found at this publishing house in Rochester, Vermont. Thank you to Jon Graham, acquisitions editor, for believing in this book (and for staying present for others even as the river took your home); to Jeanie Levitan, editor in chief—what luck of mine to have you in my life; to Jamaica Burns Griffin for her keen eye and gracious heart as editor; to Manzanita Carpenter for helping me get the word out (and to responding to my litany of questions); and to Priscilla Baker and Virginia Scott Bowman for creating a beautiful layout and design.

Finally, I am deeply grateful to the spiritual sages whom I rely upon: the Great Unknown of the I Ching, Three Crows, Black Elk, Padmasambhava, Atisha, Shantideva, Tsong-Kha-Pa, Green Tara, and Manjushri. *Om Ah Ra Pa Tsa Na Dhih!*

Bibliography

Arterburn, Stephen, and Jack Felton. *Toxic Faith: Experiencing Healing from Painful Spiritual Abuse.* Colorado Springs, Colo.: Waterbrook Press, 2001.

Baker, Ian. *The Heart of the World: A Journey to the Last Secret Place.* New York: Penguin, 2004.

Bly, Robert. *Morning Poems.* New York: Harper Perennial, 1998.

———. *News of the Universe: Poems of Twofold Consciousness.* San Francisco: Sierra Club Books, 1995.

———. *The Soul Is Here for Its Own Joy: Sacred Poems from Many Cultures.* New York: Ecco, 1999.

Bohm, David. *On Creativity.* 2nd ed. Edited by Lee Nichol. Oxford: Routledge, 2004.

———. *On Dialogue.* 2nd ed. Edited by Lee Nichol. Oxford: Routledge, 2004.

———. *The Essential David Bohm.* Edited by Lee Nichol. London: Routledge, 2003.

———. *Unfolding Meaning: A Weekend of Dialogue with David Bohm.* Oxford: Routledge, 1996.

———. *Wholeness and the Implicate Order.* London: Routledge, 2002.

Bohm, David, and F. David Peat. *Science, Order, and Creativity: A Dramatic New Look at the Creative Roots of Science and Life.* New York: Bantam Books, 1987.

Bolen, Jean Shinoda. *The Tao of Psychology: Synchronicity and the Self.* 25th ed. San Francisco: HarperSanFrancisco, 2005.

Brown, Joseph Epes. *The Sacred Pipe: Black Elk's Account of the Seven Rites of the Oglala Sioux.* As told to Joseph Epes Brown. Norman: University of Oklahoma Press, 1989.

———. *Teaching Spirits: Understanding Native American Religious Traditions.* New York: Oxford University Press, 2001.

Caldecott, Moyra. *Mythical Journeys, Legendary Quests: The Spiritual Search; Traditional Stories from World Mythology*. London: Blandford Press, 1996.

Campbell, Joseph. *The Power of Myth*. With Bill Moyers. New York: Doubleday, 1988.

———. *A Joseph Campbell Companion: Reflections on the Art of Living*. Edited by Diane K. Osbon. New York: HarperCollins, 1991.

Cleary, Thomas, trans. *The Taoist I Ching*. Boston: Shambhala, 1986.

Cowan, James. *Letters from a Wild State: Rediscovering Our True Relationship to Nature*. New York: Harmony, 1992.

Dalai Lama. *Dzogchen: The Heart Essence of the Great Perfection*. Edited by Patrick Gaffney. Translated by Thupten Jinpa and Richard Barron. Ithaca, N.Y.: Snow Lion, 2004.

———. *Essence of the Heart Sutra: The Dalai Lama's Heart of Wisdom Teachings*. Translated and edited by Thupten Jinpa. Boston: Wisdom Publications, 2005.

———. *Ethics for the New Millennium*. New York: Riverhead Books, 1999.

———. *How to See Yourself as You Really Are*. Translated and edited by Jeffrey Hopkins. New York: Atria Books, 2006.

———. *Stages of Meditation*. Translated by Lobsang Jordhen, Losang Choephel Ganchenpa, and Jeremy Russell. Ithaca, N.Y.: Snow Lion, 2001.

———. "Womb of the Buddha: The Heart Sutra." Lecture, Indiana University, Bloomington, Ill., May 12–14, 2010.

Douglas-Klotz, Neil. *Prayers of the Cosmos: Meditations on the Aramaic Words of Jesus*. New York: HarperCollins, 1990.

Ehrlich, Gretel. *A Match to the Heart: One Woman's Story of Being Struck by Lightning*. New York: Penguin Books, 1995.

———. *The Solace of Open Spaces*. New York: Penguin Books, 1985.

Emerson, Ralph Waldo. *The Essays of Ralph Waldo Emerson*. Cambridge, Mass.: Belknap Press of Harvard University Press, 1987.

———. *Self-Reliance and Other Essays*. Mineola, N.Y.: Dover Publications, 1993.

Fincher, Susanne F. *Coloring Mandalas: For Insight, Healing, and Self-Expression*. Boston: Shambhala, 2000.

Gandhi, Mahatma. *The Essential Gandhi: An Anthology of His Writings on His Life, Work, and Ideas*. 2nd ed. Edited by Louis Fischer. New York: Vintage Books, 2002.

Gangrade, K. D. *Gandhian Approach to Development and Social Works*. New Delhi, India: Concept Publishing, 2005.

Ghose, Sudhin N. *Tibetan Folk Tales and Fairy Stories*. New Delhi: Rupa, 1993.

Gottman, John. *Why Marriages Succeed or Fail: And How You Can Make Yours Last*. New York: Simon & Schuster, 1995.

Grof, Stanislov. *The Adventure of Self-Discovery: Dimensions of Consciousness and New Perspectives in Psychotherapy*. Albany: University of New York Press, 1988.

Hague, Michael. *Aesop's Fables*. New York: Holt, Rinehart, and Winston, 1985.

Hamilton , Allan J. *Zen Mind, Zen Horse: The Science and Spirituality of Working with Horses*. North Adams, Mass.: Storey Publishing.

Hanh, Thich Nhat. *The Heart of Understanding: Commentaries on the Prajnaparamita Heart Sutra*. Berkeley, Calif.: Parallax Press, 1988.

Hassan, Steven. *Combatting Cult Mind Control*. Rochester, Vt.: Park Street Press, 1990.

Huang, Alfred. *The Complete I Ching: The Definitive Translation*. 2nd ed. Rochester, Vt.: Inner Traditions, 1998.

Huang, Chungliang Al, and Jerry Lynch. *Mentoring: The Tao of Giving and Receiving Wisdom*. New York: HarperCollins, 1995.

Jung, Carl. *The Undiscovered Self*. New York: Penguin Group, 1957.

Kahneman, Daniel. *Thinking, Fast and Slow*. New York: Farrar, Straus, and Giroux, 2011.

Kain, John. *A Rare and Precious Thing: The Possibilities and Pitfalls of Working with a Spiritual Teacher*. New York: Random House, 2006.

Khenpo, Nyoshul, and Surya Das. *Natural Great Perfection: Dzogchen Teachings and Vajra Songs*. Ithaca, N.Y.: Snow Lion, 1995.

Kleon, Austin. *Steal Like an Artist: 10 Things Nobody Told You about Being Creative*. New York: Workman Publishing, 2012.

Kongtrul, Jamgon. *The Teacher-Student Relationship*. Translated by Ron Garry. Ithaca, N.Y.: Snow Lion, 1999.

Kramer, Joel, and Diana Alstad. *The Guru Papers: Masks of Authoritarian Power*. Berkeley, Calif.: Frog Books, 1993.

Kyabgon, Traleg. "Depression's Truth." *Shambhala Sun Magazine*, March 2003.

———. *The Practice of Lojong: Cultivating Compassion through Training the Mind*. Boston: Shambhala, 2007.

Ladinsky, Daniel. *I Heard God Laughing: Renderings of Hafiz*. Oakland, Calif.: Mobius Press, 1996.

Leopold, Aldo. *A Sand County Almanac*. New York: Ballantine Books, 1966.

Levine, Stephen. *A Gradual Awakening*. New York: Anchor Books, 1989.

Loy, David R. *The World Is Made of Stories*. Somerville, Mass.: Wisdom Publications, 2010.

Machado, Antonio. *Border of a Dream: Selected Poems of Antonio Machado*. Translated by Willis Barnstone. Port Townsend, Wash.: Copper Canyon Press, 2003.

Macy, Joanna. *Mutual Causality in Buddhism and General Systems Theory: The Dharma of Natural Systems.* Albany: State University of New York Press, 1991.

Mails, Thomas E. *Fools Crow: Wisdom and Power.* Tulsa, Okla.: Council Oak Books, 1991.

Masterson, James F. *The Search for the Real Self: Unmasking the Personality Disorders of Our Age.* New York: Free Press, 1988.

Matthiessen, Peter. *Zen and the Writing Life.* Audiocassette. Louisville, Colo.: Sounds True, 1999.

McLeod, Ken. *Wake Up to Your Life: Discovering the Buddhist Path of Attention.* New York: HarperCollins, 2002.

Mehl-Madrona, Lewis. *Coyote Healing.* Rochester, Vt.: Bear & Company, 2003.

———. *Narrative Medicine: The Use of History and Story in the Healing Process.* Rochester, Vt.: Bear & Company, 2007.

Miller, Alice. *The Drama of the Gifted Child: The Search for the True Self.* Rev. ed. New York: Basic Books, 1997.

Mitchell, Steven, ed. *The Enlightened Heart: An Anthology of Sacred Poetry.* New York: Harper and Row, 1989.

Mohatt, Gerald, and Joseph Eagle Elk. *The Price of a Gift: A Lakota Healer's Story.* Lincoln: University of Nebraska Press, 2000.

Moore, Dinty W. *The Mindful Writer: Noble Truths of the Writing Life.* Somerville, Mass.: Wisdom Publications, 2012.

Moss, Jeff. *The Other Side of the Door.* New York: Bantam Books, 1991.

Neihardt, John G. *Black Elk Speaks: Being the Life Story of a Holy Man of the Oglala Sioux.* As told through John G. Neihardt. Lincoln: University of Nebraska Press, 1932.

Newland, Guy. *Introduction to Emptiness: As Taught in Tsong-Kha-Pa's Great Treatise on the Stages of the Path.* Ithaca, N.Y.: Snow Lion, 2008.

Nietzsche, Friedrich. *Basic Writings of Nietzsche.* Translated by Walter Kaufmann. New York: Modern Library, 2000.

Odes of Solomon. Translated by James H. Charlesworth. The Gnostic Society Library. Accessed May 31, 2013, http://gnosis.org/library/odes.htm.

Ouspensky, P. D. *The Psychology of Man's Possible Evolution.* New York: Hedgehog Press, 1950.

———. *In Search of the Miraculous.* New York: Harcourt Brace Jovanovich, 1977.

Pabongka Rinpoche. *Liberation in the Palm of Your Hand: A Concise Discourse on the Path to Enlightenment.* Edited by Trijang Rinpoche. Translated by Michael Richards. Boston: Wisdom, 1991.

Padmasambhava. *Natural Liberation: Padmasambhava's Teachings on the Six*

Bardos. Commentary by Gyatrul Rinpoche. Translated by B. Alan Wallace. Somerville, Mass.: Wisdom, 1998.

Pagels, Elaine. *The Gnostic Gospels.* New York: Vintage, 1989.

Paine, Thomas. *Common Sense, The Rights of Man and Other Essential Writings of Thomas Paine.* New York: Signet Classics, 2003.

Palmer, Parker J. *The Active Life: A Spirituality of Work, Creativity, and Caring.* San Francisco: Harper and Row, 1990.

———. *Healing the Heart of Democracy: The Courage to Create a Politics Worthy of the Human Spirit.* San Francisco: Jossey-Bass, 2011.

———. *A Hidden Wholeness: The Journey Toward an Undivided Life.* San Francisco: Jossey-Bass, 2004.

Perkins, John. *Shapeshifting: Shamanic Techniques for Global and Personal Transformation.* Rochester, Vt.: Destiny Books, 1997.

Pressfield, Steven. *The War of Art: Winning the Inner Creative Battle.* New York: Rugged Land, 2002.

Prochaska, J. O., C. C. DiClemente, and J. C. Norcross. "In Search of How People Change. Applications to Addictive Behaviors." *American Psychologist* 27, no. 9 (Sept. 1992): 1102–14.

Reps, Paul, and Nyogen Senzaki. *Zen Flesh, Zen Bones: A Collection of Zen and Pre-Zen Writings.* Boston: Tuttle Publishing, 1985.

Sanchez, Victor. *The Teachings of Don Carlos: Practical Applications of the Works of Carlos Castaneda.* Rochester, Vt.: Bear & Company, 1995.

———. *The Toltec Path of Recapitulation: Healing Your Past to Free Your Soul.* Rochester, Vt.: Bear & Company, 2001.

Sanford, John A. *The Kingdom Within: The Inner Meaning of Jesus' Sayings.* New York: Paulist Press, 1970.

Santideva, *A Guide to the Bodhisattva Way of Life.* Translated by Vesna A. Wallace and B. Alan Wallace. New York: Snow Lion, 1997.

Shaw, Connie, and Ike Allen. *The Tao of Walt Whitman: Daily Insights and Actions to Achieve a Balanced Life.* Boulder, Colo.: Sentient Publications, 2011.

Shermer, Michael. *The Believing Brain: From Ghosts and Gods to Politics and Conspiracies; How We Construct Beliefs and Reinforce Them as Truths.* New York: Henry Holt, 2011.

Siegel, Daniel J. *The Mindful Brain: Reflection and Attunement in the Cultivation of Well-Being.* New York: W. W. Norton, 2007.

Sloane, Sarah Jane. *I Ching for Writers: Finding the Page Inside You.* Novato, Calif.: New World Library, 2005.

Sonam, Rinchen Geshe. *Atisha's Lamp for the Path to Enlightenment.* Translated and edited by Ruth Sonam. New York: Snow Lion, 1997.

———. *The Six Perfections.* Translated and edited by Ruth Sonam. New York: Snow Lion, 1998.

Sopa, Geshe Lhundub. *Steps on the Path to Enlightenment: A Commentary on Tsongkhapa's Lamrim Chenmo.* Vol. 1, *The Foundation Practices.* With David Patt. Somerville, Mass.: Wisdom, 2004.

———. *Steps on the Path to Enlightenment: A Commentary on Tsongkhapa's Lamrim Chenmo.* Vol. 3, *The Way of the Bodhisattva.* With Beth Newman. Somerville, Mass.: Wisdom, 2008.

Stafford, William. *The Way It Is: New and Selected Poems.* Minneapolis: Graywolf, 1998.

———. *You Must Revise Your Life: Poets on Poetry.* Ann Arbor: University of Michigan Press, 1987.

Thoreau, Henry David. *Walden; or, Life in the Woods.* Princeton, N.J.: Princeton University Press, 2004.

Tinbergen, Niko. *Curious Naturalists.* New York: Doubleday, 1968.

Trungpa, Chögyam. *Shambhala: The Sacred Path of the Warrior.* Boston: Shambhala, 1984.

Tzu, Lao. *Tao Te Ching.* Translated by Stephen Mitchell. New York: Harper Perennial, 1991.

Walker, Brian Browne. *The I Ching or Book of Changes: A Guide to Life's Turning Points.* New York: St. Martin's Press, 1992.

Watts, Alan. *The Way of Zen.* New York: Vintage, 1957.

———. *The Wisdom of Insecurity: A Message for an Age of Anxiety.* 2nd ed. New York: Vintage, 2011.

Whitman, Walt. *Complete Works of Walt Whitman.* Delphi Classics, 2012. Kindle edition.

Whyte, David. *The House of Belonging: Poems.* Langley, Wash.: Many Rivers Press, 1997.

———. *Pilgrim: Poems.* Langley, Wash.: Many Rivers Press, 2012.

———. *What to Remember When Waking: The Disciplines of Everyday Life.* Audio CD. Louisville, Colo.: Sounds True, 2010.

Wilhelm, Richard, and Cary F. Baynes. *The I Ching or Book of Changes.* 3rd ed. Princeton, N.J.: Princeton University Press, 1997.

Yalom, Irvin D. *The Theory and Practice of Group Psychotherapy.* 4th ed. New York: Basic Books, 1995.

Yeshe, Thubten. *Becoming Your Own Therapist: An Introduction to the Buddhist Way of Thought.* Boston: Lama Yeshe Wisdom Archive, 1998.

Zopa, Lama Rinpoche. *Transforming Problems into Happiness.* Somerville, Mass.: Wisdom, 1994.

Index